Praise for Avi Steinberg's **RUNNING THE BOOKS**

"Steinberg's writing is funny, poignant and accessible. He's the guy you want in front of the campfire because he knows how to tell a good story. . . . The characters pop off the pages—not because they're stereotypical or overly sentimental, but because they're real. Some get saved, others get even more lost, but Steinberg brings them all equally to life—for better or worse."

—Associated Press

"A freewheeling meditation on the nature of incarceration and a moving chronicle of a population that remains, by design, hidden from view." —*The Boston Globe*

"Heartbreaking and entertaining. . . . Steinberg's compassion for those he mentored clearly comes through. Yet, this is far from a preachy memoir on prison reform. It's a young man's blundering, but touching, journey to find a place in the world. Fortunately, he makes us laugh and—sometimes cry—in the process."

—*The Seattle Times*

"Steinberg proves to be a keen observer, and a morally serious one. His memoir is wriggling and alive." —*The New York Times*

"A terrific book, hilarious enough to make you want to read its lines to anyone who happens to be around, and profound enough to have you care deeply about many of the men and women whose crimes have brought them to Boston's Suffolk County House of Correction." —*San Francisco Chronicle*

"A moving account of the boredom, deprivation and infernal bleakness of prison . . . [filled] with unexpected bits of comedy and insight." —USA Today

"[A] page-turner. . . . Wry, captivating. . . . An impressive account of a world that few readers of this newspaper will recognize." —The Economist

"A thoughtful and gifted debut author. . . . Steinberg's writing is sharp and witty throughout." —The Forward

"Running the Books presents [Steinberg's] experiences working in the prison's library as a fiendishly intricate moral puzzle, sad and scary, yes, but also—and often—very funny." —Salon

"Funny, eclectic, and ultimately moving." —The Daily Beast

"Delightfully insightful. . . . How much can we readers expect to learn about prison life through the prism of its library? Answer: Volumes." —Haaretz

"Perceptive, comic, self-deprecating, reflective, and pungently ironic à la Catch-22. . . . Running the Books is both very funny and heartbreaking, further evidence for Mark Twain's edict that 'The secret source of humor is not joy but sorrow; there is no humor in Heaven.'" —Chicago Life Magazine

Avi Steinberg

RUNNING THE BOOKS

Avi Steinberg was born in Jerusalem and raised in
Cleveland and Boston. His work has appeared in
The Boston Globe, *The New York Times Magazine*,
Salon, and other publications.

www.avisteinberg.com

RUNNING THE BOOKS The Adventures of an Accidental Prison Librarian

Avi Steinberg

Anchor Books
A Division of Random House, Inc.
New York

FIRST ANCHOR BOOKS EDITION, OCTOBER 2011

The Library of Congress has cataloged the Nan A. Talese edition as follows:
Steinberg, Avi.
Running the books : the adventures of an accidental prison librarian /
Avi Steinberg. — 1st ed.
p. cm.
I. Steinberg, Avi. 2. Prison librarians—Massachusetts—Boston—Biography. I. Title.
Z720.S827A3 2010
027.6'65092—dc22
2010004829

Anchor ISBN: 978-0-7679-3131-1

www.anchorbooks.com

Printed in the United States of America
10 9 8 7 6 5 4 3 2

To my family

February 19. Hopes?

February 20. Unnoticeable life. Noticeable failure.

February 25. A letter.

— FROM KAFKA'S DIARY, 1922

Contents

RUNNING THE BOOKS

UNDELIVERED

Part I

The up&up and low low

Pimps make the best librarians. Psycho killers, the worst. Ditto con men. Gangsters, gunrunners, bank robbers—adept at crowd control, at collaborating with a small staff, at planning with deliberation and executing with contained fury—all possess the librarian's basic skill set. Scalpers and loan sharks certainly have a role to play. But even they lack that something, the je ne sais quoi, the elusive *it*. What would a pimp call it? Yes: the love.

If you're a pimp, you've got love for the library. And if you don't, it's probably because you haven't visited one. But chances are you will eventually do a little—or perhaps, a lot—of prison time and you'll wander into one there. When you do, you'll encounter the sweetness and the light. You'll find books you've always needed, but never knew existed. Books like that indispensable hustler's tool, the rhyming dictionary. You'll discover and embrace, like long-lost relatives, entire new vocabularies. Anthropology and biology, philosophy and psychology, gender studies and musicology, art history and pharmacology, economics and poetry. French. The primordial slime. Lesbian bonobo apes. Rousseau nibbling on sorbet with his Venetian hooker. The complete annotated record of animal striving.

And it's not just about books. In the joint, where business is slow, the library is The Spot. It's where you go to see and be seen. Among the stacks, you'll meet older colleagues who gather regularly to debate, to try out new material, to declaim, reminisce, network and match wits. You'll meet old timers working on their memoirs, upstarts writing the next great pimp screenplay.

You'll meet inmate librarians like Dice, who will tell you he stayed sane during two years in the hole at Walla Walla by memorizing a smuggled anthology of Shakespeare's plays. He'll prove it by reciting long passages by heart. Dice wears sunglasses and is an ideologue. He'll try to persuade you of the "virtues of vice." He'll tell you that a prison library "ain't a place to better yourself, it's a place to get better at getting worse." He'll bully you into reading Shelley's *Frankenstein*, and he'll bully you further into believing that it's "our story"—by which he means the story of pimps, a specialized class of men, a priesthood, who live according to the dictates of Nature.

He means it. Like many a pimp preoccupied by ancient questions, Dice takes the old books seriously. He approves of Emersonian self-reliance, and was scandalized that many American universities had ousted Shakespeare and the Classics from their curricula. He'd read about it in the *Chronicle of Higher Education*.

"You kidding me, man?" he'd said, folding the newspaper like a hassled commuter, brow arching over his shades. "Now I've heard it all. This country's going to hell."

Men like Dice will inculcate you with an appreciation for tradition, what Matthew Arnold called "the best which has been thought and said." And you'll discover precisely why it is so important to study the best that has been thought and said: How else you gonna top it?

This at least is what I'm told. I wouldn't know. I'm not a pimp. I'm in a different sort of racket. My name is Avi Steinberg, but in the joint, they call me Bookie. The nickname was given to me by Jamar "Fat Kat" Richmond. Fat Kat is, or was, a notorious gangster, occasional pimp, and, as it turns out, exceptionally resourceful librarian. At thirty years old and two bullet wounds, Kat is already a veteran inmate. He's too big—five foot nine, three-hundred-plus pounds—for a proper prison outfit. Instead he is given a nonregulation T-shirt, the only inmate in his unit with a blue T-shirt instead of a tan uniform top. But the heaviness bespeaks solidity, substance, gravitas. The fat guy T-shirt, status. He is my right hand, though it often seems the other way around.

"Talk to Bookie," he tells inmates who've lined up to see him. "He's the main book man."

The main book man. I like that. I can't help it. For an asthmatic Jewish kid, it's got a nice ring to it. Hired to run Boston's prison library—and serve as the resident creative writing teacher—I am living my (quixotic) dream: a book-slinger with a badge and a streetwise attitude, part bookworm, part badass. This identity has helped me tremendously at cocktail parties.

In prison Fat Kat, Dice, and their ilk are the intellectual elite, hence their role as inmate librarians. But the library itself is not elitist. To gain entrance, one need only commit a felony. And the majority of felons, at least where I work, do make their way to the library. Many visit every day. Even though some inmates can barely read, the prison library is packed. And when things get crowded, the atmosphere is more like a speakeasy than a quiet reading room. This place is, after all, the library of "all rogues, vagabonds, persons using any subtle craft, juggling, or unlawful games or plays, common pipers, fiddlers, runaways, stubborn children, drunkards, nightwalkers, pilferers, wanton and lascivious persons, railers and brawlers." This according to a nineteenth-century state government report. I've met only one fiddler. No pipers, common or otherwise. But I do meet a good number of rappers and MCs. With the addition of gun-toting gangbangers and coke dealers, the old catalog remains fairly accurate.

Which is all to say that a library in prison is significantly different than a library in the real world. Yes, there are book clubs, poetry readings, and moments of silent reflection. But there isn't much shushing. As a prison crossroads, a place where hundreds of inmates come to deal with their pressing issues, where officers and other staff stop by to hang out and mix things up, the pace of a prison library is social and up-tempo. I spend much of my time running.

The chaos begins right away. There is no wake-up call more effective than twenty-five convicts in matching uniforms coming at you first thing in the morning.

First come the greetings. This takes a while. Inmates exchange intricate handshakes and formal titles: OG, young G, boo, bro, baby boy, brutha, dude, cuz, dawg, P, G, daddy, pimpin', nigga, man, thug thizzle, my boy, my man, homie. Then, the nicknames: Flip, Hood, Lil Haiti, Messiah, Bleach, Bombay, K*Shine, Rib, Swi$$, Tu-Shay,

The Truth, Black, Boat, Forty, Fifty (no Sixty), Giz, Izz, Rizz, Fizz, Shizz, Lil Shizz, Frenchy, P-Rico, Country, Dro, Turk, T, Africa . . .

And, yes, occasionally, Bookie. Incidentally I have other, less-used prison nicknames: Slim, Harvard, Jew-Fro (though my hair is stick straight). Mostly, people just call me Arvin or Harvey.

Next comes business. Every inmate wants a magazine and/or newspaper. Most inmates also want a "street book," the wildly popular pulp "hip-hop novels" whose titles tend to have the word *hustler* in them. I let Fat Kat handle these requests. Kat keeps a secret stash and runs a snug little business in these books, to which I—for mostly self-interested reasons—turn a blind eye. We have a mutually beneficial arrangement.

Then comes a flurry of random requests. Some legit, some not. Demands to make illicit calls to the courts, to parole boards, to "my mans on the outs," to mommas and babymommas, wifeys and wifey-wifeys. All denied. Whispered requests for information on AIDS, for information on the significance of blood in urine, for help reading a letter. All noted. I dismiss inmates' requests to use my Internet for "just one second." I deflect an inmate's charges that I'm an Israeli spy; confirm that indeed, I really did go to Harvard, ignore the follow-up question of why I ended up working in prison if I graduated from Harvard. I give serious thought to an inmate's request for me to check his rap album's website. I am, after all, the prison's self-appointed CGO, Chief Google Officer.

I field legal queries. I am asked about the legal distinction between homicide and manslaughter, the terms of probation, sentencing guidelines, the laws relating to kidnapping one's own children, of extradition, of armed robbery with a grenade. There are also clever criminals: a guy who wants to learn state regulations regarding antique guns and antique ammunition, items he hopes might be governed by laxer laws and fraught with loopholes. Out of the corner of my eye, I notice an inmate sporting a marker-drawn musketeer-style mustache, talking to himself in a phony posh English accent. Somebody might need to take his meds. I note this, as well.

An inmate thanks me for my suggestion that he listen to "Sherbert" at our listening station. (He means Schubert.) Inmates ask me for a book about the band Nirvana, about the state of nirvana; for a self-help guide for fathers; for a yoga book; a book on "how to mix chemicals"; a guide to real estate. Ignoring the chemicals request, I suggest "Dummies" guides. I do this diplomatically, since inmates have been sensitive in the past to the possibility that I may be calling them dummies. A caseworker suddenly appears—she's a crazy woman who talks nonstop and tells wild lies of dating European royals. She wants to borrow a book on tigers. Waiting patiently is C.C. Too Sweet, a mercurial, balding pimp memoirist who wants me to edit his revised manuscript.

My main challenge is to focus on the tasks at hand and not get sucked into the pimp and hustler gabfests. These are always entertaining and occasionally lead to fascinating discussions. I overhear an elder pimp tell an apprentice, "I wasn't born, son, I was *hatched*." But before I hear where that conversation is going, Ty pokes his way to the front of the line and politely demands to talk with me. Immediately.

He is a tower of an eighteen-year-old with a baby face and a jaw that can probably split a walnut shell in one clean crack. Today he looks spooked. As soon as I close my door—something I rarely do—Ty bursts into tears. His mother died last month and he was unable to attend the out-of-state funeral; yesterday his long-estranged father showed up in prison. These are not unusual issues in prison. I've encountered them many times before, but I still have no answers for him.

As he tells me his story, I look out the office window toward the library, wondering what atrocities are taking place in my absence. This is what I call Prison ADD: the inability to ever be present because there's always something potentially heinous occurring nearby, something that is probably your responsibility. Ty is inconsolable.

While he cries, I try to gather my thoughts. I've posted a sheet on my wall, next to my desk. It's a wordfind game that an inmate has created and sells to other inmates for the equivalent of fifty cents a pop. Thirty-eight terms, mixed into a jumble of letters. The words are listed, in roughly alphabetical order, at the side of the sheet. They form something of a mantra I use to orient myself in situations like this one.

Titled "Things Found in Prison," the list reads: *attitude, bail bondsman, booking, contraband, count time, canteen, cellie* [i.e., cellmate], *drama, depression, family, fence, grievance, gossip, hunger, habe* [short for *habeas corpus*], *handcuffs, indigent, ID card, isolation, lawyer, medication, meditation, mail, noise, officer, PIN number, prayer, quarantine, recreation, rules, shower shoes, sheriff, solitude, telephone, tears, uniforms, worry, yard*. I'm forced to reschedule a meeting with Ty. Right now, I have to help the guy who thought it would be a good idea to rob a liquor store with a live grenade. In the prison library, it's first-come, first-served.

. . . *hunger, habe, handcuffs, indigent* . . .

The hour has passed. The inmates in green uniforms finally leave, returning to the block to play chess and watch *Judge Judy* or *Days of Our Lives*. A new group of inmates is on its way. This will go on for two full shifts, until 9 p.m. when all the inmates will gather in front of TVs—self-segregated by race—to watch *Prison Break*. I take in a deep breath of recycled prison air.

. . . rules, shower shoes, sheriff, solitude, telephone, tears . . .

Before the next group arrives, Officer Malone saunters in. He and I undertake the regular task of scanning bookshelves, and other dark corners, for contraband, or for something that might be missing, especially something that can be refashioned into a weapon. This includes just about anything. We look for notes wedged into books by inmates, left for another inmate to pick up. Many of these notes are intended for the female inmates, who come down from their tower blocks at a separate time. I retrieve handfuls of these confessional letters every day. Taken as a whole literature, they give me an insight into the secret lives and concerns of inmates. I let some of the better ones pass under my radar.

Malone and I drop down to our knees simultaneously, Muslim prayer–style. We're not entreating a deity, though, but sweeping under the shelves for contraband.

. . . mail, noise, officer, PIN number, prayer . . .

Malone likes to talk. He tells me about his time in the service, about working in a paper mill. He advises me to trade in my bicycle for a Ford S150, like his. He tells me about his wife, who went back to school. She's smarter than he is, he admits. He resumes a line of conversation we've had off and on for months: he wants to help me out. I seem like a good kid, he tells me with a shrug. I should get a raise, more vaca, better retirement. My union is shitty. He urges me to join his, to become a prison guard.

I am, he says, already most of the way there.

Prison Fever

And that's exactly my problem. After working almost two years full-time in prison, it was finally dawning on me that I was a *jailer*. The book-slinging sheriff persona still worked charms at cocktail parties, but the reality of it was starting to give me acid reflux. I wasn't a visitor in this prison. I held a key and was beginning to feel infected by it. I was frankly falling apart, headed toward something of a mental and physical breakdown.

You know you're not doing well when a prisoner regards you with pity. Blue Line was a heavy-lidded man who'd been addicted to heroin since he was thirteen years old, in and out of foster care, group homes, sober houses, shelters, and prisons. He could narrate the gruesome entirety of his life through the scars on his body. When a man like Blue gives you the once-over and says, "You okay, pal? You don't look too good," this, if you're keeping score, is the exact moment you know there's trouble.

And he was being kind. To be precise, I looked like hell. I didn't admit it to anyone, but prison was kicking my ass. I'd taken the job largely to get health insurance but, the truth was, I hadn't *needed* health care until I took the job. And once I did, I subsisted only by the grace of a dream team of health care professionals: allergists, infectious disease specialists, ophthalmologists, dermatologists, orthopedists, off-duty nurses, chiropractors, Internet quacks, back doctors, front doctors, head doctors. I was even getting meds from an ob-gyn.

Every day my body passed through the prison gate, but my mind was getting caught in the mess of high walls and barbed wire. I was getting severe pains in my back. My landlady, the ob-gyn, mentioned casually that men sometimes experience menopause. "Rare," she noted, sipping her chai, "but it does happen."

Why was she telling me this?

People were beginning to dislike me. My friends were starting to find me lame. "When we hang out," my friend and prison colleague Mary Beth told me, "I feel like I'm visiting my great-grandfather." My ex-landlady was leaving passive-aggressive phone messages accusing me of not spending enough time with her; my longtime, recently long distance girlfriend and I were losing touch. And, of course, Blue Line thought I didn't "look too good."

On top of all that, I found myself having to watch my back for trouble from an emotionally stunted prison guard. A schoolyard feud between the officer and me had spiraled out of control. Suddenly I found myself facing disciplinary action for, of all things, "laying hands" on him.

That's right: I, the prison's librarian, stood accused of *assaulting* a veteran prison guard, a man trained to subdue violent felons. An improbable charge, certainly. But in prison, nothing is really improbable. That the accusation was false—okay, mostly false—was irrelevant. Prisons overflow with people claiming they've been charged falsely. Now I'd officially joined their ranks, another chump who'd caught a case.

Caught a case is prisonese for getting in trouble with the law. The expression echoes common idioms like "caught a cold." It implies passivity, inevitability. There's something distinctly casual in it. For many in prison, this is indeed the point: catching a nasty little case of gun possession, murder in the first degree, or selling heroin in prison, assaulting an officer—*hey, shit happens*, goes the refrain among those who catch a case, *wrong place, wrong time*. Criminal cases float in the air like pathogens and might infect you at any moment. People catch cases all the time. It's part of everyday life, common as the cold. Now I had caught my own mild case. Prison has always had its own diseases. In the early modern period it was called "prison fever" and it infected inmates, jailers, and even visitors who had come to reform the place. Nobody is immune.

The essence of my strain of prison fever wasn't mysterious, just persistent. It boiled down to this: I was, according to a shrink, "having trouble leaving my work at work." I was assured this was "mostly in my head." I just needed to relax a bit.

And that was precisely why I'd decided to see a movie after my last shift during a particularly bleak week in January. Something completely escapist. As luck would have it, *Jackass 2* was in the cheap theater. I called the stupidest person I knew (at the time). We were to meet at the theater. He had trouble finding it.

Perhaps it was my exhaustion with prison, or my low expectations, or the disarmingly childlike enthusiasm of my companion that evening, but the movie delivered. Happily ignoring its deeply nihilistic undertones, I gave myself over to a night in the land of *Jackass*, readily accepting the fantasy of buoyant and freewheeling guyness. Who can quibble with a dude running his skateboard full speed into a brick wall, or a blindfolded guy, in only his underwear, crawling on all fours through a giant room of armed mouse traps, or a group of stoners driving a golf cart through a golf course, crashing it repeatedly and with increasingly shocking violence? This was great fun. It was as if the id had driven the superego deep into the woods and abandoned it there. It was a world free of moral seriousness, of crime without consequences, without prison.

After the movie, I took the T home. I got lucky, just barely catching the last train. The car was full of happy drunks and couples in love for the night. I arrived at my stop, the Green Street station on the Orange Line, feeling sufficiently groovy. But it was always at those moments that my thoughts switched to the inmates and

guards: while I'd enjoyed a night on the town, stopping in ten different locales all over the city, they hadn't moved an inch. Still sitting
under the same fluorescent lights, still staring at the same cinderblock walls painted institutional colors. Still breathing that prison
air. Another few hours lost to the abyss. Prison never closes.

I remember what Boat said. He was an old Boston wiseguy, a former bank robber and mobster recently hired to the library's inmate
staff, joining Fat Kat, Dice, and the rest. Boat liked to give me advice.
"There's plenty a shit to go around here, kid," he'd said one day,
while we were stamping books. "The windows in here are sealed
shut. No circulation. You breathe the same fuckin' diseased air we
breathe." I really didn't need to hear this. "You stay in here long
enough," he continued, "you take in that air? It gets all up into your
cells and shit? You'll take it with you. You'll *never* get it out of your
system." I thanked him for the public service message. He was, I suspect, trying to be helpful.

I emerged from the subway station into the chilly evening.
Jamaica Plain, my neighborhood of less than two months. Through
the crystalline winter air, downtown Boston glistened in the east.
There I spotted a sign. That single cautionary word—PRUDENTIAL—
glowed high in the heavens, beaconing from the crest of the sky-
scraper. *Prudence*, an antiquated word that sums up my hometown's
patrimony of dread and pessimism. I promptly wrapped a scarf
around my neck, adjusted my hat, zipped up my coat.

As I turned left to walk home, I heard a voice behind me. Barely
audible. Muffled.

"Go into the park," it said.

He shoved me.

"Don't *fuckin'* run," said the voice. "I got a gun. Walk normal,
give me the money in the park."

I tried not to look at him. I took a deep breath. There was a police station around the corner. This guy's audacity worried me. But I stayed calm and so did he. At least, for the moment.

"I'm getting my money out now," I said, putting my hand into my pocket.

There was no cash. Any semblance of calm drained out in a cold sweat. I reached into my other pocket. There'd been an ATM stop outside of the theater. Forty bucks. I could breathe again.

"Let's stay calm, okay," I said, speaking more to myself than to him. He didn't respond.

I stopped in the park and held out the money toward him, two crisp twenty-dollar bills, plus a few singles, all folded up to seem like more. I was calm, but my hands were shaking. I looked at the ground and caught a glimpse of his weapon, not a gun, but a six-inch knife, slightly rusted along the edges, concealed under a long shredded sleeve. I sensed he was looking at me. He took the money. But didn't move.

Why isn't he leaving?

"Hey," he said suddenly. There was a new, unidentifiable tenor in his voice. "You work at the Bay?"

Every single joint in my body tensed. My throat locked. It was true: my work *was* following me home. It wasn't in my head.

Here is what I should have said: *The Bay? What's that? A seafood place? Never heard of it.*

But I didn't. Instead, I turned to him. He was tall and thin. Long arms, steady shoulders. He wore a blue ski mask with a worn-out black hood over it.

"Yeah," I said, "I run the library there."

"Yeah, *shit*!" he said, his Spanish accent coming on strong now. "I *remember* you, man. The *book guy*!"

"Right," I sighed, "the book guy."

If this were an inspirational prison movie, this would be the point at which he would have given the money back to me, cried, and thanked me for believing in him (just as "Lean on Me" cues in on the soundtrack). I, also in tears, would grab him just as he was about to leave and tell him that he didn't have to do this anymore. There would be more tears. He would turn his life around; I would have learned an important lesson about the power of books to transform lives, about the inherent goodness of people, or whatever. The last scene would show me in a stupid tweed jacket, a few more wrinkles in my face and a sprinkle of white in my hair, as I take my seat at a UN ceremony honoring my reformed mugger for a lifetime achievement in humanitarian causes. But that's not what happened.

A long second passed. I got the distinct feeling that he was smiling behind his mask. He signaled to someone in the distance, turned away, and jogged briskly into the park with my forty-three bucks, earned at the prison that had, until recently, held him. Perhaps this was justice. I'm not one to say.

He however did have something to say.

"Hey," he yelled, from about twenty feet away, "*I still owe you guys two books.*"

And then he disappeared, laughing, into the night.

In his careworn, gravel-voiced, is-he-doing-a-Pacino-impression way, Boat continued laughing at me for weeks afterward. (I shouldn't have told inmates about the mugging, I later realized.) At every opportunity he'd repeat the line, "Hey, you work at the Bay?" With the help of his cane, he'd drag his shot-up legs across the library, and interrupt me with a mock earnest, "Hey, you work at the Bay?"

He told me that I shouldn't dwell on the fact that the mugger robbed me of my money and mocked me.

"Bottom line," said Boat, leaning on his cane, getting serious, "this cocksucker didn't stab you in the throat, right? He's got a personal beef with you, he woulda. *Believe* me. You gotta focus on the right facts here."

I didn't quite agree. And, in any case, soon there were some new facts to contend with. My anxiety had caught up with me. As luck would have it, it happened in the library one afternoon. While moving cartons of books, a sudden, crippling back spasm buckled my knees, sending the contents of an entire box, dozens of books, cascading out of my hands. The books had been destined for my pet shelf, the Classics section. My back was clenching like an angry fist. I couldn't breathe without sending a scalding pain through my lower back, legs, and arms, right down to my fingertips and toes. I couldn't even reach for my glasses sitting on the floor next to me. I couldn't move. Over a year and half in prison and now this, the floor.

I looked up and saw a young inmate in a tan prison uniform. He was licking a bootlegged prison lollypop and regarding me with detached curiosity.

"*Daaaamn*," he said, swiveling the lollypop from his mouth and shaking his head in what was, perhaps, sympathy. "That's a bad hit, cuz."

Was I just knifed?

It certainly felt that way. In prison, you can't rule it out. Alas the stabbing pain was internal, self-generated. The mind can do this. My former friend and mugger didn't need to stab me that night in front of the train station. He needed only propose the idea. My body gladly finished the job. Before Boat, Dice, Fat Kat, or any of the other loyal men on my staff could rally me to my feet, I had a moment alone, flat on the floor.

I understood why religions conduct prayers from down there. There's a certain irrefutable eloquence to a floor. You can't help but adopt an honest perspective. I recalled something an inmate had recently told me. As a laborer he had actually helped construct the current prison facility in 1990. He had laid down steel for the very building in which he was now imprisoned, the 3-Building.

"That's a hell of a mind fuck," he told me. "You're sitting there locked in this small fuckin' cell, feeling like shit and about to go out of your mind, and you're thinking: *Christ, I built this.*"

We build our own prisons. Usually, by accident. And so it was that, lying on a polluted prison floor, incapacitated and half-blind, surrounded by a messy pile of the Great Books, I was forced to consider the existential question. The question that takes on a peculiar twist for a prison worker who, unlike an inmate, *chooses* to spend his days in prison. That deceptively simple question buried deep in *The Jailer* by Sylvia Plath, in a book lodged somewhere in the pile next to me on the prison floor.

How did I get here? asks the poet.

Signifiers of Bunnyness

Two years earlier, on a warm April afternoon, as the sun cast long shadows over the Massachusetts Bay Colony, as slim trees stretched out in their cottony pink and white delicates, I arrived at the Hyatt Hotel in Cambridge, Mass. A friend from high school was getting married—almost all of my former classmates were married, many with children. All I had to my name was a haircut that resembled a bad toupee and a stalled novel, *Easy Go*—a title chosen, after weeks of deliberation, over *Easy Come*—whose first line went, "I sing of legs and the woman," an homage to the opening of Virgil's *Aeneid*: "I sing of arms and the man." The novel was pretty much downhill from there.

Under the toupee-hair, my brain was in commotion, afflicted by half-cocked ideas: To start a cable network that played nonstop bar mitzvah videos, complete with commentary. To open a business renting puppies by the hour to help people attract dates. New plot twists for *Easy Go*. These schemes left me more than spaced out; I was functionally senile.

That spring day, I walked, slightly dazed, up to the hotel, an edifice along the Charles River that bears a strong resemblance to a ziggurat, a striking sight, even to one who is not strung out and stoned. I, however, was both. A few years out of college, I was still contemplating my future. Let me amend that: I was having the early stages of a drug-induced panic attack about my future. Short of breath, a bleak strain of agoraphobia and doom rising in my chest, I pulled out a wrinkled yarmulke from my wrinkled jacket pocket, clipped it to the toupee-hair, and proposed to myself but one modest goal for the evening: to avoid my former rabbis.

Deep in indirection, I was anxious about appearing before my former community. In the past, these weddings left me feeling crappy and rejected. As an unabashed breaker of Jewish law, I was no longer permitted to take part in the serious, legally binding tasks at the Orthodox weddings of my friends. Not permitted to serve as a witness and sign the *ketubbah*, the marriage contract. Even at close friends' weddings, at which I would certainly have been given this duty, I was instead given nominal tasks designed to make me feel included but which actually served to remind me that I was a persona non grata, relegated to the Talmud's club of second-class losers: children, slaves, hermaphrodites, the mentally deranged, and women.

But in my community a sin graver even than religious treachery was professional inadequacy. My yeshiva high school's basketball team was named not the Tigers or the Hawks, but the MCATS. As in, the Medical College Admission Test. This was a joke, but not a joke. If you weren't on a track to becoming some variety of lawyer, businessman, or doctor, if you weren't en route to grad school or a post-graduation job at a bank, you were guilty of something worse than worshipping Baal (which is at least an ambitious pursuit). From the various weddings I'd attended in the past months, I already had a reasonable idea how the small talk would go. A chat with the father of a former classmate a few months earlier had provided a rough template:

RICH BALD GUY: Now what is it you do? You write death notices?

ME: Obituaries.

RBG: Isn't that the same thing?

ME: Obituaries are articles; death notices are lists of dead people.

RBG: But the articles are about dead people.

ME: Yeah.

RBG: Well, you seem like a nice guy, I'm sure something will come along.

ME: Thanks.

RBG: Can you make a living off writing death notices?

ME: Obituaries.

RBG: Right.

ME: Well . . .

RBG: How are you going to afford to send your kids to Jewish schools?

ME: I don't know, maybe I won't have kids. Or maybe I won't have Jewish kids.

This suitably horrifying answer had done the trick—but I didn't know how many more times I could put myself through the emotional strain. I considered walking around wordlessly as hors d'oeuvres were being served with one of those long-winded panhandler signs: *Hello, I am living in sin. I have forsaken the Torah and strayed far from the Orthodox community. My rabbis were right about Harvard. All I did was chase girls, do drugs, and write a carefully argued, typo-ridden satire of a senior thesis paper on Bugs Bunny. "This essay," I wrote, "will explore the iconography and signifiers of Bunnyness in the context of wartime cinema, that is, in the wartime theater as both a capitalist venue and aesthetic-ideological spectacle." These days I earn poverty wages as a freelance obituary writer. I know I need a haircut.*

My college career had run exactly like the morality plays drilled into me at yeshiva, the kind of cautionary tale that illustrates why "secular college" was thoroughly *treyf*, or unkosher: Sure, a *ben torah*, a learned and pious Jewish kid, goes to college with the best of intentions, determined to pray three times a day, keep kosher, keep *shabbes*, the holidays, the fasts, learn Torah for *x* hours a day, wear his yarmulke and *tzitzis* with pride, stay away from girls—and especially, Heaven help us!, from *shiksas*—before long, though, even this *ben torah* will be drunk, on all fours in Dunster House on a Friday night, on Yom Kippur, unlatching the stately bra of a junior from rural Pennsylvania, whom he met in a core class on Islam. As the rabbis say, the rest is commentary.

It's not as if there weren't warnings. On a junior year trip to see my grandparents, I had overheard my beloved grandfather, a shtetl-born grocer, "whisper" to my grandmother, in his agreeable Midwestern accent, "You know, he's reading these Shakespeare books. I'm worried he has no, you know, direction."

"You might be right," said Grandma Edna, flipping through her *Hadassah* magazine.

"And," added Grandpa, "he's dressing like some kind of beatnik."

There'd been earlier warnings. In the "Destination" section of my yeshiva high school yearbook, my fate was described in these terms: "Avi's destination . . . is to be a shepherd in the Negev desert." As a seventeen-year-old religious nut, this warmed my heart, vindicated my adolescent spiritual yearnings. Now, in hindsight, I could see the designation as it had been intended: that I was a bit of loner and romantic, destined neither for gainful employment nor a useful role in the twenty-first century.

In a worrying recent development, my good friend, Yoni, who was even more aimless than I, expressed concern about my direction. As we prepared for the wedding with a pipe of medicinal pot, he asked if I was happy writing obituaries.

I paused to consider this question. Yoni grew impatient.

"I mean," he said, "obviously that's not *really* what you wanted to be doing now, right? I'm assuming that's not what you hope to be doing with your *life*."

I expected this from the bald rich man—but Yoni? This was a guy who'd sent me hallucinogenic emails from Amsterdam, during his infamous layovers: *I've lost track of time,* he'd written in one. *That's what happens when you don't sleep regularly and nab various half-hours on park benches. My body is weary. I need dignity. The Van Gogh museum was an unbelievable experience. There were some real lows but some real highs. I am writing down where I need to be otherwise I'll get lost. I have to remind myself at times that I am not clinically insane. My flight is at 2:50. I'd say 95% chance I'm on it.*

I wasn't sure what to say to his question about writing obits. Unsatisfied by my continued reflective silence, Yoni listed, for my dispassionate consideration, various mutual friends who were, he noted, outperforming me in my chosen field of writing. He detailed those who had better jobs, better insurance plans, better party invites, major awards, people who were getting serious book deals, selling screenplays to major studios, getting raves in the *New York Times*. And here I was, he observed, writing freelance articles about people who, in addition to being obscure, were now also dead.

"You're not exactly 'living the dream,'" he pointed out. "How does that feel? Does that *suck?*"

A word about Yoni: It's true he wasn't great at reading social cues or anticipating/obeying basic sensitivities in others. But he meant no harm. He was just curious. Yoni subsisted on a diet of six to twenty cups of coffee a day and canned string beans stir-fried in a witch's brew of ranch dressing and massively ill-proportioned dry spices. He spent most of his college years dazed and unshowered, wandering Harvard Yard in filthy hot-orange sweatpants pulled up like pantaloons. His current job involved wearing a six-foot-tall cougar costume at high school football games in the Deep South, where he tried in vain to ward off platoons of middle schoolers who assaulted him with kamikaze fervor. Yoni was a man convinced a hemorrhoid affliction was explained by his grandmother's childhood diagnosis that he had "an unusually small anus"; who was once ejected from

Fenway Park for heckling; who was literally moved to tears by a slow, acoustic version of "Ob-la-di, Ob-la-da" he performed in the subway during a period of unemployment.

Yoni didn't judge others. There was something about his transparence, his vulnerable blend of impatience, suggestibility, and ardor that inspired me to tell the truth.

"Yeah," I said, "it sucks."

"Aw, man. That's some heavy shi—," he said, swallowing the end of his thought with a giant gulp from his water pipe.

I had to concede the point. My job was freelance, meaning I got paid almost nothing per article, forced to hustle hard to make rent. I had neither job security, nor health benefits. I was effectively broke.

To compound matters, I had recently suffered a bit of a demotion, even within this humble station of mine. I had been writing metro news and features for my hometown paper, the *Boston Globe*. Yet for quixotic reasons—namely, that I enjoyed writing obits— I had decided to scale back on articles about city life in order to write exclusively about the city's dead. For even less money. It was a strange and inexplicable career move.

And there was other bad news from the front. Newspapers weren't hiring. I was told not to expect a promotion at the *Globe*, regardless of how hard I worked. The rickety ship of newspaper journalism was rapidly sinking. Everyone was telling me, Get out while you can. An editor told me that if I stayed too long, there would be only two obits left to write: the *Boston Globe*'s and mine. I dealt with his joke with characteristic aplomb and a mild case of stress-induced hives.

I knew that writing obits would be short-lived. But, since I enjoyed the work, I'd delayed searching for something new. Then one day, while helping a sweet but disorganized young anarchist, a friend of my family, find a job, I came across an unusual ad on Craig's List. It was brief: *Boston, Prison Librarian, full time, union benefits.* I certainly hadn't known that prisons hired full-time librarians. To me, libraries and prisons seemed like polar opposites. Perhaps even at cross-purposes, like a pie-baking class at Marine boot camp. Something about it sounded fishy. Out of sheer curiosity I inquired about the job.

The more I learned, though, the more interested I became. At first, I'd assumed that switching from the corpse beat to prison work would be, from an existential perspective, a lateral move. But as a woman from the prison described the position to me over the phone, I became aware of the things absent from my current work life: there was a strong social dimension to this new job, I'd be working as part of a big staff and doing some teaching. Working as an obituary man, I was starting to get lonely, disconnected.

Best of all was the promise of job security and health insurance. But, still, I was on the fence. Was this another half-baked scheme, like the All Bar Mitzvah Network?

These were the questions churning around my feverish brain as I made my rounds at the wedding. It was the hors d'oeuvres hour—affectionately known in Orthodox circles as "the shmorg," which, though short for smorgasbord, is actually more like fifteen pornographically proportioned smorgasbords.

Through my uncut bangs, I observed my former classmates. They were becoming bankers, doctors, lawyers, professors, rabbis. They were getting married, and many already had their first children. They were landowners, budding philanthropists, pillars of their communities. They had retirement funds, and college funds for their infants. They were busy with serious commitments. And religious.

In the midst of my panic-attack doom-and-gloom, I reaffirmed my commitment to not becoming a good Orthodox Jewish doctor or lawyer. The most notorious Jewish terrorists of recent times, Baruch Goldstein, who gunned down twenty-nine Palestinians at prayer in Hebron, and Yigal Amir, the man who murdered Prime Minister Yitzhak Rabin were a good Orthodox Jewish doctor and a good Orthodox Jewish lawyer, respectively. You didn't see formerly Orthodox obituary writers gunning anyone down.

But aside from not engaging in religious-fueled political violence, I wasn't sure what I wanted. And, to my dismay, the yearbook prediction made by these very people was surprisingly accurate. *Avi will be a shepherd in the Negev.* Here I was, seven years hence, out to pasture, living hand-to-mouth. Even more disturbing was the fear that this figurative sense of being out to pasture might, eventually, lead to the quite literal version. If a shepherding position had opened up, I probably would have sent in a résumé.

To my great relief, these waves of anxiety were kept at bay by the simple comforts provided so generously, so systematically, by the shmorg. The unbridled, unrepentant American Jewish optimism that finds expression in the cocktail weenie dipped in a whole mustard sauce; skyscrapers and oceanliners of sushi; small piles of the flaky, the spinachy, the mushroomy; skewers of barbecued Korean steak tips and Hawaiian chicken; corned beef, pastrami, and turkey carving stations; breads, egg rolls, crepes, pastas, salads, fishes, tofus, fruit baskets the square footage of medium-sized New York City apartments. And booze. All of it served as a softening agent to conversations about what *shul* I belonged to or what product just became kosher and made it fun to listen to gossip regarding a certain married woman's Orthodox-mandated wig ("you wouldn't *believe* how much she paid for it"). There were worse ways to pass a Sunday evening.

But, still, I was sticking to my mission. Avoid rabbis. I'd already been to too many events in which I'd ended up in heated debates, condemned for my move to irreligiosity.

I had disappointed my teachers, many of whom I still admired. I obeyed none of the Jewish laws. Nothing. I was a complete heretic. Their displeasure was magnified by the fact that I had once been a promising, or, at least, devoted, yeshiva student.

Some highlights from my youth as a zealot. At age fourteen, I quit my yeshiva high school basketball team—the mighty MCATS—to dedicate myself to the study of Torah. I walked around with a pocket edition of the *Mishna*, the central Jewish legal text, codified in the third century, and studied the cover off of it. During any lull in the day, and I mean *any*, I'd whip it out. Whenever there was literally a second to spare, walking down the hall, waiting for a bus, for five minutes between classes, for fifteen seconds while a teacher paused to find his place in a book. I took the rabbinic injunction of "not wasting a moment for the study of Torah" literally.

I didn't stop there. Unhappy that my school, whose schedule was a mere 8 a.m. to 6 p.m., offered only one and a half hours of Talmud a day, I lobbied successfully for an extra, voluntary Talmud class on Wednesday nights that met until 7:30. I passed on Dylan tickets to attend a weekly Saturday night Torah discussion group (that I had organized). I founded and ran a Torah-studies journal. Refused to shake women's hands. Won an award at graduation for commitment to Torah study. Spent an inordinate number of teenage hours in silent prayer.

During summers, I'd jet off to a yeshiva in a West Bank settlement and study for fourteen hours a day. Talmud Camp in the ancient Judean heartland, a.k.a. the Occupied Territories—this was my paradise. Even my parents, who were religious, were concerned about my fervor.

For my senior year project I didn't get an internship at a newspaper or a research lab. I didn't volunteer at a soup kitchen. Instead I sat in solitude and studied the volume of the Talmud dedicated to corporeal punishment. As indicated by its refreshingly straightforward title, *Lashes*, this legal volume explores, in pitiless detail, the dozens of instances in which the rabbis reserved the right to arrest an offender and flog the crap out of this person (literally, as they note in chapter three). And how it was done. The strangest part about my careful study of *Lashes* was that I didn't find it strange at all. Neither did my rabbis, who were in fact quite encouraging.

After high school, I spent two years in yeshiva, first on the West Bank and then in New York City. But now I neglected the whole thing. I was a big-time Orthodox failure.

I n the bathroom at the wedding my plan came to an abrupt end when a stall opened and Rabbi Blumenthal emerged. I'd never fully appreciated how much like a pygmy owl Rabbi Blumenthal looked. He was short, compact, with a fine, close-cropped beard that seamlessly blended into a close-cropped haircut, forming a white halo around his remarkably round head. This frame offset a small dark face, two large unblinking eyes, a sharp efficient little nose. It might have been an image of diminutive cuteness were it not for its air of menace. The mouth was nowhere to be seen. The eyes just looked and looked and looked and observed and gave nothing away.

Years ago, he had taught us the sublime, morality-intoxicated poetry of the prophet of Isaiah. The class was utter chaos. Nobody had paid attention. Students goofed off incessantly, some sat with their backs to the rabbi, chatting and laughing. People walked about freely, forgetting entirely that there was a teacher at the head of the classroom.

The only students who listened were me and another boy, a Torah prodigy and math wiz whose name was also Avi. We, the two zealots with identical names, sat all the way up front, our two desks pressed right up to the rabbi's and to each other's—a three-bulbed potted Torah plant swaying in the wind.

Now here was Rabbi Blumenthal in the bathroom, unblinking and thoughtful as ever. He washed his hands meticulously, like a surgeon, and made guarded small talk, gathering information about where I'd been these past few years since graduating high school. I told him about Bugs Bunny and obituaries and about my hazy aspirations. In my drug-induced state, I added some weird asides about how nothing really mattered since the sun is going to die anyway. Then I mentioned the possibility of working in a prison library.

The rabbi assumed his raptorial gaze. His eyes narrowed. The killer bird spoke.

"A prison?" he said. "Why would you do that? Don't do that."

"Why not?" I asked.

"You should be involved in the Jewish community. Why would you waste your time with that?"

He adopted an annoyed, but professional, manner and ticked off a litany of questions, which I answered in order. *No*, I confessed, I did not pray or put on *tefillin*. *No*, I did not observe Shabbat or keep kosher. And yes, I added, unprompted, I loved shrimp. *Loved it!* They should serve it at shmorgs.

"What happened to you?" he said.

What *happened?* It's the first question a reporter tries to answer. For an obituary writer, the question is, What happened in this person's life? What were the facts, and what did these facts amount to? Every morning a fateful message would appear in my inbox, an email whose subject line was simply a person's name. McMahon, Kovar-Sletten, Montague, Goolkasian. These were the names of the dead. I would inhabit their realm until bedtime. Often I'd dream about them.

The email from my editor would say something like, "This person seems kind of interesting, why don't you check her out." This message, in which an entire life was reduced to "kind of interesting," was the first of many poignant moments in my day. I spoke to as many people as possible. Each interview expanded the story of the life, threw in a new twist. Sometimes there were tears, or laughter. Sometimes bitterness, the disclosure of secrets, of regrets. People would confide in me, speak to me for much longer than they'd intended. It sometimes felt as though I were a rabbi or priest making a pastoral call, helping people cope with the issues of life and death and mourning, especially when I made housecalls for interviews. I would sit with the mourners, look at photographs, old letters, and try to piece together the life.

But, ultimately, my deadline loomed. I was forced to cut the conversation short, sit down, organize competing versions of the biography, the disparate details, the secrets and semi-secrets, inconclusive plotlines, mysteries, coincidences, and moments of truth, and make sense of an entire life in a thousand words. The conclusion of the obituary, a person's life story, was a simple, deceptively neutral list of names, the survivors. The omissions to this list and its length — extended or brief — often articulated more than any quotation could.

When you write obits it is impossible to avoid thinking of death—or more precisely, of the totality of a life: why it turned out the way it did, how it might have turned out differently, how one thing led to the next (usually by accident), what decisions and crucibles a person faced, what was left behind. I had pieced together the lives of many people, but hadn't dared do it for myself.

In the hotel ballroom, the music started.

The joy at an Orthodox Jewish wedding borders on desperation. Before long, it gives way to fits of mania, first individual, then collective, culminating in widespread hysteria and, finally, in small-scale acts of violence. It is the ultimate release of the community's worst fears, stewing for millennia: the never-ending sense of persecution, a feeling so dense and often justified that it itself is a form of persecution. The wedding is a celebration of a new young family with its promise that at least another generation, a new guard of Jews, will help stem the tide of history, repel the constantly impending genocide at the hands of notable haters, Pharaoh, Haman, Hitler, Stalin, Ahmadinejad, and Mel Gibson—and, worse, the self-haters within the community who aid this cause by marrying gentiles, eating shrimp cocktail, criticizing Israel's right wing, or making Holocaust jokes.

This outpouring, coupled with the effects of alcohol on people who are of below average height and don't tend to drink, can be dramatic. Which is to say, things get rowdy.

It doesn't take long before the trappings of a Western wedding ceremony, with its stifling pageantry, fall by the wayside, and the truth emerges: a Jewish wedding is a hoedown, sweaty and tribal. Buttoned-up outfits—designed for cocktails on moonlit verandahs—

quickly become a hindrance. Men loosen their black ties and toss away their jackets, women hike up their gowns (modestly). Respected physicians and CEOs juggle, lift each other onto their shoulders, throw each other in the air, break-dance, wrap their arms around each other, catcall, hug strangers. Meanwhile, the waitstaff stand by and exchange looks.

The music is low-klezmer, the lyrics high-biblical. Still divided by sex—men on one side of the floor, women on the other, a physical barrier set down between—the dancing is manic and intensely circular. These are not polite circle dances. This isn't a lazy Sunday morning "Hava Nagila" through the park. These are hard-driving, frenetic, Darwinian merry-go-rounds of testosterone.

There is a lot of pushing. The circles get tight and competitive. People push to get things moving forward. Inevitably some guys will try to get to the inner circle. They too begin pushing. For reasons pertaining to physics, psychology, and theology, the inner circle is the most aggressive and dizzying dancing the human body can endure. In order to get that circle moving, you push.

I'm not saying the community of my youth is loud and pushy. Only that they're in earnest. They don't half-ass things; they mean business. When the rabbi says, "You *must* make the bride and groom happy," it means you make them delirious until they're pummeled within an inch of their lives and left for dead by the side of the dance floor. I understand this well because I've been an active participant in this enterprise.

At my best, I was more sincere than ten bearded Hasidic men combined. I've been to scores of Orthodox weddings. I've pushed. I've been pushed. I've pushed hundreds, possibly thousands, of my fellow Orthodox Jews. I've pushed on the Sabbath and I've pushed during the week. I've had people pushed into me, I've pushed people into other people. I've been pushed by children, by the elderly. I've pushed children, pushed the elderly. This is how it goes. I don't regret it. I'd do it again. But I'd lost the touch long ago.

Perhaps it was the drug, which had now run its course, or the stress from running into my old rabbis and classmates, perhaps it was the cumulative sense of having had enough of monotheism, but that day I was incapable of jostling and being jostled. You might even say I was feeling a bit vulnerable. I let my guard down. This would be a big mistake.

The punch that came blind from my right was in no way predictable. The first split-second was characterized by the almost obscene slap of a sweat-drenched hairy fist to my cheek, next to my nose, followed by a bone-to-bone, knuckle-to-face whip crack. My head snapped. The room upended. I was cheek to parquet floor, at a ninety-degree angle from the world.

Nobody cared. It's not that they were callous. They simply didn't notice. Onward, in an endless cycle, they marched. Dressy legs and shiny shoes stomped next to me, a few on me. There were too many people, too much pushing, for someone to stop and help. If a guy were to stop *he* might get pushed down or, like me, clocked. Who would risk it?

I knew the rules: on the carousel of testosterone, there are winners and losers. I had lost. Only the well-adapted survive. I got exactly what I deserved. Knowing this, however, did not make me feel better.

I looked up. Dancing expressionlessly was Rabbi Blumenthal. I was seized by the suspicion that it was he who had popped me, in fulfillment of the rabbinic dictum for dealing with the Bad Son, "you strike him in the teeth . . ." For a moment, I entertained the thought of jumping up and taking him out. Then I realized this was an awful idea—one of my worst. Then I realized he'd have been right to punch me.

I had to admit that my head-pounding could have a pedagogic function. In the past it had.

On a school trip to Toronto senior year of high school we had played laser tag (what else does one do in Toronto?). The major rule of laser tag at the laser arena/funzone place in Toronto was *no running*. We were told again and again. "Absolutely no running." When I heard this, I guffawed to myself: No way I'm following *that* rule. Toronto had been godawful and now, given a chance to let off some steam, I was amped, raring to do battle, eager to get into the field, scout out a perch or two and commence the laser carnage. I wanted nothing short of the fucking lasertag battle of Midway.

I was all over the place, blasting people right and left. I was runnin' and gunnin' like a disgruntled Texan. Late in the game, when only a few fighters remained, I scoped out a nice high spot, called for cover, got it, and, of course, ran to get there. At that point, I'd completely forgotten that there was even a rule against running.

I saw the danger only once it was too late. The guy running directly at me was moving quickly and unrelentingly forward. I remember my last thought, right before we collided head-on, at full speed: *Jesus Christ, who's that crazy asshole running* right *at me?* As I fell back, my glasses busted on my head, my nose exploded in blood, and my sensor unit buzzing after sustaining a direct shot from an opponent, I looked up and saw my own beat-up face staring back at me. In my thirst for laser dominance I'd disregarded the tenets of basic optics. I'd run headlong into a mirrored wall. Turned out the crazy asshole running at me *was* me.

But this is how I learn: by stubbornly doing things my own way until I run face-first into a wall. Frankly, I'm grateful for that wall.

Back in the bathroom at the wedding I looked at my face in the mirror. There wasn't that much blood and I soaked up what there was of it. My head ached but I felt lucid for the first time in a long while, possibly years, and was struck by an urge to make decisions about my life.

Got to get a haircut. Go to the dentist. Get in shape. Get more organized. Pay my taxes on time. Figure out my life. Stop being a damn beatnik. Get my shit together. Perhaps let Easy Go *go.*

Looking at myself in the mirror, an old, favorite prayer returned to me. It is said when the Messiah arrives or when you see a long-lost friend:

Blessed are you God, who revives the dead.

The punch to the face, which may or may not have been delivered by the rabbi, had knocked me off of the fence. I lingered for a moment in this marvelous clarity of mind. Clear about what I knew and did not know.

Rabbi Blumenthal had educated me well. He had taught me to take the prophets seriously. Yet, earlier at the wedding he'd said, "You should be involved in the Jewish community." Why, he'd argued, waste time working in a prison? Is this any place for a good Jewish boy?

But, as he knew, the prophets had spent time among outcasts and criminals. Many *were* criminals—and not just for their revolutionary ideas. Isaiah, like many brilliant preachers, had a weakness for indecent exposure. Elisha committed first-degree murder when someone made fun of his hair. Abraham did time; Joseph did time;

Jeremiah did time; Daniel did time. So did Samson. Jacob was a con man who spent most of his life on the lam. Both Moses and Elijah were fugitives for committing murder. And so was David, until he returned with a loyal gang of outlaws. The prophet Hosea had a notorious predilection for hookers. Nearly every single one of the prophets was either a criminal or had spent time among criminals. Clearly the prophets themselves believed there was something to learn in prison, even if Rabbi Blumenthal did not.

I decided to apply for the job as a prison librarian. The idea of it had been with me for weeks. Now was the moment to admit it was something I wanted, perhaps needed, to do. I wasn't sure why, exactly. It probably had something to do with my education. Harvard was a lovely assisted-living facility from which I'd emerged, like my classmates, stupider and more confident. I still had a lot to learn. When I imagined grad school, though, all I could see was long, passionately argued footnotes on the iconography of Bugs Bunny's carrot—I wasn't going to be of any use to a university, and vice versa. And so the choice crystallized in my mind: It was either law school or prison. The decision was clear.

I ran back out into the wedding celebration and found Yoni. Bathed in sweat, wearing some type of tribal headdress, his tux in tatters, he was bellowing a rowdy Hebrew fight song that called for the Messiah to immediately restore the Great Temple in Jerusalem on the site of the Temple Mount.

"I think I'm going to apply for that job," I said.

"What?" he shouted. The music was blaring.

"I think I'm going to prison," I shouted into his ear.

He flashed a big grin.

"Nice," he shouted back. "And honestly, dude? It'd probably do you some good."

The Hair Test

"While I don't have a degree in library science," I reasoned in a cover letter, "I possess both the skills and motivation to be a successful prison librarian." This was résumé talk. The truth: I had never stepped foot in a prison nor worked as a librarian. Until I'd come across the listing, I hadn't even known such a job existed.

I was interviewed by three people. The director of the prison's Education Department—which sounded ominous to me—the union boss, and the head of personnel.

The blunt questions came from the union boss, Charlie (pronounced the Boston way, *Chah*lie).

"Where'd you grow up?" he asked.

"A bit in Cleveland," I said, "but mostly in Boston."

"Oh yeah, where?"

"Cambridge."

His eyes narrowed. "Cambridge," he said, "is *not* Boston."

Coming from a man raised in the Irish projects of Dorchester, a proud union man, this comment had a particular resonance: he was calling me out as a child of Cambridge privilege who either didn't know the difference between an Ivy League enclave and the big working-class city or, worse, was posing as a city kid.

"Yeah," I said, "but we have excellent views of Boston from our condos."

Charlie seemed to like this answer.

"You know," he said. "We don't like newspaper reporters, especially those know-it-alls at the *Globe*. Why should we let you in?"

He said this with a smile. But he was serious. And it was a good question. I danced around it and mentioned that, having recently quit reporting on living people, I didn't pose too much of a threat.

After Charlie finished his routine, the head of the Education Department presented me with some scenarios and asked how I would deal with each one. The answer was the same each time: I'd defer to the security personnel.

"We need team players here," she said.

"I could do that," I replied, realizing immediately that my answer subtly revealed a deeper truth, a psychological insight that, until that point, I myself had only faintly acknowledged: I'm not much of a team player.

Finally, we reached the last question. *Is there anything else you'd like us to know about you?*

I tried not to allow my eyes to widen before this delicious feast of a question. There were so many possibilities. Did they want to know that I read *Cat Fancy* magazine? That my feet are flat and duck-like? That my initials are A.S.S.? Were they angling at something specific? Were they asking if I'm gay? A Zionist? I decided not to chance a reply. Instead mustered up a "No, I think that just about covered everything."

This seemed to do the trick. I was told the position—which included working as a librarian and a creative writing teacher—was mine. That is, on condition my background check was clean and that I passed a drug test.

"No problem," I said.

And I had thought it wasn't. But, as it turned out, I was wrong. I realized after the interview that my pre-wedding smoke with Yoni—roughly two months earlier—would most certainly pose a problem.

What would happen if I failed the drug test? This wasn't a typical employer. It was, after all, the Sheriff's Department. The guy who'd sold Yoni the marijuana might be sitting in a cell in this very prison. I had a bad feeling about this.

When the head of personnel called to discuss benefits and payment plans she asked me point blank, "Are you going to pass this test?"

"Yes," I replied reflexively, "of course."

How did she know to ask, I wondered. Was there something about me? The nefarious moptop? Did she really want to discuss this issue openly? Blissfully ignorant of the prison's internal investigative division, and their habit of tapping phone conversations, I decided to level with her, thinking perhaps she'd give me a break.

"Well," I said, "I did . . . smoke. Once. I mean most recently, a while ago though—at a party. I mean, it was a wedding, actually. And it was obviously *before* the wedding. The party at the wedding, I mean." I winced. "But that shouldn't be a problem, right?"

Dead silence.

"Hello?" I said.

"It's a heya tess," she said finally.

On the phone, and thrown off balance, I was having trouble with the Boston brogue.

"A what?" I asked.

I heard her sigh. She didn't want to discuss this further.

"Heya tess," she said and quickly changed the subject to dental plan options.

That night I searched online for information on drug screening. Within two clicks, I understood that the woman from personnel had been trying to tip me off: I was facing a *hair test*. I delved into the minutiae of this screening method. In addition to being alarmingly accurate, it also covered a longer period of time than the imprecise, tamper-prone urinalysis. Apparently hair, even more than urine, is articulate of its master's misdeeds.

This didn't surprise me. I'd always held quiet beliefs about hair, vague but persistent suspicions of a treacherous, even demonic, aspect, the more sinister for its allure. It grows beautifully even though it's dead. That's creepy. I'd always sensed it wasn't to be trusted.

Now was the time to act. The incriminating data was hidden at a certain point in every strand of hair on my head. I had to locate, then remove, evidence—a wonderful start to a job at the Sheriff's Department. There was only one surefire way to accomplish this: to shave my head completely. But I'd been taught etiquette, and it was bad manners to arrive at a hair test with no hair. I'd have to take a risk, tell Manny the barber to go as short as possible, and hope the evidence ended up on the floor of his shop.

I emerged from the barber's—my exposed scalp cool to the breeze—with a chill of doom. Even if I passed the test, I was marked as guilty. The moment my new bosses saw my drastic haircut on the day of the hair test, the sequence of events would be plainly obvious. I was a criminal applying for a job in a prison. I might as well walk into the joint festooned in oversized dollar-sign pendants, wearing an *I ♥ Drugs* T-shirt. I felt so exposed I actually wore a baseball cap on the way to the prison, as though my guilt were apparent to all. I couldn't shake the feeling I was making a misstep in pursuing this. Maybe the woman from personnel had been trying to tell me to quietly drop out.

The thought of turning and fleeing was unavoidable as I neared the front entrance. But before I could weigh this option, I was already walking fatefully into the lobby. Within a second, an officer told me to remove my cap. That was the rule, apparently. No headgear in prison. There was no anonymity, no hiding here.

I sat down on a bench, cap in hand—a gesture that felt comfortingly Victorian—waiting for my potential boss, poised to catch her reaction to my radical new hairdo. Would she smile? What type of smile would it be? Would it be better or worse if she said nothing? This was no way to begin a new job.

But the boss took her time. I had a moment to absorb the surroundings. The lobby was an accumulation of wide gray pillars, like somber votives, which alerted you to the immense weight bearing down from above, the concrete and steel tower balancing overhead. This was a very heavy building. From the moment you entered, you were being watched. You were on record and were meant to know this. You were dimly aware of a control room, which flickered and buzzed behind heavily tinted windows next to the door to the prison—or was it the door to the door of the prison?—located at the far end of the lobby. The officer guarding this door, identified by his name-patch as Grimes, fidgeted with his pistol holster and toyed with the metal detector. He kept a well-worn book of Zen Buddhist philosophy at his post.

It was the three o'clock shift change. Large groups of officers came and went, ribbing each other loudly, dodging children who were running around, doing silly dances, playing hide and seek, while their mothers or grandmothers sat by nervously. The children seemed intimately acquainted with the prison lobby, well-versed in the fun-making dimensions built into the wide pillars. This was, I gathered, where they waited to see daddy or mommy.

A few officers stood nearby, next to a *No Fumar* sign by the front steps, puffing cigarettes and ogling women. Speaking in semi-code, they gossiped about union matters.

"Hey, ya hear Fitzy's taking some heat?"

"Really? For . . ."

"Yup, that."

"No shit?"

"Yah, no shit is *right* . . ."

Both laughed.

An officer approached me with a message. The boss was skipping our meeting. He told me to follow him. What was going on? Had my boss seen my crew cut on a closed-circuit security TV and decided I was a criminal? And if so, where was I being led? I followed the officer, though not without trepidation, into a back hallway. He directed me to some guy named O'Shea, who would administer the hair test. Nothing was wrong—the boss was merely overbooked. I would be spared the awkward encounter.

The hall led to the clubhouse of Local 419, the officers' union. It had vending machines, an empty lounge with a giant sheriff's badge painted on the wall, and a TV that beamed in a daytime talk-show in which a studio audience scrutinized a messy family drama.

Further on were unmarked offices, men's and women's locker rooms. A transistor radio blasted classic rock from an unoccupied weight room. A glass trophy case displayed artifacts and photos from the old prison at Deer Island: a dusty set of nineteenth-century-era handcuffs, shackles—both of which called to mind Harry Houdini— an old-fashioned mug shot number sign, a billy-club and tear gas canister from the neolithic age. Nearby, plaques honored officers from the prison who were serving in the wars. And next to that, a handwritten sign: *Inmates do only as much as you let them.*

I waited a few minutes in front of O'Shea's office, cap in hand. There was no turning back now. Finally, the door swung open and a large man with a buzz cut and a mischievous smirk emerged. He winked at me and said "g' luck" as he walked by. He'd just taken the hair test himself.

The office was cramped, though there was nothing in it. O'Shea was a short, aggrieved man. After a quick *how y'doin'*, he took a few snips of my hair, and sealed it in an envelope. It was an oddly intimate gesture, like he was taking a lock of my hair as a romantic keepsake. Perhaps that was why the conversation turned to sports. We reviewed the Red Sox's prospects. O'Shea was openly disdainful of my optimism.

"I don't care what they did last year," he told me, referring to the Sox World Series title. "They're still the Red Sox and they'll always fold in the clutch. Any asshole can get lucky once in a while."

Sitting in that office, anxious and radically shorn, I readily agreed. I myself was just such an asshole, hoping to get lucky this once.

Two weeks of low-grade dread passed. Finally I got a phone call from personnel. I was to begin ASAP, she said. There was no more talk about the hair test, no *congratulations, you passed the drug screening!* It was official. I was now on the side of angels. The Po-Po. The Fuzz. The Heat. The Big Blue Machine.

The transformation was immediate. Over the weekend, I couldn't help spinning around quickly, scowling into a mirror and saying, "I'm with Johnny Law." Or simply, "Whada *you* lookin' at?" This act was first performed for the benefit of my girlfriend, Kayla. But pretty soon I was doing it all alone, for the benefit of no one.

"I *heard* that," Kayla shouted from the next room, during one of these supposedly private performances. "You better not freak out on me. I know you."

The next Monday I headed off to the prison—or to work, I wasn't sure how I'd refer to it—with a brand new sheriff's badge in my pocket. The photo on it had been taken by O'Shea the day of the hair test, when I hadn't known the outcome, when I was feeling exposed, still feeling as though I were sitting for a mug shot. In the photo, I am captured with the buzz cut and a crooked, bewildered grin. This photo—which I was required to wear at all times—was to be my official image in prison.

The Tour

In Boston, justice is a mom-and-pop shop. Bob throws you into the joint, Patti takes it from there. Patti, director of the prison's Education Department, was my supervisor. She is married to Boston's number-two cop, a perennial candidate for the police commissioner job. Patti agreed with the general perception that Bob was "too rough around the edges, too much of a street cop, not enough of a politician." She said this with some resignation but mostly with pride.

Patti herself was much smoother. She was friendly, smartly dressed, bobbed and highlighted, clearly the hip lady in her weekly fifty-plus knitting group in Dorchester. On my first day, I was an observer. Patti was my tour guide. After drifting through the classrooms, we entered the library. We immediately ran into an inmate, or rather he nearly ran into us. He emerged from the back room, walking briskly with a giant stack of papers tucked under his arm. Patti gave him a skeptical look.

"Hello, Mr. Coolidge," she said.

Coolidge was a tall, stout man with a quick, peckish grin, and a pencil mustache mismatched, or perhaps, overmatched by a large, square head. Wide, intelligent eyes passed judgment with each blink. The tan prison uniform, from the 3-2 unit, was worn as though it were a business suit. Reading glasses dangled from the collar. A fragrant puff emanated from the square head. Could it be? *Le parfum*, in the joint?

As soon as he saw me, he stopped in his tracks, a grand cartoonish gesture, almost hurling his papers into the air. He threw back his head demonstrably. To my surprise, he had a goofy, high-pitched snort of laugh. Patti shot him a look.

Still composing himself, he said, almost shouted, "Are you *kidding* me?" And then to me: "How *old* are you? You in school?"

"No," I replied. "I'm done with school."

"Done with school already? Hey, *congratulations!*"

Patti began to nudge me in the other direction. Coolidge took the cue.

"Awright, awright," he said. "Let's be serious now. How do you feel about black folks? Ever spent time with black people?" This was making his day.

"Um, I have," I said awkwardly, unprepared for this much more pointed second interview. "I grew up in a mixed neighborhood in Cleveland. And at different times of my life. And a lot with my work as a reporter."

I sensed Patti fidget. I was divulging way too much personal info and walking into a variety of traps.

"I've been around a bit," I concluded, "Even though I'm young."

Coolidge desisted.

"Just kiddin' with you," he said. He offered his hand, "Robert Coolidge . . ."

With the handshake Patti shifted with noticeable discomfort. Did Coolidge notice this? Was that his intention? He flashed a warm, professional smile. His demeanor made me certain he would say, "attorney at law." And I wasn't far off. What he actually said was, "I work in this library. I run legal affairs."

Patti rolled her eyes.

Coolidge proceeded to point out the salient features of the operation. The different sections of books, the organizational principles, the law library in the back, which he referred to as "the most important part of the library."

"It's mandated by law," he said of the legal shelves. "I'll show you the case law sometime. I remember it personally." He lectured us on the finer points of the library's system of circulation. On the quirks of the daily schedule. But when he began to walk forward to continue his tour into the next room, his "office," Patti put her foot down. "That's okay, Mr. Coolidge," she said. "I'll show him around. You can go back to what you were doing."

Coolidge pursed his lips. The mustache twisted into a tiny, angry knot. I got the distinct impression that he was struggling to control his temper, which, judging from the rising tension in his shoulders, was considerable. As I'd later learn, years of hard time had taught him to pick his battles carefully, though rarely carefully enough. But, at that moment, he kept his cool and flashed us a false smile.

"Okay," he said. "Now if you'll excuse me, I've got some motions to fill out. We'll talk later. Alvie?"

"*Avi*," I said.

"Halby?"

"No, A*h*-vi."

"*Ah-vi*. Got it. What is that, French?"

"No, Hebrew. It's a Jewish name."

"Uh-oh. We *definitely* have to talk later."

As Patti's tour continued out of the library, to other corners of the Education Department, the fragrance that had radiated from Coolidge lingered. It was definitely cologne, and it was clinging to my right hand. The handshake. A minute in prison and I'd already been scent-marked.

Job Training

During my first week, Patti alternated staff people in the library to keep an eye on me. They had their own agenda: to earn comp time.

My first tutor was Linda, a flirtatious (dyed) blond Italian-American woman who resembled a polecat cub and wore a leopard-print, faux fur-lined frock coat. There was talk of mafioso ex-boyfriends. ("Oh, Dino, Dino, nobody knew but he really was a teddy bear even though he had a *terrible* temper.") Tilted at a clever angle, her mouth decanted gossip gently into your ears. She bore no grievance against inmates, nor much interest. Her job in the prison was to administer reading tests.

Diana presided from afar. She was a tough, older, Albanian-American teacher, a formerly groovy 1970s feminist who now wore a windbreaker printed with pro-parenting slogans. She was a quirky matriarch with a wry smile—unless she got angry, and then she breathed fire. She didn't discourage dissent as much as strongly encourage assent. When she spoke, she'd grab my arm. At the imminent approach of a punchline, she'd squeeze my wrist with surprising might and wrench me, judo-like, toward the ground.

During my first days, Diana would pop her head into the library to "check my status." Which I took to mean, to see whether I was being beaten and/or stabbed. It was Linda, however, who was charged with babysitting me. But when the inmates came filing in, her affability evaporated. She sunk into a chair behind the library counter with a pile of *Star* and *Us* magazines, immersing herself in a report on Tori's shocking weight gain. I was left to fend for myself.

The next day, a new prison staffer showed up to help me. She looked like a friendly pigeon, middle-heavy, a small, smiling head. She was a butch woman who inhabited a crisp, tucked-in polo shirt and roomy khakis. An ID lanyard dangled from her neck, a plastic coffee cup was glued to her hand. From a hundred yards away, one could tell she was a prison caseworker. Her demeanor was business casual. She deployed a firm handshake, but otherwise didn't clutch my arm or confide past loves. I doubt she dated mobsters. My guess was school principals. She didn't divulge much. What she did tell me was that I had to be tougher than a prison guard to work this job.

"You're in a bind here," she informed me, "you don't have that uniform. Your authority comes from *you*, your actions alone. In my opinion every staff person in here should wear a uniform."

The first few seconds of every prison library period were crucial, she told me. That's when you establish your authority. She showed me how to stand. Back straight, chest puffed out, arms crossed.

"Don't smile," she said. "This isn't The Gap."

That made me smile.

She had me practice. I put on a super-mean face. My much-rehearsed Johnny Law scowl. After considering my style with a critical eye, she had only one suggestion.

"You want to look serious," she said, "not *sad*. You look like you're going to cry. No good."

Also, she wasn't happy with my height. I might want to wear clogs, she advised, or some shoe with a tall sole. I imagined throwing caution to the wind and coming into prison with a leisure suit and platforms. When she spotted the inmates en route, her smile faded. She tapped me. I knew what to do. Battle stations!

When the inmates stormed in, we were already standing in formation, shoulder to shoulder—or, to be precise, my shoulder a couple of inches below hers—our arms folded. She mowed down the first wave of inmates, sending them back to the block for running. When they protested, she clenched her teeth and said, "You either turn around or I'll send you to the hole."

The rest of the hour proceeded from there. She made a big scene with one of the inmate library workers. His uniform top was inside-out. She commanded him, loudly and in front of other inmates, to change it. In a clear effort to save face, he told her he'd do it when he went back to his cell.

"No," she said, "now."

They glared at each other for what felt like a full minute. Finally she said, "You want to go to the hole?" He continued glaring. I heard him mutter, "You can't treat me like a damn child."

"And why don't you show me what you have in that pocket?" she said, referring to the bulging, now-concealed inside-out chest pocket.

He reached into his shirt and pulled out a little volume of Psalms. He smiled smugly. But before he could gloat, she said. "Go into the back and flip your shirt the right way, right now."

But he didn't go into the back. Instead, he walked to the middle of the library and, with dozens of inmates now stopping to watch, removed his uniform top, stood there for a moment pitiably half-naked—a silent protest—and finally flipped it the right way. He continued his protest by abandoning his post behind the library counter. He went to the other side of the library to shelve books, which he did furiously and, from what I could discern, in no particular order. Meanwhile, my caseworker tutor held her ground, arms crossed, jaw clenched. But the red in her face betrayed her.

The advice came from all sides. My friendly union boss, Charlie—a.k.a. *Chah*lie—popped his head in one day during the first week. Though technically Patti's assistant, in reality he was no such thing. Charlie was what parliament-run governments call a "minister-without-portfolio," a staffer-at-large. He was an old patronage hire, part of the former system who arrived on the scene before the staff had professionalized, back when the prison was merely a junket of government jobs—when it was about who you knew, not what experience or training you had. He also happened to be a lovably politically incorrect grandfatherly gent. Charlie knew everybody by name and was a unifying presence, friends with officers and civilians alike.

On my third day, he pulled me aside. He'd seen me from the hall, he said, through the library's picture windows (for security reasons, everything has to be as literally transparent as possible, every room in the prison has large hall-facing windows). He shook his head disapprovingly.

"You're moving around *too* much, and you're moving *too* fast," he told me. "You trying to set a record? *Don't* work so hard."

Charlie was a relentless jokester, but he actually wasn't joking. I was on union time, union pay scale. I got paid the same amount regardless of how hard I worked or how well I performed. More important than achieving anything, as far as he was concerned, was to arrive and leave on time. Not a second earlier or later.

"Don't get fancy," he told me. "Just do your job, stay healthy, and keep your nose clean."

And take your union-protected break. Charlie had demonstrated this last one for me himself, during my initial job interview. In the midst of his tour, we'd stopped for a spell at the front gate. At the time, I had no idea why we were standing there, just staring at a chain-link fence and the sky. After about a minute of silent reflection, he'd announced, "This is where you come for your break. It's in the contract. So you take it." Running around like a waiter and "trying to set records," however, was not in my contract.

Gilmore, the night-shift officer stationed outside of the library at the time, also had advice.

"You need to have open eyes in this place," he said. "It's like boxing. The punch that knocks you out is the punch you don't see."

He'd taken measurements, he told me. The space was outfitted with giant security mirrors, designed to see around corners. If you stood in a certain spot behind the circulation counter, you could see almost every inch of the space. He even offered me pieces of tape to mark the spot on the floor.

"This is your post," he said. "Just stand here for the next thirty years and you'll retire a happy man."

He gave me a friendly pat on the back.

The opinions I encountered pointed to a larger question: What *was* the role of the prison library? Almost everyone I asked during those first weeks had a different answer. Some thought it was a sham that, at best, served no function; at worst, coddled the inmates and gave them a place to plan and commit crimes. Some thought it was an effective way to numb inmates to the reality of captivity, to calm their nerves. The library made the prison safer for everyone, I was told. One senior officer mentioned that it was a good place to gather information from inmates who didn't realize they were being watched. As Coolidge liked to point out, the heart of the prison library, strictly speaking, was the law collection: Inmates had a legal right to it.

Some staff believed it was a place to awaken, not numb, inmates. A place inmates might be able to change their lives, pursue an education, do something productive—though few actually did. There was the model of Malcolm X, who underwent a major transformation in a prison library, in the same Massachusetts system in which I worked. In his autobiography, which sat on our shelf, he wrote, "Ten guards and the warden couldn't have torn me out of those books. Months passed without even thinking about being imprisoned . . . I had never been so truly free in my life."

A young black officer told me he believed that prison libraries were lost on 99.9 percent of inmates, but for the chance of producing another person like Malcolm, it was worth it.

On the other hand, there was the model of James "Whitey" Bulger, the murderous Boston Irish crime boss—whose $2 million reward puts him second on the FBI's Most Wanted list, behind Osama bin Laden. Bulger refined his notoriously ruthless tactics, and his method of systematic, brutal repression, by making a careful study of military history. This also happened in a prison library. The FBI's wanted poster for Bulger indeed notes that he is "an avid reader with an interest in history. He is known to frequent libraries." Whitey, like Malcolm, first discovered books in the prison library. And it was there, in the quiet of its shelves, that he made his first and most diligent intellectual efforts. Both men had entered the prison library as unread young street thugs but emerged as leaders—with opposing visions of power.

During my first days of work I noticed that the names of Whitey and Malcolm came up often. People wanted to read about them, to read what they had read. Or just to talk about them. For each person seeking spiritual guidance or the development of his political conscience, like Malcolm, there was a cold materialist, studying how to employ violence more efficiently in the service of brutal criminal endeavors. Just like Whitey.

O fficer Gilmore, and others, had told me to *be on the lookout*. That was the phrase he used. When I asked him what it meant, he indicated that it was a broad comment.

"I know," he said, "that this probably seems messed up, right, to be constantly watching other people." He shrugged. "I mean, it *is* messed up. But you get used to it. There's no getting around it, though. In here, privacy is a problem."

In prison, where privacy is a problem, reading is considered a just bearable form of self-seclusion. And yet, after a few days, I was beginning to detect that there was a problem even with this abstract form of privacy—the kind that occurs when a mind sits alone with a book. It wasn't obvious, and certainly not to me, how to distinguish a Whitey from a Malcolm.

This was precisely the source of some of my coworkers' skepticism regarding the prison library. And it wasn't anything new. Writing in 1821, prison chronicler George Holford noted that he couldn't discern "whether the prisoners are working, or gambling, reading history books or Psalm books furnished by the chaplain, or legends and songs of a very different description." The charged relationship between books and prison was probably as old as the institution.

During lunch in the staff cafeteria, I asked Diana what she thought was the purpose of the prison library. She smiled.

"Oh no, silly," she said, grabbing my wrist under the table. "Don't think about it too much. These guys have a lot of time on their hands. Reading is just a good way for them to pass the time. That's the way it's always been in prison."

As she tightened her grip on my wrist, her silver rings slowly digging into my radial artery, I nodded in complete and utter agreement. But her answer seemed too easy and left me even more curious.

The Hobbes Girls

My first impression of the creative writing class for women inmates, held up in the tower, was less than positive. I was looking at a pretty rough bunch. For a moment, I wondered if I'd accidentally walked into a neck scar convention. I counted three. The one who didn't have a neck scar had a neck tattoo. The one who had neither sported a lewd cupcake-shaped hairdo and looked just plain mean.

I was reminded of the famous line from *Leviathan*, in which Thomas Hobbes envisions a grim world without a strong central sovereign, a "war of all against all," in which the life of a person is "solitary, poor, nasty, brutish, and short." Here they were, reunited in one room, sitting right in front of me: Solitary, Poor, Nasty, Brutish, and Short.

The first to speak was Short. Short was both short and wiry, especially in her prison uniform, which appeared roughly five sizes too large. As is common for her kind, Short balanced a massive chip on her shoulder. When I asked her to please join the small circle of seats, she leaped up, threw her chin forward, and said, "You gonna make me?"

With my response, an equivocal "uh," she smiled and loosened up.

"I'm just playin' with you," she said and bounded over to the circle.

But she wasn't. I already knew Short routinely looked for, and usually found, fights. In preparation for my class, I had read her litany of prison disciplinary reports, many of which attributed to her such winning quotes as, "Bitch, I'm gonna cut your damn titties off." And: "You fucking cunt ass ho, you got the stinkiest damn pussy in this whole place. *Bitch.*" This woman was a perfect fit for a creative writing class. She had me at *titties.*

And then there was Nasty. Nasty, unseemly cupcake hairdo upon her head, really was rather nasty. But mostly just morose. She'd stare ahead for periods of half an hour without saying a word, her face waxing bitterer with each passing second. I could tell time by watching this woman's loathing grow. She usually said only one thing during a class, always at the end, as a sort of summary statement, and always genuinely mean-spirited.

I have to admit I had a soft spot for Brutish. Sure, she was brutish. She behaved like a frat boy, displayed little to no socialization. She'd slump in her chair, drop her hands deep into her prison-issue pants, probe the region, make a little adjustment, cop a little feel. She said whatever came to mind. The profane, the foolish, the casually defamatory. "Your shirt is old," she'd say. Or "Your hair looks like shit." (At least, that's what she'd say to me.) Everything was shit—shit was her currency and her compass. Negative developments were *bad shit*; positive were *good shit*. Her winters were cold as ___, and her summers hot as ___. She picked her nose, passed gas, betrayed confidences. But she meant no harm, and it was a testament to her irrepressible good humor that somehow people forgave her for acting like a prize hog at the state fair.

She and Poor were pals. They were an odd couple: Brutish, fat and carnal, Poor, a stick figure—though sturdy in her boniness—constantly grubbing, ever fearful. A permanent expression of doom in her eyes. Brutish abused Poor's neediness, but also watched out for her. Or so it seemed.

Solitary intrigued me. She sat at the far end—alone, of course—staring out the window. Later, after everything that happened, I still held on to that first image of her: sitting very upright, legs crossed, hands folded neatly on her lap, squinting in the sun, a frowning, pre-occupied Betsy Ross–at–work air about her (if Betsy Ross had been a washed up ex-stripper). She was hard, proud, and prim. Didn't utter a peep during our first meetings.

The first words out of Solitary's mouth, however, immediately endeared her to me. For the first two classes, I had brought in three short readings—poems by Philip Larkin and Amiri Baraka and a passage from *Beloved* by Toni Morrison. We read and discussed each in class. I did this mostly to get a sense of where these women were in terms of their reading skills and interests. The discussions were a bit forced but not entirely discouraging. Solitary, for her part, kept mum.

Finally, I decided to up the ante. For homework—which, Poor corrected me, should not be called homework but "cellwork"—I asked them to read a short story by Flannery O'Connor.

Solitary raised her hand.

"Can we see a picture of her first?"

"You won't read it until you see a picture?" I said.

"That's right," she replied, unsmiling.

I flipped to the author's photo in the Library of America edition of O'Connor's collected works, and forked it over. Solitary examined the photo.

"Okay," she said, handing it back, "I'll read it."

What in Flannery O'Connor's countenance met with Solitary's approval?

"I dunno," she said. "She looks kind of busted up, y'know? She ain't too pretty. I trust her."

Details, Details

On my first day flying solo in the library, I was met by five men in prison uniforms—one in a prison-issue fat-guy T-shirt—facing me, awaiting instructions. Only then, and with some dryness of mouth, did I realize what my job entailed: I was, first and foremost, a prison boss. My main task involved not books or teaching, but running a prison inmate work detail. I'd never been a boss to anyone, let alone a staff of convicted felons. During my initial interview I'd been informed of this responsibility, but hadn't known what it meant.

What it meant, at least at first, was that I stood helplessly behind the inmates, observing them do their jobs. The library detail was a group of six to eight inmates: four or five men, two or three women—of course, never remotely in the space at the same time. For this detail, inmates were compensated to the tune of two dollars a day, funds that were deposited directly into their personal inmate accounts (unless they owed money). Inmates could use this account to order items from the prison's canteen, to pay medical co-payments, and court fines, and, if they pleased, to disperse funds to parties outside of the prison. Outside parties could deposit money there for them. This was also the channel for illicit transactions.

The library offered the cushiest detail. Working the prison library—with its stock of books, magazines, movies, and company—was an understandably more attractive option for the inmates than mopping the floor alone in their unit. To get the detail, one had to have some education, or at least relevant skills. In the words of the head classification officer—a man who, incidentally, spent his spare time authoring erotic prison thrillers—the prison library was "the elite detail." Often an inmate came recommended by other staff members. Sometimes an inmate put in his own application.

I generally worked a 1:30 to 9 p.m. shift; the day shift, which began at 7:30 a.m., went to Forest, a man who, unlike me, was actually trained as a librarian and had worked in the New York City Public Library system. The library's daily schedule consisted of consecutive one- to one-and-a-half-hour periods organized by prison unit, from 3-1—i.e., the unit from the first floor of the 3-Building—to 4-3. (The units in the 1-Building, the Tower, were constructed to have more than one unit per floor, and went by numbers like 1-2-1, or 1-11-2.) During their designated period, up to thirty inmates were permitted into the library at once, which meant they had to get onto their unit's list ahead of time. Sometimes the demand was too high and inmates would have to wait a day or two until it was their turn.

At 3 p.m.—and, as Charlie ensured, not a second later—Forest and much of the civilian staff blew off for the day. Occasionally Forest and I would swap shifts, usually as the result of his charitable donation to my Friday night social life. But I was mostly in prison during the afternoon, evening, and night. Perhaps I felt more comfortable during the night shift—all of my later problems occurred, or at least originated, during my rare stints on the early shift.

It was the night shift that brought me into daily contact with the women inmates. Every evening at 6:30 p.m. the men would be locked down in their cells, and the women would descend from the prison tower. For logistical reasons—namely their status as a minority population—the women were rarely permitted to emerge from their units and had very limited time away. And once out they were fired up. For an hour and a half each night, the library was engulfed by lively crowds of women inmates.

The women were much more social and talkative than the men. You could document on graph paper the cultural difference between the sexes by the way in which each used the library space: women would sit together in two or three big circles, while the men retreated to private corners, with only a small group surrounding the counter. There was a thick sense of group among the women—they didn't balkanize like the male prisoners. Same-sex dating was common and openly accepted. Interracial friendships were the norm. There was less gang activity, if any. Unlike the men, the women were all deeply involved in each other's business. Gossip was the standard currency. Even in the first few sessions, I could discern the differences. I had to break up a few sex-acts in the corners of the book stacks, a few physical fights. The drama among the men did not play out openly like this, and certainly not in the space of the library.

When I arrived on the scene there were two women working the library detail, a young pregnant woman and an older "madam" who went by the name Momma D. During my first week there, the pregnant woman tried to persuade me to hire one of her friends for the library detail. If I failed to do so, she threatened to name her child after me.

"You don't want people to start talking, do you?" she said, in what I believe was a joke.

She also informed me, in praise of her friend, that "hoes make the best librarians." Why? "Because they know how to be sweet but they will bust yo' ass if you get out of line." I agreed that this pro-file fit the qualifications of an effective librarian. Overhearing this conversation, Momma D, however, demurred. Madams are the best librarians, she argued. They know how to "run an operation." It all sounded plausible to me.

The men's library detail was also already in place when I began working. Coolidge—veteran thief, flimflam man, and law clerk—was the self-appointed elder statesman of the group. He helped me steer the ship at the beginning. Coolidge was a large-scale talker and four-time religious convert. He'd alternated between various streams of Christianity and Islam. He was an autodidact and prison diploma holder. The staff member who actually ran legal affairs, a certified lawyer, told me that Coolidge truly did maintain an impressive grasp of the law. Coolidge's vocabulary was extensive, though he often stretched it beyond its limits. In conversations, he quickly turned bully. But I enjoyed talking to him—at first.

His knowledge of the library and of the prison was indispens-able. He knew more than my bosses about the actual, day-to-day operation of the library, and he took the time and interest to explain things to me. As a result, I was slightly under the sway of his paranoid delusions.

"Everyone's gonna want a piece of you in here," he warned me. "Watch yourself."

When I asked him what he meant, he just said, "You'll see."

In addition to his current sentence, Coolidge was facing another robbery charge that could tack on a few decades to his countless years as an adult in captivity. He was busy preparing a vigorous, full-scale legal defense.

"It's not a legal defense, Avi," he said, as we waited for a legal brief to print. "It's a legal *offense*. I *will* be taking umbrage, you understand? It's gonna be like Napoleon's invasion of Russia, except I'm gonna win."

I wasn't sure what a Napoleon-complex would look like in a man over six feet tall, but was confident I would find out.

Coolidge's focus on his own legal matters kept him removed from the rest of the detail, an arrangement that seemed to suit everyone. He'd set up shop in the back room, the computer room. Other inmates were not to interfere with him back there. He was magnanimous, though, and held office hours to help inmates with their legal questions.

Fat Kat was over ten years younger than Coolidge, but probably a generation or so removed. He was a child of the chaos of 1980s Boston, the first generation to run serious drugs and guns on the streets. He and his buddies had been rounded up in the nineties by the Feds, in a historic sweep of Boston's street gangs (meanwhile, Irish Southie mob boss and FBI double agent, Whitey Bulger, continued running his rackets miraculously unabated). Many of Kat's friends had done or were doing serious time. Some of them were beginning to hit the streets again. Kat had a couple of years left.

Coolidge and Kat got tight and bonded over a shared passion for case law. Coolidge once told me that he viewed Kat as a son. It wasn't clear to me that Kat saw it this way.

Cherubic and clever in equal measure, Fat Kat never boasted, but also never bothered to conceal his large aspirations. He could tell you which boutique designed which NBA players' plus-sized custom-tailored leather tailcoats. He could expound upon the logic of each cut, button, and stud, could make the structural argument for fusible interfacing, for the need of contrast stitching. Kat's collection of couture sneakers went into the hundreds of pairs. He could talk shop about yachts. But, touched by the curse of self-awareness, his flourishes of connoisseurship always amounted to sorrow.

"I grew up poor," he told me, with a sigh. "I *need* this stuff. At least that's how it feels."

Fat Kat also said he wanted out of "the game." How these wants and needs would sort themselves out in the future was unclear. If there was a way, he was certain he'd find it. The respect accorded him by both inmates and staff was real. His playfulness, his vegetarianism, his love of *National Geographic*, his fantasies of relocating to the woods of Quebec, all complicated the stereotype of the street thug.

Elia was a quiet, lumbering man in his mid forties. Hair pulled back into a tiny ponytail, deep creases in his forehead. A shy smile, missing some crucial teeth. There was a faded bohemian smoothness to him. His demeanor was gentle, courtly. Born in Alabama and shuttled to Boston at a young age, he used to hang out with the musicians of Harvard Square, where he helped found *Spare Change*, the local street newspaper written and sold by homeless people. He wasn't ashamed that he'd stayed in shelters, he told me. Or that he struggled with a drinking problem. He was trying to patch things up with his wife. He missed the way she dragged him to ballets and plays. A photo of their beautiful four-year-old daughter was always with him in his prison uniform.

From prison disciplinary reports, I knew of his cycle of violent behavior. Although he was quiet and I never saw him in full throttle, his underlying rage didn't surprise me. I could imagine how he'd react if his delicate pride were defiled, even in a small way. It would provoke a holy windstorm.

Elia spoke in hushed tones and didn't hang around the library's counter, where the brash talking happened—the loud conversations, political debates, pimp verbal jousts, religious disputations, chess trash talk, and other varieties of bullshitting. Instead he retreated into the library stacks, where he quietly reshelved books.

Pitts, on the other hand, loved to be in the fray. Somehow, even in his prison uniform, he was a sharp and flamboyant dresser. Handsome and pampered, Pitts was a high-roller. Raised in North Carolina, where he picked tobacco as a child, he was now a thirty-five-year-old bachelor and ex-Navy man. No kids: not unless he gets married, he said. This had been a vow taken by him and his siblings in an effort to end generations of familial disorder.

Pitts's closest drinking buddies were cops who liked to party hard. They had taught him, among other things, how to bullshit his way through a Breathalyzer test. When it came to vice, he tended toward the classics: women, gambling, and booze. And all-you-can-eat buffets. He almost cried once upon arriving at the airport in Vegas. He was just so happy to be there.

"Honestly man," he said, "my eyes got misty."

Pitts was on a quest to discover the true nature of the early Church. He read extensively on the Apocrypha, on the redaction of the Bible. He was in search for the authentic Christianity. Nothing he read satisfied him. A born salesman, Pitts rejected Judaism on the grounds that it "didn't offer a good plan for Redemption." When I had suggested that religion didn't function like a cell phone company he replied, "Well maybe it should."

He'd sit at the library counter, plumbing the depths of some heavy theological tome, ignoring the mundane requests of our inmate library patrons. Invariably he'd slam the book shut, shake his head, and say something like, "Ain't that a *bitch*." He wasn't getting the answers he needed.

Pitts, who also worked as the prison's barber (for black inmates), was witty and affectionate; we quickly became close and had many fascinating discussions on the nature of faith. He was wrestling with the question of getting baptized. He even spoke of studying in a seminary and asked for my advice, as a lapsed seminarian myself. His search for truth in the Bible eventually subsided, however, and he channeled his considerable passions into chess and trash talk.

Thomas was round-headed, fair-minded, and impatient. A slight man with thick, circular spectacles, and a pinched, perpetually affronted countenance. He was a clean-shaven older Muslim convert, a stickler for etiquette who never failed to call an older inmate *OG* (old gangsta) and younger inmate *Young G*. Details of his biography were not divulged. Least of all, to me. He was stationed with Kat and Pitts behind the counter.

John, high-spirited and garrulous, was the white guy. He would narrate freewheeling sagas of various concerts and sporting events attended and of the various drugs taken before, during, and after. When he spoke of the old days, back when he used to get "fuckin' *re*tarded," his eyes bulged and twinkled and you got the sense he was, in the retelling of the story, able to rekindle just the tiniest bit of the old high. Addicts will smoke even the ashes. His stories were always upbeat, full of madcap near-death exploits and fights gloriously lost—and they always culminated in a request to undertake some personal favor for him. He tried to ally himself to me as the lone white guy. He was a quick study with the law and would often huddle with Coolidge.

And so it went. The roles people played in the library matched their personalities/criminal vices: the operators and crime boss types ran the front desk, the con man ran his own small law firm, the gregarious drug fiend had no place and bounced around hustling whatever he could muster, the depressive homeless alcoholic found a private corner for his own reveries. The library, it seemed, was big enough to accommodate many types.

And then there was me, standing with my arms crossed, taking it all in, wondering what my role would be.

Diana had said that the library wasn't complicated, that it was just a place for people to pass time with books. Perhaps that was true back in the old days, when the prison would simply deliver books to inmates in their cells, a practice that had lasted hundreds of years. But the library was different: it was a *place*, a dynamic social setting where groups gathered, where people were put into relation with others. A space an individual could physically explore on his own.

This seemed important, even though I wasn't sure yet what it meant. But I was about to get a hint.

The Great Amato

During lulls, Officer Gilmore would drift away from his hallway post and into the library for one of a few reasons: to read the sports papers, to give me security updates, to warn me that the big boss was coming, to use a dictionary or thesaurus—as aids to writing incident reports—or to chat. Often it was some combination of these. On a certain Tuesday afternoon, he was on a mission to recover a word. It had been driving him mad. After a minute with *Roget's Thesaurus*, he found it: *precarious*! His sanity was restored.

"I *love* that book," he said, slipping it back onto the shelf. "Never fails."

Something in the hall caught his eye. He leaned back, tapped me on the shoulder, and nodded in that direction.

"By the way," he said. "There's your man right there."

"*That* guy?"

"That's him, all right," he said, "the famous Don Amato."

I'd heard a great deal about this Amato. The former prison librarian. But I had to admit, I didn't expect him to look quite so . . . conspicuous. The get-up was more *Il Padrone* than neighborhood librarian. In a gleaming gray double-breasted suit and cufflinks, he was, without a doubt, the flashiest librarian this side of Palermo. The hair was meticulously barbered and combed-back. The hard, leather-soled balmorals clicked a snappy little beat on the prison linoleum. He nodded slightly as he walked, as though conferring, just slightly, his much-desired approval onto his surroundings. Amato cruised by the library, fists in pockets, pouting and dapper, humorless as a tire iron.

"You *sure* that's him?" I asked Gilmore.

"Oh yeah," he replied, with a snort. "Who else could it be?"

I hadn't realized the infamous Amato still worked at the prison. As I soon discovered, his promotion to director of inmate vocational training had opened the librarian position. I'd seen him before without guessing his identity. But it was true. This man with the cufflinks was a certified Master of Library Science. Perhaps it wasn't as incongruous as it looked. Perhaps in a prison library being a tough guy was as much a professional credential as a degree.

It wasn't until relatively recently that the prison had created a home for books. In the 1980s a room was cleared out in the previous facility on Deer Island, marking the first time inmates could make a proper library visit. The blueprint of the current facility, completed in 1991, included a permanent library space.

But as soon as a space is carved out in a prison, it becomes a safety concern. The library, in particular, posed security headaches. It was one of the few places, aside from the prison yard, through which so many inmates passed and its layout made it difficult to monitor. Every shelf—some reached floor to ceiling—offered cover, every book a drop spot. The library was well-suited to prison mischief, for leaving notes or contraband, for passing gossip to inmate librarians to propagate within their respective prison blocks.

For these reasons, the library had always been run by a strongman. Fu-Kiau Bunseki, now retired, had founded the library at Deer Island. He was a scholarly man, certainly not loud or mean, but he commanded respect. In an attempt to contact him with questions about how the library functioned, I discovered everything I needed to know in his outgoing voice mail message, which consisted of two words, deeply intoned in a heavy Congolese accent: "Be brief." There was something dreadful in that baritone, and in that message. Something that really made you want to be brief.

And then there was Amato. Amato took charge of the library after Bunseki and was the library's second strongman. Unlike Bunseki, however, he was anything but quietly domineering. He was a pinky-ring autocrat. According to everyone, Amato was sometimes loud, always direct, and often confrontational. I'd heard a good deal of talk about Amato from both inmates and staff. The word *territorial* came up a lot. He was a character of legend. Just mentioning his name usually provoked a smile of recognition and a personal tale of fear and trembling. One caseworker told me she used to literally hide under her desk when she heard those shoes tapping on the linoleum. It wasn't a positive development if Amato alighted upon your office doorway. It meant one thing: he was about to tear you a new asshole—and then a new asshole for that asshole. And without so much as loosening his tie. Now that I finally got a look at him myself, I understood. This was a gentleman who played hardball.

According to the inmate librarians, Amato had whipped the

library into shape, vastly increasing the collection and organizing it with care. Although his communications skills may have been questionable, his ability to impose order was not. One had to respect that. Forest and I were new to all of this. Neither of us had any experience in a prison. Even worse, we were both mild-mannered and bookish by nature. Forest was a painfully shy, sweetheart of a man, and I was a reedy, poetry club type. We were far from prison tough.

Amato's reign had been literally marked by the propagation of rules. His laws were posted, in capital letters, all over the library, on some manner of demonic, industrial-grade sticky paper. Impossible to remove. From day one, Forest and I neglected to enforce these rules. Amato's permanently affixed signs stood as aging monuments to a former golden age of decorum and, by mocking contrast, as markers of our new, lax regime.

The week after Officer Gilmore had pointed him out, Amato paid me a visit. Through the library's big windows, I watched him pass through the door from the yard and stroll down the hall. Hearing those hard-leather soles tapping in my direction, I have to admit, I felt a spasm of panic. I seriously considered diving under my desk. But before I could execute any sort of drastic evasive action, Amato was standing before me, the prison lights glaring heavily from his shimmering suit. There he stood, in fluorescent splendor, adjusting his cufflinks.

It turned out he hadn't come to see me, but to procure a certain legal form from our collection. He was doing this favor, he explained, for "one of my guys." We had a little chat.

"You the new guy?"

"Yup."

"How's it going?"

I shrugged. "Okay, I guess."

He seemed concerned by this answer.

"Let me give you a piece of advice," he said. "It takes a lot of work to keep this place looking right, working right."

"I'm learning that," I said.

"Just don't forget where you work," he said. "I'm serious, now. Don't let it become an anything-goes zone in here. I know you're just a college kid or whatever, but you've got to control stuff in here or there could be some serious problems. This is a prison. Don't forget that for a second."

Amato then launched into a story of what happens when the library is not guarded well. The story involved gangs, knives, shields, and possibly spears. I wouldn't know. I wasn't actually listening at that point—too distracted by the top of this man's head. With the benefit of a close view, it was now safe to draw conclusions: the hair was impressive. Soft, kitten-soft, yet combed to a satisfying sturdiness. Such hair merited the word *coiffure*. It was a professional job. Had there been a way to inquire where I might find the stylist, or what products were used, without sounding like a smartass, I would have.

He was wrapping up his tale. There was a grave nod of the head, some clicking of heels. Then he was gone.

Once the coast was clear, I walked up to one of his signs, the one that warned inmates not to loiter by the front counter. I tried to peel it off. Then I tried harder. But the damn thing would not budge. Amato's legacy wasn't going anywhere.

Solitary Departs

Back in the tower, I was making some headway with the women inmates' creative writing class. The practice of examining authors' photos before reading their work had become a firmly established practice. I would pass around a photocopied author's portrait and have the women spend the first or last five minutes of class composing a little response to it, putting in their vote at the end. It became a writing exercise.

Regarding Toni Morrison, Short wrote, "Dats what I'm *talking* 'bout Harvey." Of a young photo of Lorca, "That boy is Trouble. My vote Yes." Brutish had strong views on Marquez. "That man is a *liar*," she wrote. Nasty said, simply, "No." For Whitman, Brutish wrote, "Hellzz ya!!"

The women were especially taken by a self-portrait of the photographer Arthur "Weegee" Fellig, peering from behind his giant Speed Graphic camera, a lit cigar dangling from his mouth.

"That is one greasy-ass motherfucker," observed Short.

This was a compliment—and one Weegee would probably have appreciated. We looked at his photos from late-night 1930s New York City: hookers, strippers, society ladies, circus freaks, crime scenes, and a series of tenement fires. One photo showed a man running down a fire escape in only his boxers, holding a pair of pants. He wears the hyperalert look of a man stunned into consciousness and seems amused by his good fortune. Another, which I flipped through quickly, pictured two women wailing as their family dies in a fire.

The final photo depicted two firefighters clutching a statue of a heaven-gazing angel playing a dulcimer. The angel had been pulled from a burning church. I asked the women to write about the fire series but to focus on this last photo, which Weegee had captioned "Two firefighters rescuing angel," a print from 1939. The women seemed to like these photo response essays and eagerly got to work.

But Solitary seemed bored. After class, she walked past me and muttered, "Sorry." "For what?" I asked. She shrugged. She was just sorry. That was it.

She was perhaps apologizing for her lack of interest. Her indifference had irked me, but I forgave it. In general, if an inmate was just looking to escape the prison unit, that was fine by me. As far as I was concerned, nothing good ever came from staying on the unit. But still, I had to run a class. If I let one inmate isolate herself and stare out the window, I would have trouble keeping order with the rest.

It didn't take long for the window gazing to become a problem.

"Why does *she* get to sit by the window?" complained Brutish.

"The only reason she want to be there is to look at the dudes" — in the prison yard below — "so she's got something to remember later . . ." said Nasty, making an appropriately nasty gesture.

Brutish smiled, "Yeah, *yeah*! That's what I'm talking 'bout! I wanna look out the window too!"

Poor, the group's unofficial spokeswoman, mournfully laid out the terms of an offer. "How about you let us stare out the window for the first five minutes of class? We'll pay attention more."

I considered this for a split second. "No," I said. Even after a few sessions I already had enough experience to know that the opposite was true. If they stared out the window, they'd be distracted and gossipy for the remainder of the period.

"Damn," said Short, crossing her little arms. "I know you ain't a bad dude, but you done had a cold-heart transplant."

I couldn't have said it better myself. After this conversation, of course, I had to pull Solitary into the circle, away from the window. But now, staring at the window from the other side of the room, or perhaps at the blank sky, she grew even more distant.

As usual, she walked past me after class and mumbled an abstract apology. She skipped the next class to "meet with her lawyer." And the one after that, for a visit (an unlikely occurrence at that hour).

Then she had to go to the infirmary; then she had to take a shower. The excuses were getting weaker. She didn't show for weeks. I removed her name from the roster. I was inclined to hunt her down, but decided to lay off. From the outset, she hadn't been interested and frankly only hurt what little morale existed in the class. Without her we had now upgraded to "poor, nasty, brutish, and short." Perhaps this was progress.

Ever since she'd skipped out of the class, Solitary had also quit visiting the library. It was a shame. But that's how it went. Everything in prison was personal, especially for the women, many of whom were borderline personalities: they either loved you or hated you, and they assumed you operated the same way. She believed that she had to lay low and avoid me. And so, one of her few outlets in prison, the library, was now off-limits. I sent a message to her through a semi-reliable inmate: she shouldn't hesitate to come down to the library on my account, I wasn't mad at her and she wouldn't get in any trouble. I sent the same message through a caseworker, to no avail.

But among the women inmates there were no secrets. It was inevitable that I'd learn the truth about Ms. Solitary.

The Day to Day

The prison library was a lending library. Inmates were permitted to check out no more than three books at one time. With each checkout, they were issued a receipt that doubled as a contract obligating them to return the item. But we rarely levied fines for late or unreturned books. This was another dangerous liberalization of Amato's regime.

It wasn't mere carelessness on our part. In prison it was simply too common for checked-out books to disappear — either removed by a vindictive or indifferent officer or stolen by a fellow inmate. Fining for lost books would discourage even honest people from borrowing them. And, ironically, the prison library — whose clientele included the largest concentration of thieves of any library in the world — lacked an alarm system. In short, we operated on the miserable premise that every book on our shelves would eventually turn into prison fodder.

The library offered both paperbacks and hardcovers. Patti insisted that we had permission to lend out hardcover books but many officers fervently disagreed. An officer walked into the library one day and gasped when he saw shelves piled high with hardcovers, which could be turned into weapons.

"Are you *kidding* me?" he'd said. "You can't give these out."

In many prisons this was true. For reasons that were never clear, however, this facility permitted it. At the same time, the administration neglected to put the policy into print, so it remained open for debate. Officers often saw this gray area as license to confiscate and, in many cases, dispose of books. This was an ongoing struggle.

Other policies were much more clear. Inmates could buy books by mail order, but only direct from publishers. No books could arrive in prison from private addresses. Prison regulations permitted inmates no more than six books in their cells. Inmates who ordered books often had to get rid of old books in order to keep the number under six. Some inmates sold their books to other inmates — an illegal transaction — some donated them to the library.

The library had a tiny budget. For bureaucratic reasons we weren't permitted to buy from cheap online booksellers. Forest and I poached yard sales, laundromats, and used bookstores. Usually at our own expense. The major source of books was random individuals who arbitrarily showed up with giant shipments. These reliable donors were an assortment of hippies covered in dog hair, smiling evangelicals, and local oddballs, who did things like give you an unsolicited thirty-minute lecture on the intricacies of the formal Japanese bow ("it's a lot like setting up a golf swing"), and then peer-pressured you into an embarrassingly elaborate bowing ceremony in front of the prison, in the presence of coworkers on their smoke breaks. But I was very grateful for the earnest efforts of these donors. When they dropped off their payloads, Forest and I enjoyed an out-of-season Christmas.

I n prison, where scarcity is the norm and ownership is limited to a paltry few items, books themselves began to take on more functions. There seemed to be endless ways to use books. Hardcover books could be fashioned into body armor. Placed in a bag and wielded as a battle flail. Taped together and used as weights. Used to hide contraband. Books could be mined for paper or illustrations, or used to help prop things up around the cell. And for all of these functions, books became an item for barter.

One woman confided that she kept a book in bed with her while she slept. Its presence comforted her.

Some people even used books to read. For education, entertainment, therapy, a way of making sense of the world. Sitting at the library's circulation desk, I saw more than one woman on the verge of tears while checking out a favorite children's book that she hadn't seen in years—*Charlotte's Web* or *Curious George*. For many in prison, childhood memories were very difficult or nonexistent.

Book lending was also a means of communication with another person. An argument over a political or religious issue often resulted in inmates, and sometimes staff, drawing up reading lists for each other—often on the spot and in a huff—as a means of setting the other straight. In my first week, an inmate named Robert Jordan, upset by something I had said, told me he wouldn't speak to me until I read *The Souls of Black Folk* by W. E. B. DuBois. I told him I'd already read it.

"Read it again," he told me. "'Cause you missed the whole point."

The next time he came in, he brought the book with him and put it directly in my hands. I realized that he wasn't asking me to understand DuBois but to understand something about him, Robert Jordan. I read it again, in this light. And since we were going to let our books do the talking, I gave him a similar reading assignment, Kafka's "The Animal in the Synagogue," a story about a mysterious dusty blue-green creature that has taken up residence in the balcony of a decaying synagogue. Needless to say, a favorite of mine.

I had many similar conversations-through-books with inmates. Much of my own reading came by way of these assignments. As a result, I found myself reading a lot of conspiracy theorists.

But for the most part, prison library reading tastes tended to match those of the wider American population. We had a shelf for Oprah's Book Club selections. James Patterson, Dan Brown, James Frey books rarely lasted more than fifteen minutes. In order to keep an eye on them, we kept these popular titles displayed behind the counter. Inmates also loved reading books on real estate and starting small businesses. There were other, less concrete interests. Books on dream interpretation were wildly popular—this is actually an ancient prison genre: in the Bible, Joseph makes a name for himself by interpreting fellow prisoners' dreams. Given their unfortunate present circumstances, prisoners have a special investment in future events.

Astrology books were also much desired. After the ex-inmate mugged me—and boasted that he still had two books out—I checked to see just which Latino man, roughly five-foot-ten, recently released, still had two books due. It turns out that this profile fit one man, a certain Ernesto Casanova. And the two books he owed: *Introduction to Astrology* and *The Astrology of Human Relationships*.

The true crime genre was, obviously, also a favorite. I was asked for true crime books on a daily basis. From the wide assortment of small-time Machiavellis I got regular requests for *The Art of War* by Sun Tzu and *The Forty-Eight Laws of Power* by Robert Greene. Thanks to slain rapper Tupac Shakur, a.k.a. "Makaveli," I was often asked for books by Niccolo Machiavelli himself. In his song "Tradin War Stories," Tupac breaks it down thus:

> . . . *a legend in my own rhymes*
> *So niggaz whisper when they mention*
> *Machiavelli was my tutor*

The majority of inmates who read *The Prince*, however, returned slightly disappointed. The sixteenth-century text wasn't as user-friendly as they'd hoped.

"Urban literature" was another popular genre, but inmates were frustrated that our collection was practically nonexistent. They would complain that the library "didn't have no good books." Standing feet away from shelves that held tens of thousands of books, some inmates would inform me "you guys don't have *any* books here."

Eventually I got wise and took advantage of this scarcity. I subtly encouraged the inmates' black market for street books to find a home in the library. If inmates were going to find and read them anyway, they ought to come to the library to do it. As Fat Kat, the former gangster, noted, "We don't want no competition out there. We gotta put them out of business." I agreed. When it came to books in prison, we wanted to be the main show in town.

A few times a week, Forest and I would pack a few boxes of paperbacks, newspapers, and magazines onto a pushcart and visit those prison units that weren't permitted to visit the library. The men in the vast federal immigration wing—a giant prison unto itself—the units of pretrial detainees, the infirmary, and New Man, the unit where newly minted inmates were housed until they received their permanent classification.

These visits gave us the chance to explore different corners of prison. We would show up at the heavy door of a unit, wave to the officers on duty, wait for an eternity before the door would decide to roll open, then we'd push into the unit and place the goods in the designated spot. The first few times we made deliveries, we arrived when the cells were open and the inmates were roaming around the dayroom.

This was a mistake. There was a palpable air of desperation in these prison units, whose inmates were almost completely cut off from the world. By a force of animal hunger, something like electromagnetism, the inmates would swarm us from all corners. A few would simply start grabbing the items, right out of our hands. It was almost as though they couldn't see us or were looking right through us. They saw only what they wanted and lunged for it. Within seconds we were surrounded on all sides by burly, desperate prison inmates. It put us on edge.

The officers on duty regarded this as hilarious. From afar, it probably was. Without fail, our arrival in New Man was accompanied by a grin from the officer on duty. Before opening the door for us, he'd tap his partner, the international sign for, *Hey get a load of this* . . . They were never disappointed. Just as we were getting swarmed and gang-mugged the officers would stand at the side with big smiles. One comedian of an officer would begin flapping his arms and screeching like a seagull, *caw caw caw.* And exclaim loudly, "Look, it's like Revere Beach, the seagulls are coming down, guys!" It was a nasty comment made the more nasty because it had some truth to it. Equally nasty was this officer's suggestion that we walk in and dump the goods onto a table—without even trying to arrange them properly—like a zookeeper dumping feed into a trough.

The word *seagull* quickly gained currency all over the joint. People would ask us if we "got seagulled today" or warn us, "now don't get seagulled over there."

The short but noteworthy era of seagulling soon ended when we stumbled on the brilliant discovery that we could time our deliveries for those moments when the inmates were locked in. But I did learn an important lesson during one particularly dicey seagulling session. While the officer kept to the side, too busy enjoying the spectacle to help us, I took matters into my own hands. I shouted—something I didn't even know I was capable of doing—and told the inmates in front of me to step away. *Now.* This was directed at one particularly aggressive inmate. The young con pulled back, crossed his arms, and laughed.

"Shit," he said. "Ain't me you got to be worrying about. You got to watch the people *behind* you, man."

I turned around and saw a group of inmates standing behind me, big shit-eating grins on their faces.

That summed up how I felt during those first weeks. Every time I felt secure that a situation had come into focus, a more important fact, a new grinning variable would tap my shoulder from behind.

The up&up and low low

Mars Bar just got to prison; her pregnancy test was positive. Shizz, also relatively new to prison, accuses her of having cheated on him with a certain someone.

"Lady, you know who!" he says.

After reminding Shizz that he'd been spending a lot of time with his own babymomma, Mars Bar denies his charge, insisting that he, Shizz, is the father.

"Remember the night before you was arrested? Why do you think I TOLD you I was pregnant!"

Yes, he remembers. It was a night that started at that Jamaican joint and ended at his crib. His mood changes completely. Suddenly he's thrilled, planning their future, promising to be a better father than Mars Bar's other babydaddy, from whom she kidnapped her oldest son.

But then it turns out she's not pregnant.

Not long after the pregnancy episode has concluded, Mars Bar accuses Shizz of having HIV and not telling her. He becomes furious and demands to know where she heard this. She admits it's a rumor.

He promises to produce a document that proves he's HIV-negative and to find the rat who is spreading the rumor. Again, they reconcile and reminisce about the times they used to get fucked up, make baked ziti and play video games together.

Every day for nearly a month I tuned into this soap opera—all of which took place inside an ordinary reference book. Using volume 57 of the *Federal Reporter*, a bulky series of case law, as their ad hoc mailbox, Shizz and Mars Bar, two inmates who never came face-to-face inside the prison, maintained their stormy relationship. The correspondence ended one day, leaving me to wonder what ever became of their complicated romance.

As I made my daily rounds, I discovered notes—sometimes pages long—wedged in books. In an art book, or a guide to women's health, or a giant concordance of Lord Tennyson's works. The denser, the better.

"Ill leave you the next one in the boring books," wrote one inmate to his lady pen pal. He was referring to the *Encyclopedia Brittannica*.

As I learned from reading them, a prison letter is known as a *kite*. The word appeared everywhere. Stix, a nineteen-year-old first-time convict, always signed off his letters with a promise to "fly ya another kite next week."

I liked the connotation of the word. It was a tidy metaphor for a letter, especially from prison, a precious and precarious little creation, a physical object—unlike most forms of letters today—folded up and sent out into the world for another person to see from afar. Sometimes these letters were addressed to a specific person, sometimes they were left for whomever found them. Often, that person was me.

I didn't always intercept these missives. When a male inmate, who had just entered the prison, broke the news to his sister, an inmate in the tower, that their mother had just died, I obviously wasn't going to remove the letter.

"See lil' sis," he wrote, "you *know* you still got me. Don't never forget."

But in general, I treated even the innocuous letters as contraband, as per my job description and Amato's warning to prevent the library from becoming an "anything-goes zone." I made regular searches through the books and shelves, scouring hot spots, keeping an eye out for inmates dropping notes. I checked disks and computer desktops for e-kites. I felt bad tampering with other people's mail. One never knows what's behind even a silly letter, what the context is. Removing letters seemed more of a misdeed than the placing of one.

Secretly, I was grateful for the kites. They taught me a great deal about the language and culture of my workplace. Like actual kites, these notes came in all shapes and sizes. They were some of the best reading on the library shelves. Some were masterpieces of the genre, contenders for the Great American Kite. One guy tried to win back his erstwhile girlfriend by writing in the voice of God. "Behold," he wrote on page 5, "I give thee today the Blessing and the Curse." The takeaway lesson from his letter: if you decide to speak in the name of the Almighty, don't make so many spelling errors (". . . for I shall reek vengince . . .").

Another inmate alternated between English and Spanish, sometimes in the same paragraph: in Spanish she was sweet and conciliatory, but in English she was a raging lunatic.

But few could match the swashbuckling antics of a kite that dropped out of an economics textbook one dreary afternoon. This letter from one woman to another—unsigned, though all evidence suggested Ms. Brutish—may be the voice America has been waiting for: the diesel-fueled lesbian hybrid of Saul Bellow's *Augie March* and Snoop Dogg's *Doggystyle*:

What's good Baby girl?!
Yo, your kite was right!! Chic, ya off the hook, and on some real shit, I'm feelin' that! But anyhow, I'm never one that's lost for

words. A bitch like me can't be stuck on chuck, the boss is lost, for nada. I'm a go-getter, and I go for what I want, and usually, I get what I want. Early! . . . so you need to be dicked down and licked down? Well, ma, I can't help ya with the first one, but I've been told that my skills on the other is SWEEEEEET! Ya need ya estrogen levels balanced by a pro. Make a bitch forget reality, speak in ancient tongues and shit. . . But like I said, I aint tryin' to step on no one's toes cuz that's not the type of bitch I am. But on the up&up and low low I gots to make a proper attempt though, cuz I'd kick myself in the ass, ass backwardz if I didn't attempt to get the goodz, knowin' that I wanted a piece of the pie . . . So, ya crown jewels make a nigga rob banks. Only if ya crown jewels shine ma, like I know they do. An Italian princess like you should never be anything less, always have ya jewels shine . . . and if you feel the need to be unfaithful, then it be what it be ma. Go for yourz . . . now thatz the shiiiiit! I like the answers as usual. You keep shit rockin'. Here's some more questions girly girl.

1. When is ya man getting out of jail?
2. Have you ever had a 3some?
3. Have you ever had a 4some?
4. Would ya ever pose for "Girlz Gone Wild"?
5. Can you skip the jail house panties, and just stick with the Georgia peach (straight up and down)?
6. Have you ever seen a man cry?
7. Does your office space have room for 2?
8. Have you ever had cyber sex?
9. Do you see yourself with a future? A different future?
10. Can I get a Woop Woop?
11. Can we be friends?

12. *Can we be m.t.j.f.? [more than just friends]*
13. *"Do you understand the words that are coming out of my mouth?". . . courtesy of Chris Tucker*
14. *What's ya fave movie?*
15. *What's ya fave flavor?*
16. *You want to smoke an "L" with me?*
17. *You want to smoke the judge who sent you here?*

Her Secret

One night, Martha dropped by to say hello. A hooker hooked into just about everything, Martha was a notorious gossip who would hang out at the library counter, reading aloud from the newspaper's police log and offering a running commentary on the catalog of recent crimes, the vast majority of which were committed by her relatives, close friends, neighbors, and an endless train of acquaintances named "Timmy" and "John John."

"I *knew* that ho was headed to jail! . . . Oh Christ, not Timmy! . . . Tony, you *dumb fuck!*"

And on it went. It was hard not to like Martha. If she had been remotely trustworthy, I'd have hired her to work the library detail.

That night, Martha leaned in across the counter.

"Hey Arvin," she said. "You wanna know something?" She was smiling like a crocodile.

"Probably not," I replied.

"Your friend, Jessica," she said, using Solitary's Christian name, "she don't come to your class no more 'cause she can't look out that window."

"What a shame," I said. "When I teach a class on window gazing, I'll sign her right up."

"Yeah, funny. But she's got her reasons."

"Oh really, why?"

"She wants to look out the window cause her son's in the yard. 3-3's in the yard same time as your class. Poor girl goes to your class to catch a view of him. You get what I'm telling you?"

I must have looked incredulous because Martha straightened her back and placed her hand over her heart, as though she were about to recite the Pledge of Allegiance. This woman took her gossip as a solemn duty.

"Honest to *God*," she said, carefully enunciating her thick Boston *ohwnest ta Gowad*. "She ain't seen the kid in like ten years or something, and then, like that, her baby boy shows, wearin' blue."

The Man in the Lime-Beige Plaid Suit

Jessica's son wasn't the only unexpected arrival. My good friend Yoni had been prison-bound for a long time—possibly his whole life. Like many a rambling man before him, Yoni's adventures ended pitifully by the side of a lonesome Tennessee highway, police flashers ablaze in his rearview mirror. The officer took one look at his car, with its tinted windows and its *Support the Troops* bumper sticker (placed there in order to curry favor with cops). One look at Yoni's hippie getup, at his roguish dimples. The car was searched— an unfortunate turn of events, as the satchel stashed in the trunk, the one embroidered with a zebra-skin map of Africa, contained enough homegrown to qualify for "intent to sell," a class D felony.

Did it matter that Yoni had committed no crime? That the bag, along with the intent to sell its contents, belonged to his new friend, the man sitting in the passenger seat, a fiftysomething ex–Black Panther/out-of-work teacher/subsistence farmer? Of course it didn't matter. That was for a judge to decide. Cops have a different way of doing things. As the old Southern folksong says,

> The sheriff'll grab ya and the boys will bring you down
> the next thing you know, son, you're prison bound.

After the arrest, the holding cell, and the arraignment, after bond was posted, after a sleepless summer facing possible jail time, up to a year, Yoni had finally gotten justice. It wasn't simple. For the events of Yoni's life tend to unfold on an Old Testament scale; his god is an Angry God. It took driving his jalopy to court directly through Hurricane Katrina, through sideways rain that gave the impression of operating underwater, but his record was finally wiped clean, his mug shot expunged. His name cleared. Again.

Yoni's name had been cleared more times than a table at Big Boy—and each time, ready for the next greasy feast. The man was a glutton for trouble. While living in the Mississippi Delta, where he taught high school English, he had tried his hand at the Southern hospitality thing. When a rifle-toting cowboy drifter, wandering next to the Mississippi River, asked him if there was "anything fun to do in town," Yoni immediately invited the man home for a platonic dinner. The meal ended with the irate, sexually frustrated cowboy exposing himself to Yoni. During his own travels, Yoni saved money by sleeping on park benches instead of in hostels.

And then there was the kind of trouble that hadn't happened yet, the evil seed that might one day yield a poison fruit: writing on a housing application for graduate student housing, for example, that he had a problem with *nocturnal enuresis*, a.k.a. bedwetting. While this lie achieved his immediate objective, securing a rare single room, he still wonders if one day, down the road, this bedwetting document will somehow end up in the wrong hands. Perhaps a tenure committee, perhaps a congressional committee. When that day comes, he'll need to clear his name once again.

Yoni has lived much of his life under the shadow of false accusations. His slovenly and peculiar ways led a college administrator to interrogate him over the (completely false) charges that he was a heroin addict. On a separate occasion, Yoni was summoned to this same administrator's office, this time accused of a hate crime—again, a terrible misunderstanding. True he'd yelled, in his booming voice, out of his window and into a crowded courtyard of a college dorm, "Hey, Avi, you *fucking* Jew!" But it had been a joke, a Jewish thing, he explained to the administrator. Even at the biological level, Yoni stood falsely accused: he once tested positive, falsely, for syphilis.

But Yoni was the master of underdog brio. As an overweight Little Leaguer, his record of striking out over twenty times in a row did not prevent him from stepping up to the plate and, like Babe Ruth, grandly pointing to the outfield fence, calling his imminent home run. Years later, after reading an article on Donald Trump in an in-flight magazine, he decided to heed the great man's advice and always wear a tie in professional settings. Yoni was a stalwart optimist.

His great moment would arrive on *Jeopardy*, in front of nine million viewers. After two rounds the studio audience hadn't exactly turned on him, but they'd undoubtedly written him off. Yoni's goofball antics—blowing a lewd kiss and winking into the camera during his introduction, his funny voices, his fist-pumping enthusiasm, his lime-beige plaid sportcoat, Byronic shirt collar, his sagging, beltless trousers, his scruffiness—had announced that he was performing some sort of personal sideshow. Nobody, and certainly not his mother sitting in the studio audience, knew what to say when the

bantering segment of the show became a nationally televised session
of Freudian analysis:

> ALEX TREBEK: It says here that in college you ran naked around
> Harvard Yard, wearing only a giant orange wig, during the
> annual Primal Scream event. And that your *mother* was
> there to watch?
> YONI: My mother was a supportive mother. As was her friend.
> And my brother. And my grandmother.
> TREBEK: All of these people ran naked?
> YONI: No, they watched.
> TREBEK: What about your grandma?
> YONI: She was intrigued from the sidelines. Didn't realize how
> many shapes and sizes . . .
> TREBEK: Right, right, okay . . .

Before the largest audience of his life, Yoni had succeeded at
playing the fool. As if to give weight to this role, he'd played two
uneven rounds, entering Final Jeopardy in last place, $11,900 behind
his opponents. Nobody in the studio audience believed that this
lightweight, this clown in the loud sportcoat, had the mettle. But
after the Final Jeopardy think-music had ended and the lights went
up, it was Yoni alone who had identified the person on the Warren
Commission who later faced assassins. Thanks to President Gerald
Ford and his would-be assassins, Squeaky Fromme and Sara Jane
Moore, Yoni was on national television, $25,799 richer, dancing a
ludicrous jig as his preppy co-contestants stood by in shock. He'd
proved his point: the fool prevails.

But it took a long time to get to that nationally televised jig. Years earlier, Yoni was just a guy out on bail, with a mountain of legal debts, looking for work. After Halloween and the end of his job as a haunted house persona—a malevolent German scientist—Yoni had applied for gigs as a fruit vendor, a street musician, a bicycle tour guide, a Dunkin Donuts guy, a bar mitzvah tutor, a stripper—and secured all but the last three positions. But the money was never right, and the job search continued.

As luck would have it, the prison at which I worked had an opening. After waiting for his criminal record to be cleared, and allowing his system to rid itself of any illicit residue, he shaved and came in for an interview.

One sunny afternoon, a few weeks later, mere months after he'd barely eluded prison time, Yoni strode through the hallway door to the yard, walked past the guards, and threw open the prison library door. He marched in, a contractor's ID dangling from his shirt, a big ironic smile on his face.

"Whaddup up, pimp," he said, and gave me a goofy fist bump. This delighted the assembled library regulars.

"This your boy?" asked Fat Kat, with a big grin.

"I think *so*," said Dice.

"Um," I said, "guys, please meet Yoni, he's the new 'Life Skills instructor.'"

The Katrina Hustle

This was about the time when I found myself in the sallyport—the little limbo between the prison's front double security doors (never open at the same time)—crowded in with six or seven staff members. An older woman flashed me the overly familiar smile that invariably prefaces unsolicited comments from strangers. I get these a lot.

"You a volunteer?" she asked.

"No," I said, "staff."

I flashed her my shiny ID, the one with the photo of my incriminating haircut and befuddled expression.

"Hey," she said again, after it was evident that the officer in central control was taking his time giving us clearance. "I thought we had child, uh, labor laws in this country." She could barely get this comment out before expelling a smoker's guffaw. "What are you — twelve, thirteen years old?" This prompted grins, even among those who'd been pretending not to hear.

For the first time, I'd decided to heed the prison's "Dress-Down Friday" policy. (A policy for staff — if inmates dressed down any further, they'd be wearing loincloths.) I was sporting jeans, a Red Sox T-shirt, and chucks on my feet. This apparently lent me the look of an overgrown tween. It would be the last time I'd be observing Dress-Down Friday.

But the wheezy woman in the sallyport wasn't alone. I was one of the youngest, and greenest, staff members. People seemed to enjoy reminding me of this. After about the seventh person had told me to be careful — to not trust anyone — I began to wonder if there was something particularly naïve looking about me.

I needed to gain some prison respect. Yet, try as I might, I couldn't escape the impulses of my education: that the world's problems demanded the old college effort. Yes, I would do this the Harvard way. I would *spearhead an initiative*.

I spliced some glossy magazine photos of Hurricane Katrina refugees and designed a nice propaganda poster with it. There had been a good deal of outrage among the inmates at the government's indifference toward poor black communities in New Orleans. I would challenge inmates to do something beyond complain. To donate money to hurricane relief and to command respect for having done so.

When I proposed the idea to Patti, she balked. It hadn't occurred to me that raising money from inmates, especially as a collective, was actually a radical concept, not to mention a potential logistical nightmare. But these, I insisted, were mere technical problems. *I'll stay on top of it*, I assured her, supremely confident. I could tell she didn't feel comfortable with the idea. But, probably not wanting to dampen my enthusiasm, she gave me the green light. Or rather, the yellow light, which in Boston means slam on the gas.

Up went the poster. I rigged up a special consent form with which an inmate could authorize the transfer of money directly from his prison account to the Red Cross Katrina Fund. The consent form was photocopied as a receipt. I made up lists of inmates by prison unit. I perfected my pitch and made flyers that were to be dispersed throughout the prison.

Everything was going well until a senior staffer, a jolly linebacker-sized caseworker with a heavy black leather jacket, a thick curly mop, and even thicker Greek accent, walked into the library, clutching one of the flyers. His smile beamed through his gum-chewing.

"Eez theez for real?" he asked, lifting up the flyer.

I confirmed that *theez* indeed was quite real.

"Ho boy," he said shaking his head, laughing. "Goo' luck, my friend."

He gave me a friendly slap on the shoulder that almost knocked me square out of my Rockports.

The reaction from staff was nearly unanimous. Another caseworker, on his daily newspaper break in the library, asked me what inmate donors would get in return. A *sense of agency*, I theorized. A faint grin crossed his face as he awaited the punch line. When it didn't come, he burst out laughing.

"That," he said, "is *priceless*."

After the caseworker left, still chuckling to himself, Coolidge appeared. Sitting nearby, poring over a volume of the *Massachusetts General Laws Annotated*, he had overheard this exchange.

"Don't listen to them," he said. "You know you're doing a good thing."

"Thanks," I said.

"I can help you, you know. I can go into the unit, get people to sign. No problem."

"That's okay. I'm all set."

"No, really, I can help you. I know how things get done in here."

"No, really," I said. "All set."

And I was. Despite the skepticism of my coworkers I'd actually begun attracting a few donors. Even a few who were almost broke themselves. I was feeling good. If it was radical to raise money from inmates, then I guess I was a radical.

The truth is, I'm nothing of a radical. I wouldn't be caught dead displaying a picture of Che. And though I was amused by a Wesleyan student I once met who told me that she funded a prison education program with the proceeds of her swift drug dealing business, I wasn't one for revolutionary action.

But I did have fits of ambition. Though the goals for fund-raising were modest enough, once the project was under way I wanted to do it right. To make as much money and reach as many inmates as possible.

Coolidge's offer intrigued me. He was right. He could reach

those people who never came to the library and speak to them in a way that would be more persuasive than I, a fourteen-year-old-looking white boy. With his help, I could double (or more) the reach of this effort.

After a week of watching the donations continue to trickle in, fewer every day, I decided to give him a shot. I approached his "office," the back reference/computer room. Coolidge caught me hesitating at the entrance, wondering whether it was wise to proceed.

"Please come in," he said. "I'm not too busy."

"Right," I said. "I've got a job for you."

This was the formulation I'd chosen over *I need your help.*

"Oh really?"

"I thought about your offer to help with the Katrina thing and I've decided that I want you to collect signatures in the units."

"I told you."

And with that, he opened up a folder and pulled out smudgy sheets full of signatures.

"Already started," he said. He was pleased to the point of nausea. "How do you like that?"

I didn't like it at all. He'd gone behind my back. But I had to admit he'd secured an impressive number of donors.

"Good," I said, "keep it up."

Prison Doors: A Brief History

The prison occupies a former dump and incinerator site. It is nearly impossible to reach by car. You must first navigate an Escher-like labyrinth of streets, in which a turn west lands you east, and a turn east lands you nowhere. To get onto Bradston Street, where the prison is located, you must make a sudden, impossibly sharp right turn. If you miss the turn, you're sent directly onto the interstate. It's as if the city planners are warning you: *Trust me, you don't want to turn here, get away, far away, from this place.*

Not that I drove. I took the Mass Ave. bus line, which ferried me from the gates of Harvard Yard, near where I was living at the time, to the Boston Medical Center. From there, I walked fifteen minutes across the giant highway interchange, into the netherland of South Bay.

A street sign identified the area as Newmarket Square—though I'd never heard anyone call it that—an industrial zone sandwiched between some of Boston's toughest and fastest gentrifying neighborhoods: Roxbury, Dorchester, the South End, and South Boston, or Southie. Most of my friends and neighbors in Cambridge had never heard of South Bay even though it was a twenty-minute drive down the road.

It turned out the common metaphor of prison as a warehouse was actually not a metaphor. South Bay was a warehouse district. There were auto-body shops, mason depots, a methadone clinic, sundry bombed-out buildings, the headquarters of the Boston Fire Department, the Transit Police. But mostly just streets of warehouses and a chorus of beeping, produced by the backing up of delivery trucks. Sometimes it felt as though the entire place was inching backward.

And in a way, it was. South Bay is rumored to be sinking into the sea. Although a landmass for generations—having been filled in a century ago—seagulls still swarmed the skies. Perhaps they sensed the rising tide.

Signs of the End were everywhere. In a large storage lot in front of the prison, an urban cemetery: street signs—some from familiar city thoroughfares, Commonwealth Ave., Beacon St.—twisted into tortured poses. Splintered telephone poles strewn about in haphazard mounds, battered streetlights, busted-up traffic signals, a perfectly new Fisher Price Talking Chef Magic Kitchen set.

The area around the prison didn't do a good job concealing its former use as a shipping yard. Antique train tracks asserted themselves at odd intervals all along surrounding streets. The streets themselves appeared to have sustained a mortar barrage. You had to drive around the prison at a respectful pace. There were no quick getaways.

The current facility was designed in "pods"—smaller cell blocks, or "units," organized around dayrooms that allow the inmates to interact—and replaced the old Deer Island prison's Auburn architectural model, the notorious linear design of long corridors stacked into tiers intended to maximally isolate inmates. When this new, "state of the art" prison was built in 1990, William Weld campaigned against it.

"This Taj Mahal of a jail," then candidate Weld declaimed, "is an obscene symbol of everything that is wrong with state government and stands as a permanent insult to the taxpayers of Massachusetts. I'd like to reintroduce our inmates to the joys of busting rock."

He was taking a traditional perspective of prison architecture. An encyclopedia entry from the early nineteenth century explains that a prison's design should involve "an effectual method of exciting the imagination to a most desirable point of abhorrence . . . the exterior of a prison should, therefore, be formed in the heavy and somber style, which most forcibly impresses the spectator with gloom and terror."

To Dr. Benjamin Rush—who in addition to signing the Declaration of Independence was also a prison reformer, and a bit of a drama queen—the door wasn't just a visual but an auditory feature: "Let the avenue to this house be rendered difficult and gloomy by mountains and morasses. Let the doors be of iron, and let the grating, occasioned by opening and shutting them, be increased by an echo that shall deeply pierce the soul." At the time, this was a progressive position. Piercing souls was a more humanitarian approach than carving up bodies.

The designers of the South Bay prison had a different perspective. During the initial stages of design, architects at Stubbins Associates—the firm responsible for the Federal Reserve Bank in Boston, the Citicorp building in New York City, and the Reagan Presidential Library—posted various images of old prisons in their sunny offices in Cambridge. All were too depressing. One stood out. The highly mythologized Bridge of Sighs in Venice. As a senior architect told the *Boston Globe*, the Bridge "connects a public building to a prison in the back of the Doge's palace and it points to the civic role of buildings like this . . . a bridge between the public face of justice and the reality of incarceration and punishment."

Though they disagreed on the purpose of the building's design, both the governor and the architects did share an old assumption: that a prison's architecture should affect the citizens on the outside as much as the prisoners on the inside. Both agreed that the prison's exterior matters, that it's an essential public symbol of . . . *something*.

One day before my shift started, I stood in front of the prison, looking at the façade. Probably hoping to put off work for another few minutes, I decided to do a little experiment: to close my eyes and open them, to allow the architecture to work its magic on me, to produce some emotional reaction, some sensation.

Here are my findings: nothing. No gloom, no terror. No echo.

My soul was not pierced deeply. It wasn't a Taj Mahal of a jail, an obscene symbol, as the governor had quipped. Nor was it the architect's highly conceptual Bridge of Justice. There was no "effectual method of exciting the imagination" in any direction at all. The structure repelled all imagination. It was two cereal boxes. It left no impression, and asked to be ignored. It was purely functional. But what function—this was not made clear.

It wasn't always like this. In "The Prison Door," the memorable first chapter of *The Scarlet Letter*, Hawthorne describes, or imagines, how this very same institution, the Boston prison, appeared in its earliest incarnation, the very first prison in the New World. These are the opening words of the book (which sits on both the Classics and Fiction library shelves in the prison's latest incarnation):

> A throng of bearded men, in sad-colored garments and grey steeple-crowned hats, inter-mixed with women, some wearing hoods, and others bareheaded, was assembled in front of a wooden edifice, the door of which was heavily timbered with oak, and studded with iron spikes.
>
> The founders of a new colony, whatever Utopia of human virtue and happiness they might originally project, have invariably recognized it among their earliest practical necessities to allot a portion of the virgin soil as a cemetery, and another portion as the site of a prison. . . . Certain it is that, some fifteen or twenty years after the settlement of the town, the wooden jail was already marked with weather-stains and other indications of age, which gave a yet darker aspect to its beetle-browed and gloomy front. The rust on the ponderous iron-work of its oaken door looked more antique than anything else in the New

World. Like all that pertains to crime, it seemed never to have known a youthful era.

The prison's door, the most ancient-seeming entity in the brand New World, was such a potent symbol that Hawthorne began his story about the nature of sin and punishment by focusing the reader's attention on it, even before introducing his main character. The prison door itself is the protagonist as much as the criminal who walked through it.

From a dreadful symbol of sin, the prison had evolved into this: a building that doesn't say anything coherent, does nothing to announce its function, a prison designed to blend in, to be sped by on the highway. Was that progress?

In today's prison, there are no spikes, no grim iron-work, no castellated towers. And no ponderous door. Hawthorne's prison door, it would seem, exists only in words on the shelves of the prison library. The space where this actual prison door used to stand is now a hollow entryway into a lobby.

In the absence of a symbol as concrete as Hawthorne's prison door, everyone is free to fill this hollow space with private meanings. The literacy teachers and "re-entry" counselors, like Yoni, had their resource books. The officers and support staff had their retirement funds. Jessica, it turned out, had family drama. And what did Coolidge have? He filled the empty space left by the prison door with, as usual, conspiracy theories. Like many inmates, he wondered aloud what this place was *really* about. He would mock the American penal system's vaguely Orwellian nomenclature of "corrections": *Department of Correction, House of Corrections, Correctional Facility*, and his favorite, *Correction Officer*.

"What does that even *mean?*" he said once. "Let me show you what a *correction* is."

On the back of one of his legal briefs, he scribbled: *I like to right.* Then he crossed it out, and rewrote it: *I like to write.*

"*That's* a correction," he said. "This here is a damn prison."

There were often grains of truth in Coolidge's ramblings. Nobody knew what "corrections" meant. It was a hollow word. Just like that empty space where the prison's door once made its presence known.

In this prison, the door can be found safely out of public sight, inside of the building. One must strain to locate it. In the lobby, behind the metal detector one can see the steel and glass sliding double doors, transparent and inconspicuous. And yet heavier than the Puritans' oak by several orders of magnitude. This prison's door is a good deal more gloomy and a good deal less visible than the old door.

Charlie, taking his union-protected break, caught me staring up at the tower.

"You're late," he said, as always, half in jest. "What're you looking at?"

"Nothing, actually."

We walked through the hollow space and back into the lobby.

Coolidge at the Helm

Even before the Katrina fund-raising drive, Coolidge had been an exceedingly busy man, always the first in, the last out, of the library. In addition to being one of the great legal minds of his inmate generation, he held various self-appointed positions, complete with homemade titles: *Law Coordinator*, which he sometimes called *Legal Aid* or *Law Advocate* or *Law Clerk*. *Education Counselor, Re-entry Advisor, Baptist Services Coordinator*. Coolidge had enough fictional titles to compete with any cooked-up Harvard senior's résumé.

All of these (non)positions qualified him for a yet higher (non) position as something of a prison chieftain, the representative of the inmate collective. *El Presidente*, as some inmates called him in disdain. Coolidge's political moves were well documented. When he wasn't drafting legal briefs, he composed various official memos, op-eds, formal queries, letters to the editor, progress reports. On special occasions, he'd put out a press release. If cameras had been permitted in prison, he would have arranged photo ops. Under the circumstances, he contented himself with the written word.

Though not the best writer, Coolidge always came out swinging. He was the Mark Twain of the memo, attacking even pedantic forms with verve and occasional wit. He'd ask me to edit his latest writings, then proceed to reject every single suggestion I made. When I advised him to spread the *!* lightly, he became exclamatory.

"C'mon now!" he said, throwing up his hands. "I *invented* the damn exclamation point! I made it a household name! I got it trademarked, man. I make royalties off it!"

With his schemes and his exclamation points, Coolidge pestered the courts, parole boards, newspaper editorial boards, noted authors, the prison administration, City Hall, celebrities, the clergy, and pretty much anyone with a mailing address. None of this bothered me. He was bringing in sheets of inmates' signatures. Money was rolling in to the Katrina fund-raising project. Everything was great.

My first hint to the contrary arrived, appropriately, by way of a memo. Or, to be more precise, a draft of a memo Coolidge had accidentally left lying around the library. It concerned the Katrina project. *His* Katrina project.

In the document, addressed to the prison administration, Coolidge "respectfully requested permission to solicit donations in the units housing the female inmates (the Tower)." I couldn't help but smile at this modest proposal. Coolidge knew this request was both illegal and laughable. A male inmate requesting to visit the female prison blocks was like an inmate asking to be let out for the night to attend his buddy's bachelor party.

As "Program Organizer," Coolidge continued, he humbly offered his services—with, he conceded, proper "accompaniment of prison staff." This effort, he argued, would significantly increase the amount of money and the profile of the project, all of which would be great PR for the prison administrators themselves. On a more menacing note, he pointed out that it was imperative that inmates—who were furious at the racial injustice of Katrina—had a "peaceful outlet for their justified anger." And that failure to include the women might be perceived by many inmates as an attempt to stifle this effort. The implied threat of violence was clear enough.

Coolidge concluded the memo by stating that he was very proud to have conceived and planned this initiative and would like permission to organize a "media event" upon completion of the project. Again, he would be happy to offer his services and work up a press release. A list of expenses was included.

It was a thoroughly entertaining proposal, a masterpiece of delusional deadpan. Entertaining enough that I hardly cared that he was taking credit for my idea.

That Friday, during the morning shift, my office phone rang. I picked up.

Fire Coolidge.

It was Patti's voice.

Why? I asked.

Silence.

That's the order I got from above, she said finally. *Fire him from the library detail. Effective immediately.*

What do I tell him?

That he's fired.

Right, but . . .

And that he's got to go back to his cell immediately.

And what if he asks why?

There were noises of displeasure. A sigh, a sniffle, a tapping pen.

Tell him it's an order. He'll find out when he finds out.

This last comment was directed at me, as well, which I found irritating. But I had a more pressing concern: I'd never fired someone, let alone a violent felon. It was at these moments that I realized I hadn't undergone any training. That this *was* my training.

When Coolidge came into my office, he knew something was wrong. Even before I uttered a word, he pointed his big gloomy square head at me and made a bid.

"I don't need to be a part of the project," he said. "You can take all the credit and smile for the cameras. I'll sit on the side. It don't matter."

"Thanks for the offer," I said. "But there aren't going to be any cameras." Before he could say anything else, I just blurted it out.

"I got a call from the higher-ups," I said. "They told me to fire you. And they said you have to go back to your cell immediately."

Coolidge's face twisted into a snarl. I tabulated the odds he was going to rip the head off my shoulders. Perhaps it'd hurt for only a second. Perhaps it would be painless. A swift death: Always a good Plan B. But I needed a Plan A. I scanned my office for weapons. I'd pick up my giant computer monitor, crash it on his head, and run. Or use it as a shield. The trick would be in hoisting up the monitor and pulling the cord out of the electrical socket in one deft motion.

Coolidge assumed a variety of extreme poses in rapid succession. He jumped out of his seat, paced, punched his palm, ran his hand roughly through his hair, slumped back in his chair. Finally, he sunk his face deep into his hands.

"Why?" he asked.

"I don't know. They didn't tell me why. I figured you'd know."

He glared at me. I put a hand on my computer monitor.

"Please don't do this," he said, almost in tears. "I need this. I gotta work on my case or I could go away for a minimum of seven years. Minimum! It could be up to twenty. This isn't a joke, man. This is my life. I got a right to defend myself."

I thought about the promise he'd made to his daughter, to be there when her daughter, his granddaughter, was born. I remembered the inmate Coolidge had taught to read, and how he'd helped me during my first weeks.

"It's not my choice," I said, miserably.

As he walked out, he said, almost in a whisper, "If you don't stand up for yourself and your detail, man, everyone's gonna walk all over you."

Later that day, another inmate told me that Coolidge had gone into his cell and wept.

. . .

After a few days, I finally discovered the reason for the sacking: the notorious memos. Coolidge had finally crossed the line. He was sounding more and more like a staff member. The prison administration had become alarmed. The final straw was a letter—in which he wrote "Internal Memo" on the header— requesting an extension of religious programming, complete with extra towels and white bathrobes for the Baptist services that he had (supposedly) planned. The staff minister who was paid to organize Baptist programs was furious that Coolidge had gone over his head. Apparently it hadn't been the first time.

I was mostly amused by Coolidge's memos, annoying as they sometimes were. Coolidge could be a bully and wannabe, but at least he was actually trying to do *something*. That was more than could be said of other inmates and some of the staff. I couldn't help but feel that Coolidge was, in effect, being punished for showing initiative.

I also felt bad for him. It was true, he had been working tirelessly on his case. For the robbery charges, he could do serious time—the law is not lenient with "career criminals" like him. I saw inmates who were on trial for murder, facing possible life imprisonment, who spent their library time playing chess or watching Ben Stiller movies. Coolidge had made a mess of his life. But at least he had pride enough to give himself a serious defense.

And I had to admit there was some truth to what he'd said to me as he walked out: I'd been a bit of a dupe. After firing Coolidge, I'd walked over to Patti's office and made the case to restore Coolidge's job, on the grounds that his knowledge of the law was a major asset to the library. But this had been rejected without a moment's deliberation. I didn't appreciate that the administration would fire a valued employee of mine without my input, without even the courtesy of an explanation. I mean, it was like I was working in a prison.

But, at the very least, I'd made some headway by raising a couple thousand Katrina dollars—thanks largely to Coolidge's legwork. At least I could point to that success.

As I readied my final report for the Katrina project, an inmate handed me a typed note. He said it was from an inmate in his unit. The note claimed that Coolidge had engaged in some funny business during the fund-raising drive, that he had stolen funds and some inmates' ID information for illicit purposes. That he had strong-armed some inmates into donating money. The note ended by offering to detail these claims—if I were willing to put some money in *his* prison bank account.

I wasn't about to pay this guy for information. But his claims were disturbing. I recalled my conversation with Coolidge a couple of weeks earlier. Our business had been running swiftly.

"This isn't a con, is it?" I'd said. This was meant as a joke.

"Ah man," he'd replied. "You serious? I wouldn't bring that shit in here, man. Into the *library*? C'mon! Please."

I now turned to some of the other guys on the detail. I asked them if the charges were true. None of them answered. They were bound by the convict code of silence. But they didn't deny it, nor offer up any defense.

Later that day, a member of the detail walked into my office and told me that he "didn't know nothing" about what Coolidge had done, but advised me with a knowing sort of nod that it'd be wise to not finalize the transfer of the inmates' funds. Thus my Katrina donation drive was officially tainted by corruption. All my remorse over firing Coolidge left me in a split second.

"That's the way it goes in here, man," the detail member said, trying to console me. "Can't trust nobody in here."

"Can I trust you?"

He shook his head, laughed, and walked away.

"Just trust *yourself*," he said over his shoulder. "That's hard enough around this place."

A New Sheriff in Town

I did trust myself. I think. At least, I was pretty certain I did. I was confident, for example, that I wasn't anything like Mike De Luca, the daytime officer posted next to the library. He was a short, hot-tempered fellow, who bore more than a passing resemblance to Napoleon, with a hint of Mr. Bean. De Luca liked to sing commercial jingles and to answer trivia questions. Wherever possible, he combined these interests into a round of *Name That Tune*, a game he played with gladiatorial zeal. De Luca's emotions were terrifying—but predictable. When the Red Sox had won the night before, he was charming; when they lost, he was Ivan the Terrible. It was that simple. You needed only check the sports page for the De Luca forecast. He held court at his post, usually flanked by a pack of fellow union buddies. The co-cantankerous. A prison gang, one of the oldest around. They called themselves "the Angry Seven."

In doing his job keeping order and directing inmate traffic in and around the education wing, De Luca had a tendency to work himself into an eye-bulging mouth-foaming frenzy. This he called his "style."

At the end of each period, De Luca would throw open the door and charge into the library. He'd stand there like a trapped fox, eyes darting around. He had no patience for inmates who had ignored his first call of "That's a wrap!" Arms in full swing at his side, fingers a-flutter, as though itching to punch someone, he'd rush at lingering inmates yelling, *Get out, get out, getout out, out, out, right now, ri' now, ri' now!* His advantage was always in the surprise heavily caffeinated attack. The inmates hated him, but for the most part, he was effective.

Months later, after he'd been deposed, I overheard him sullenly tell another officer that "the bigwigs don't like my style but they can't say I don't get the job done." This was true.

A number of inmates and staff told me that De Luca would not have dared blitz the library during the Amato era. He respected Amato—and in any case, there hadn't been a need during Amato's iron reign. De Luca's rabid incursions pointed to a lack of leadership in the library: Forest and I weren't commanding enough authority and the inmates were doing as they pleased. De Luca filled the gap with his verbal assaults, leaving Forest and me looking even more powerless, and the library more like a prison block. Coolidge, now just a library patron, routinely mentioned this situation in order to needle me. When I finally told him that I had a different way of running the place than Amato, he raised a lawyerly brow.

"Yes, Avi, that's my point," he said. "And that's exactly what's gonna get you in the end. Listen, De Luca ain't your boss. But you don't take control, he will be. Yeah, Amato was an asshole but he understood control; you ignore it and you'll get a hundred De Lucas in here carving the place up for themselves and having a big ol' barbecue right up on your desk."

Of course, Coolidge should know. He had done just that, which was his point. Ever since Amato had paid me a visit and warned me not to spare the iron fist, I had noticed some slippage. Both inmates and officers treated the library like a truck stop. Things were getting sloppy. There was occasionally an utter lack of decorum. Materials were disappearing right and left, including a good deal of materials that could be made into weapons. We were discovering a greater volume of graffiti, of notes relating to drug deals, prostitution, and other illicit activities. After each period, there was a lot of trash left behind on the tables and floors. I noticed that some of the beefs from the prison units were playing out within the library space itself. If the place was, at its best, a neighborhood pub, it was, at its worst, a frontier saloon. Something had to be done. The library needed a sheriff.

As luck would have it, one of the inmates had just returned our well-worn edition of *The Prince*. His bookmark slipped out. It was a list of the 48 Laws of Power, a distillation of the Machiavelli-inspired 1998 Robert Greene book of the same title. Possibly the most requested book in the library. I read the list of the 48 Laws of Power and flipped through *The Prince*.

Hmm, I thought.

A fter the rousing success of my creative writing class for women in the tower, I decided to inaugurate my class for men. The class met every Monday and Wednesday in the back-back room of the library. Ten inmates signed up.

On a Wednesday afternoon, I was standing in front of the circulation desk, waiting for the inmates to file into the classroom. Just then, the front door swung open and one of the inmates, Jason, strode in, looking straight ahead and perturbed. Officer De Luca appeared behind him, arms swinging, according to his style. His head shook as though it were about to detonate.

"'Ey, get back here!" he shouted.

Jason glanced behind him. "I'm here for my class," he said casually and proceeded to enter the room.

"Oh no you don't . . ." De Luca said. He was almost running now.

I decided to try to defuse the situation. "It's okay, Officer, he's in the class. His name is on the list."

Without so much as glancing at me, De Luca said: "No, no, no, no . . . this guy punked me out, he's going back up to the unit. Or maybe the hole."

This was not what I wanted to hear.

I hadn't seen what had happened. Jason probably had said something stupid to him. On the other hand, De Luca's bellicose "style" no doubt provoked him. I knew Jason well. He was mild-mannered and perfectly respectful when respected. I also knew that the inmate had every right to be in the library and that by giving him a hard time and now kicking him out, De Luca was pulling a macho power play that had nothing to do with any immediate security concern. And if there was a security situation, it was because De Luca was escalating the situation.

I could feel myself getting angry. The edges of my ears began to tingle. I was sick of De Luca's style turning my library into Gitmo. Nor did I appreciate how he'd just blown me aside, without any attempt to give respect—you don't do that in prison. There were less rational things churning through my head, as well. I was still annoyed that Coolidge had conned and embarrassed me. That my bosses had fired my employee without any regard for my position. I was generally sick of being messed with. And so, as my class of ten inmates and the four members of the inmate library detail stood by, I was suddenly overcome by a spirit, the impulse to *go rogue*.

Every piece of prison swag I'd heard suddenly swirled into my head, and was absorbed directly into my bloodstream. The 48 Laws of Power. Law 17—Keep others in suspended terror; cultivate an air of unpredictability. Law 37—Create compelling spectacles. And the boasting of the kite writer: *I'm never one that's lost for words. A bitch like me can't be stuck on chuck, the boss is lost, for nada. I'm a go-getter, and I go for what I want, and usually, I get what I want. Early!* And not only that: The spirit of Don Amato himself descended upon me. My lips curled into a faint sneer, the haughty gaze of the prison's newest wise guy, the Sheriff Librarian. *On the up&up and low low, you go for yourz.* Law 28—Enter action with boldness.

I looked squarely at De Luca.

"Okay," I said. "But now *you're* punkin' *me* out. He's in *my* class."

De Luca looked at me as though for the first time. It wasn't a look of anger but of abject confusion, as though I'd just assumed physical form out of thin air. It suddenly occurred to me that he hadn't ever really noticed me. And now, out of nowhere here I was, some stranger, dressed like a first-week college freshman, talking at him like a tough guy. It must have been a bit puzzling.

"What? No, no," said De Luca. "He's coming with me." And to Jason: "You, up. You're going right back."

And that was that. I wasn't going to escalate things any further. I had made my point. (Law 47—Do not go past the mark you aimed for; in victory, learn when to stop.) It was important to let the officer save face. He was, after all, the officer; in prison, it was his ass on the line.

As soon as De Luca had escorted Jason out, the other inmates commended me. "You go, Artie!," "You tell that mutherfucka!" "We got yo back, bro"—all of which made me cringe. Nevertheless, it was respect, political capital that I could store away. And perhaps De Luca, the Angry Seven, and the inmates would think twice about crossing the Sheriff Librarian.

The Life-Skills Instructor's View
of the De Luca Incident

Yoni was getting rave reviews as a teacher in the 1-2-1 unit. The irony of his role as a "life-skills" instructor was of no consequence. When it came to teaching classes on résumé writing, job interview skills, task management, organizational methods, or any subject for that matter, he was a natural. Yoni's classroom charisma, his native smarts, and his abundant dedication to his students compensated for his own loose organizational methods. He quickly won over his reluctant students. The inmates appreciated his ten-minute improvised stand-up routine on the potential drawbacks of listing "jizz_baby@yahoo.com," as the contact information on your résumé, as one inmate had proposed.

Outside the classroom, he was having a bit more difficulty. The two women with whom Yoni shared an office were put off by his habit of clipping his fingernails at his desk, of listening to the Grateful Dead on his desk speakers, his tendency to conduct loud, badgering, interminably long, speaker-phone negotiations with box office managers, credit card people, bank tellers, and family members.

One of his officemates noted that Yoni seemed like a guy who might benefit from a severe beating. This was prison, after all; if you got out of line, someone would probably slap you down. For Yoni, it happened sooner rather than later.

He'd had a particularly egregious week. While on the phone with an important contact, Yoni had struggled to find a scrap of paper with a phone number on it. Rifling his desk, he'd muttered, "Fuck me." The contact had been offended and reported him.

But that was just the appetizer. Trying to make friendly conversation with his officemates, he'd asked one of the women who she thought was the sexiest inmate in the 1-2-1 unit. She didn't appreciate the question and reported him, too.

But the low moment came when Yoni used the word *nigger* in his classroom. He was teaching a class on the economics of crime, trying to persuade the students that crime literally didn't pay. To make this point he read aloud from the chapter in *Freakonomics* that explains why so many crack dealers live at home with their mothers. The book quotes a black crack dealer who uses the word *nigger*. Yoni simply read these passages in what was a clear educational context. But when a disgruntled inmate complained that he hadn't signed up for a class in order to be called a *nigger* by some white guy, Yoni, like so many times before, realized he was in trouble.

No prison administrator would come to his defense. "You don't ever use that word in prison," he was told, "educational context or not." The director of the Offender Re-entry Program, the NGO who had hired him, was furious: he had inadvertently compromised the entire outfit.

Yoni was formally reprimanded, forced to sign an official document of censure that listed his offenses—from cursing on the phone, to the inappropriate question, to his use of the word *nigger*. The document would be placed in his employment file for eternity. It was that kind of week.

The punishment served its purpose. Yoni reined in his behavior, and his officemates were willing to forgive and forget. Things were just beginning to quiet down, and his coworkers and students were starting to like him and to appreciate him as a lovable eccentric. Then the garlic incident happened.

Yoni had recently bought a gallon tub of peeled garlic. This was done to save money. But of course he hadn't succeeded in eating it all, and the garlic had begun to turn. Ever eager to get his money's worth, Yoni fried the remaining garlic cloves in oil. Once sufficiently browned, he poured them into a bowl, sat down, and gobbled up every last one. Upwards of thirty cloves of garlic. That was his dinner, a pound or so of fried not-quite-fresh garlic, and nothing else.

He didn't die in his sleep. But he came close. On his way out to work the next morning, after a long, turbulent night, he emailed me a one-line update, "i smell quite putrid. interesting."

Perhaps to him, a future anthropologist, it was. To the rest of humanity, however, it was insufferable. Roughly twelve hours after his garlic feast, Yoni showed up to work at prison, where the windows are sealed shut, the air recycled. He walked into the prison lobby, the sallyport, up a few halls, through the 1-2-1 prison unit, into his small, shared office. Everything seemed fine.

Everything was not fine. Yoni did not appreciate the extent of the problem. The stench pumped out from every pore, follicle, and orifice of his body, and hovered around him in a hazy poisonous aura. Nor had the smell diminished over the hours. On the contrary. Yoni was a walking radiator of toxicity, filling every space he entered with a wretched odor.

He walked into his office, sat at his desk, smiled, said good morning to his officemate, Peggy. She just looked at him in disbelief, covered her nose with her hand.

"Oh. My. God," she said. "Are you *kidding* me?"

Less than a month after he'd been formally reprimanded, he was called back into his boss's office. He was certain this was it. Holding her nose, a look of deep despair on her face, his boss said, "Yoni, I don't know how to have this conversation," and then quickly added, "You know what, we aren't even going to have this conversation." He assured her that this was really it. He was finally going to get his act together.

That afternoon, Yoni, with his toxic reek, thankfully did not make his usual visit to the library to say hello. But we spoke over the phone. He told me the pitiful tale of his day. The most surprising part, for me, was the moral of the story.

"The garlic was a really bad move," he admitted, "but you were much stupider, and fuckin' *crazy*, for getting into a beef with De Luca."

I argued the point with him. But it was academic. A man who's recently consumed thirty fried garlic cloves has crossed over into some mystical realm few have entered and has achieved some kind of Zen-like understanding of human folly. You cannot challenge the master's authority. When he criticizes your behavior, you heed his words.

And he was right. I'd jeopardized my relationship with De Luca, who was after all a necessary ally. With a day's introspection, and Yoni's metaphysical guidance, I was able to admit that I not only behaved rashly, but out of weakness. And that De Luca, despite his contentious "style," and regardless of his association with the seedy likes of the Angry Seven, was really after all a decent guy who liked to sing jingles. I had to smooth things over with him. But before I had a chance, De Luca approached me.

I was standing behind the counter. No one else was around. De Luca seemed very uncomfortable, almost as though forced to talk to me. He addressed me by name—having clearly asked someone what to call me—and apologized for removing one of my students and for "stepping on your toes." He explained that he had to take action against the inmate. I agreed in principle, apologized for my rude comment, and reiterated that we needed to work together to avoid misunderstandings. It was all very statesmanlike.

For the next few days I maintained my Sheriff Librarian persona, enforcing the rules with gusto, banishing inmates, speaking with authority to officers, and basically taking no shit from anybody, Amato-style. Fat Kat pulled me aside and gave me some advice.

"I know what you're doing," he said with a smile. "And I think it's a good idea. But watch yourself. And don't ever, never, do what you did with De Luca again, or you're asking for some serious trouble. And De Luca's okay, you know? Don't go crazy here."

I shrugged.

"Listen," said Fat Kat, "you might think you're a badass. You are not a badass, my friend. You're, *at best*, a punk. So why don't you just stick to being a librarian?"

De Luca and the inmates in the library probably thought of me as an overeducated young brat who didn't know the first thing about the real world of tough-guy prison combat. And they were completely right. But if they feared me a tiny bit or thought I might be a loose cannon, that was fine with me. I now knew the 48 Laws of Power.

"To quote Dirty Harry," I replied, "*I work for the city*."

"To quote Dirty Harry? Okay, Avi," Kat said, walking away, laughing, "I'll remember that."

Jessica Returns

After the public embarrassment of my tainted Katrina drive and of my scene with De Luca, I decided to keep a low profile. I turned to a quieter matter: Jessica. I'd been mulling over her situation for weeks, wondering what it was Jessica was really after. If she wanted to connect with her son, she could. She knew where he lived. She could send him a note. Perhaps she had. She may have left him a letter, a kite, in the library books, just like everyone else. But my guess was she hadn't and that her need to look out the window came in lieu of actually contacting him.

But what exactly was she doing in that window? Did she simply want to see what he looked like after all these years? Was she tormenting herself? Was she looking for some clue, some insight, some way to understand him? Everything about this scenario, this type of longing, was entirely beyond the scope of my life experience. It was inscrutable to me.

One thing was certain. When I saw her that first day, squinting in the sun, sitting with her perfect posture, hands folded in her lap, she seemed almost hypnotized by whatever it was she saw through the window. She was oblivious to the other people in the room. I'd had to rouse her. I'd been curt with her. I'd felt immediately bad for my impatience, and doubly so for wielding my authority crudely over someone older than I. But I think my regret originated from a less palpable source, from a sense that something else, something imperceptible to me, was happening. Even before I knew the truth, that I was interrupting her in some way.

But this remained a vague feeling. Even by the standards of this class, I barely knew her. She'd spoken maybe twice in the class, and almost always refused to hand in her writings. When she did, she rarely offered up more than a few stingy lines and was totalitarian in self-censorship. *I remember the day I first got arrested*, she once wrote for an essay assignment. *It was cold and cloudy. I don't remember much else.* She didn't bother including a fourth sentence in this essay (which was more of a haiku).

But still, I knew her silences were not for want of perception. This after all was the woman who'd examined Flannery O'Connor's photo and, even before reading a word, clairvoyantly summarized

O'Connor's sensibility: *She ain't too pretty. I trust her.* The little I knew of Jessica indicated that she had a sharp eye and that she trusted her vision. Perhaps that's why I wanted to know what she saw through that window. I thought about this often. So often, in fact, I had to wonder further: Why did I care so much?

I decided to pay her a visit in the Tower. That was one advantage of teaching in prison. The inmate students could run but they couldn't hide. It was impossible to play hookie in the joint. But as I stood in the elevator, I still wasn't sure why I was pursuing this.

Even as the door to the 1-11-2 unit rolled open, I still didn't know what I was planning to say. Before I could think about it, dozens of eyes turned my way. The women inmates, suffering from annihilating boredom, began to approach me. In seconds I was surrounded. My first reaction was, *Cool, I'm a rock star.* My second reaction was, *Get me out of here. Immediately.* I found myself in yet another seagulling situation. This time, it wasn't reading material inmates wanted, but attention.

Somebody leapt out of the crowd—Short.

"Whaddup Harvey!" she said.

Another inmate, whom I recognized only by face, shouted toward me. "Hey library guy," she said, waving a women's magazine, "I'm learning how to be *Forty & Fabulous!*" She beamed a big, semi-toothless grin. Short suddenly turned serious and began working crowd control. She jostled her fellow inmates and said, "Let the man through, let the man *through.*" She escorted me. The world's smallest bodyguard. Finally, I managed to slip through the crowd.

I found Jessica playing checkers. I thanked Short for her services and asked her for privacy. Jessica was not happy to see me. I cut straight to the point, even though I still wasn't sure what my point was.

"I want you to rejoin my class," I said.

She shrugged.

"I know why you left."

She gave me a doubtful look.

"You wanted to see your son, right?" I said.

Again, she shrugged. Inmates rarely answered pointed questions, never sure if they were digging a grave for themselves or someone else.

"Okay, listen, I don't care if your son is out there or who he is or anything. But I'm willing to make a deal with you. You can sit by the window, but you can't stare out the whole class. You need to look at me as much as you look outside, you need to do it quietly and not draw attention to yourself. And you need to participate in class. That means speaking up and putting real effort into your assignments. And do me a favor," I said, with a sigh, "don't tell anyone, *no* one, or I'm going to get every single person asking me to make deals. Got it?"

She smiled faintly. We had a deal.

The Green Light

Written words continued to wash up in the library. Each wave of inmates that crashed through brought forth more prison literary detritus.

At the end of a period the library would be littered with notes and shards of notes. I would walk around like a shell collector on a beach, gathering up legal documents, love letters, queries, manifestos, grievances, marginalia, scribbled receipts, remnants of illicit transactions, wrap dates, rap sheets, rap lyrics, business plans, country songs, handmade advertisements for "entertainment" businesses, journal entries, betting lines, greeting cards, prayers, recipes, incantations, and lists. Many lists. The found poetry of the everyday:

T-shirts
socks
the divorce
US v. Ferguson
M&Ms

In their brevity, some of these notes possessed a wise cryptic quality, like a message from an oracle. A single suggestive word or phrase: *No!* or *Please* or *It was his heart*. One that gave me pause: *Take Heed*.

And plenty of new kites—aborted, shredded, completed. The inmate who described the terror of a recurring dream, a reliving of an actual trauma, in which he is caught in a house fire—only to wake up, in a fright, and realize, "Thank God, I'm only in prison." Sometimes a line or two would stay with me for days: "To Whom It May Concern: I am a 36 year old mother, grandmother and addict. The latter I'm not proud of."

The kites also brought new insights. That in the world of inmate dating, for example, a full set of teeth was a prized enough possession that it was often mentioned along with other relevant measurements. And as always, the kite writers introduced me to new, dizzying patois: "I miss u so much remenicen about them summer days buggin out bottles of henn purp hayes burning in the dutch us and the goonies . . . I wanna get dipped out and make my rounds yo! Saly laided up 40's bagged will actin up like he was contributing to me popin my tags . . ."

Among the staff, the library was synonymous with inmates leaving letters for each other. It was common for me to come across an officer in a far-flung corner of the prison—usually when I was making deliveries—who would smile upon learning that I was the prison's librarian. I always knew exactly what he was about to say: "Read any good letters lately?" And I told him the truth. "Yes, always."

The letters had clearly vexed hardline Don Amato. He had posted an enormous sign on the door leading out of the library. Like all of his signs, this was impossible to remove:

BE AWARE!
LIBRARY BOOKS
ARE NOT
MAILBOXES.
IF CAUGHT,
WE WILL TAKE AWAY
ALL
YOUR
LIBRARY PRIVILEGES.

Although Forest and I didn't exactly allow letters, we didn't hand out punishments either. And so this was another immovable Amato sign unheeded. As usual, our semi-relaxed attitude was perceived as a green light, and we were left with a steady flow of missives from the shadows.

CHAPTER 2

Books Are Not Mailboxes

I couldn't help myself. I saw an opportunity for Jessica. She was a woman in her late thirties; her son was an eighteen-year-old kid, her only child, whom she had abandoned when he was almost two, and when she had been roughly his current age. Their lives had brought them to this place, to this self-enclosed world, visible to each other through the window.

And they were even nearer to each other than that. There was a portal through which they could almost touch. The library. It was a space they shared, though not at the same time. The place-ness of the library—that dynamic physical quality that made it somehow different than a pushcart of books wheeled to cells—created many unforeseen possibilities.

For a Sudanese woman awaiting deportation, for example, the library was a place for prayer. She'd find a quiet spot between the shelves, facing Mecca, pronounce the *shahada*, and prostrate herself before Allah. I asked her why she chose the library. There were two reasons. First, it was simply that time of day. And the second reason:

"This," she said, indicating the library with a sweep of her hand, "book place, holy place. Good place for pray."

Perhaps, like creating a mosque, or using books as mailboxes, this was one of the unique improvisational properties of a library in prison: a space in which to reconnect, in some way, a mother and son.

When Jessica showed up to class again, I adjusted the seats so that the group was situated closer to the windows, and Jessica seated strategically. As the session went on, she gazed down eleven stories, watching her son walk circuits around the prison yard, shoot hoops, crack jokes with the officers. She kept her end of the agreement, humoring my assignments and bringing her attention into the discussion.

I rolled with the window-gazing concept, even integrating it into the class. I asked the women to observe and describe the view through the window. A similar assignment had previously borne some fruit with the men, when I had asked them to describe the scene through their cell windows. With a painterly eye for detail (the single perk of being a jilted lover) one inmate described a crushing scene. It was a late afternoon in February. The city was enveloped in a bright white cloud. It was beginning to snow. Big, succulent, slow-drifting flakes. It must have been at just the freezing point. From his cell window, which faced the front of the prison, he saw his woman, who had just brought their five-year-old son to visit. Her new boyfriend walked with her and the boy. They stopped momentarily. She said something to the new boyfriend. He leaned over, unzipped the purse she was holding, and pulled out a scarf for her. A scarf that he, the inmate watching this, had given her. Then the new boyfriend combed back her hair with his fingers, wrapped the scarf around her neck, and zipped up the purse. The three of them walked away. Witnessing this tiny moment of intimacy destroyed him, he said. He cried, he confessed, "like a little bitch."

Jessica dutifully described her view through the window. The pigeons, the seagulls, the tiny birds whose fearlessness she admired. (Sometimes too fearless for their own good.) She described the sky, the moon, the clouds. Anything but her son in the yard below.

Short said she "wasn't in no mood" to look out the window. This was not uncommon. Inmates were often ambivalent about windows facing the world. Window gazing in prison is not neutral. From up in the Tower, one could see not only the yard but the world beyond prison, the city's buildings, and even some details from the city streets. It was just too tantalizing to be reminded of what you couldn't have. In the library, Pitts had told me he was happy to have a cell window that faced the yard. He didn't want to look at the world while he was in prison.

And then there was Tanisha, a nineteen-year-old gang member and library regular. A window view inspired her to begin writing a book. It happened during her first week in prison. From her cell window in the prison tower she could see her entire neighborhood in the distance. She'd never had a bird's-eye view of it. But there it was—the whole picture, her entire life framed in a single window. A prison window. Perhaps it was the sudden experience of objectivity, of seeing the familiar places of her life at once—the churches, the corners where she used to hang out, the high school where she'd nearly graduated, the houses of friends and enemies, streets where she'd witnessed shootings, the building in which her mother, a homeless addict, once showed up to buy drugs from her, unaware that this particular drug operation belonged to her own teenaged daughter. Seeing everything suddenly small and silent. Something about this new vantage point, this literal new perspective, made her life and those places seem like a *story*—and she, standing in that tower, its narrator. After seeing her neighborhood from up there, she told me, she'd immediately opened up a notebook and didn't stop writing until lights out. Four hours straight. And then every day since.

In one of her window-gazing assignments, Poor noted that the prison looked like a hotel. Sometimes she liked to imagine that she was on a trip, staying in a nice hotel, waiting for room service, like in the movies. She'd never actually stayed in one. I was amazed at how many different perspectives could be brought out of one prison window.

As an introduction to these assignments we read Plato's Allegory of the Cave from *The Republic*. Socrates imagines the world as a cave and all its human inhabitants as chained prisoners who "see only their own shadows, or the shadows of one another, which the fire throws on the opposite wall of the cave." These prisoners' view of reality is fundamentally skewed, and yet they cannot realize it. In class, we discussed this problem not as a general allegory but more literally, as a description of actual prison life. It wasn't hard for the prisoners in my class to relate to the problem. They lived their lives right on the edge of the "seeing problem," as one of them described it.

And yet, this prison did have a few windows. The window writing assignments turned out to be an addendum to Plato's seeing problem: that, given a window, a person's sense of sight might actually be *heightened* in captivity. That's why some inmates refused to look. But those who did tended to see the world more vividly, and certainly differently, than a visitor to the prison.

All of this served only to increase my curiosity about what Jessica was seeing.

So I asked her. It happened one afternoon after class. I was reluctant to quiz her on it but she seemed to want to talk. We stood in front of the window. She pointed her son out to me. He was playing basketball. I asked how she knew it was really him. She had friends on the outside who knew the boy, she said. They'd told her he'd be showing up in prison.

She didn't write about him for class, she told me, because she didn't trust the other women to "check their mouths." But she was happy to tell me. He hadn't changed at all. He'd been a happy child, friendly, physically precocious, affectionate, mischievous. Just from watching him in the yard, she could still see all of these qualities on display: the way he talked and laughed with the others. People seemed to like him. She'd always known he'd grow up to be that kind of guy. And he was so handsome. She choked up a bit. She thanked God that he was still a happy person after all he'd been through. She didn't want him to end up like her, in prison forever. That was all she could say. She cried.

And then, in a brutal, self-lacerating gesture, she swallowed up her emotions. There was something else she wanted to say. She dreamed about him. "In the dream," she told me, "he's playing basketball in the prison yard."

There is no one else there. He may or may not be wearing a prison uniform. It is a peaceful scene. The boy is in no rush. There is an indefinable sense of his somehow existing happily in this place. He glides in long, savory motions, as though skating gently over a frozen pond. The light is purplish and lush. He dribbles the basketball, fakes out invisible opponents, makes shots, misses shots, collects his own rebounds, leaps up—as though floating for a moment—and gently tips the ball into the hoop. It's like a dance. His body is pure joyful movement, unconstrained. The ball itself seems to move of its own volition, floats into and through his hands, weightless. The sound is the boy breathing, the ball bouncing, a satisfying rhythm. Inhale. Ball to pavement. Exhale. Ball to pavement. A deep humming silence as the ball arcs through darkness. And as the ball meets the net, a swoosh, like wind in trees. She hears it, feels it pass through her lips. His breath is her breath.

That shared breathing sensation is familiar to her from dreams she'd had when she was pregnant with him, she said. Until now, she'd forgotten about those dreams. Every night she goes to sleep and prays that God will send her the breathing dream. Sometimes he does.

Skywriting

Kites continued falling out of library books, bringing me messages almost by the hour. Eavesdropped bits. The occasional saga. Commentary on the latest prison incidents, geopolitical events. The notes also continued to fill gaps in my knowledge of prison culture.

Skywriting, for example. Starting from my first week in prison, I'd noticed the phenomenon, though I wasn't sure what it was. As I walked through the prison yard, I'd spied male inmates standing at their barred windows, furiously signaling skyward. The signals involved large sweeping hand motions—formal, almost nautical— that I later learned were letters scripted backward. I followed the invisible trajectory of these messages and found their recipients standing in barred windows way up in the Tower—the women inmates. Through the silent darkness of the prison night, there were at least five conversations soaring back and forth. This was skywriting, sometimes known as window-writing. Along with gambling, fighting, basketball, chess, and sending kites, it was the biggest prison pastime.

As with *kites*, the word *skywriting* had a poetic sound to it. Indeed the word sometimes appeared in inmate poetry. One of Nasty's haikus:

cell in late winter
skywriting to skinny dude
darkness in the yard

That darkness in the yard, together with backlighting from the cells, made skywriting a dramatic spectator sport. Or perhaps more like a puppet show or silent movie. It was a dialect as mesmerizing to observe as sign language. I often recognized the skywriters. But they rarely noticed me. Too busy reading the signals and responding, which, I was told, takes a great deal of concentration. Though aware of the existence of skywriting—anyone working the night shift would be—I could only guess what was being said.

That's where the kites helped. They were full of references to these nightly window dramas. As I learned by reading the kites, these airborne conversations were full of passionate promises, jealousies, quarrels, and reconciliations. From the earliest inklings of courtship to the bitter residue of breakups.

Lady Dee to Bill, says: "*Well let me say yes I was upset cause I thought you was writing someone else at the window, but who am I to get upset cause we're just friends.*"

Another woman to Papa Duck: "*One of my celly's just told me you were sky writing her in May, so know one thing my friend, I'm on to you Mr. Loyal!*" In case her point hadn't been clear enough, she concludes, "*Stay the fuck out the windows, I know everyone here.*"

A woman of conflicted emotions: "*You are so sweet to me I love you baby. Why are you talking smack in the window. I'll bite ya dick off, don't play.*"

Mario to T-Baby: "*I did see you in the window last night (Sunday July 23) again getting your flirt on. Why? Daddy ain't enough for you!!! You act as though I'm second hand smoke. Please check my pedigree. For the last time, I'm a thoroughbred. Well I trust & demand you got the message and the dumb shit stops now. I know your window. It's the busiest window upstairs. You obviously ain't writing me because you ain't sure what cell window is mines yet or if it's me you've made contact with. And if you did notice me last week you couldn't understand me or I couldn't understand you because I'm new to this shit and honestly if it weren't you upstairs I wouldn't play myself out with this window writing bullshit!! My window writing skills suck so we must go slow and be patient with eachother until we get better. On Wednesday, we have a window date. Be there! Fuck who's outside in the yard! ;) Post up in your cell window. When I see you I'm gonna click my lights five times (5) and then shape two hearts. Wait for you to do the same back to me (5 clicks,*

2 hearts). Feel me! Then to be exactly sure it's us and to throw off any possible pranksters & haters who may be playing the window after you signal me back I'll do two more clicks and one more heart and wait for you to do the same (2 clicks, 1 heart) and then you'll be sure it's me and we can start to show love."

A lady: "I like putting on a show for you, but I hope you know I ain't just a show, daddy."

Killa Kim, who is actually a killer, reflecting on a past window love: "I really did fall for him hard. But I couldn't stay out of the window forever."

On page 9 of his letter, one of Killa Kim's numerous pen pals indulges in some window nostalgia: "I'm thinking about the closeness we share and all the good times we've spent in the window."

Shaheed: "Please don't deny that you ain't been in the window talkin please. I was in the yard waiting and I KNEW you were there in the window looking. Now, any other time you'd be there signaling your ass off, but today nothing. But you know what, I understand, your friend may get mad. It's cool."

Lauren to Baby Boy: "If you sit on the last bench near the 4 bldg. gate I can see you. I'm the second window from your left when you look up at the towers."

A pimp: "I ain't with that window writing shit, leave that for those niggas who got nothing better to do."

Iyssyss to Big Willy, on a change of address: *"Oh, and babe, just to let you know I moved out of the window. I am in the brown unit now. 1-11-1. So, holla!"*

Again, Shaheed: *"Anyhow baby how can you question my fidelity? Don't you know I ain't studdin none of those women in the window. So they telling you I'm saying 'let me c'? See what?! They out of shape asses need to stop. It ain't nothing to 'c'. Like I told you already, they envy what we got. They don't understand or comprehend how what we have is very real. It ain't window talk & just something to do."*

A worried woman: *"I guess this will give us time to work on ourselves cause God knows I was real busy in the window! I might lose my child to DSS for crissakes. I need to get my head together."*

K*Shine to Lady D: *"You just opened up to me on Sunday the day we was dancing in the window."*

Killa Kim on evolutionary selection in skywriting: *"He wasn't good at skywriting. I couldn't understand a word he said. He's not as good at it as you daddy."*

Prison Windows: A Short History

Like everything in prison, window-gazing has a long history. In the old days, prisons were designed to bring the attention of inmates toward a focus in the yard. Based on the design of monasteries, some eighteenth-century prisons placed an altar or a chapel at the center of the yard. Some prison cells had no windows at all, only a long shaft that blocked out everything from view—everything but the altar.

This was intended as an object lesson: criminals are alone in the world, cut off in the dark cell of their sin. But not completely. The way of God and repentance was represented literally as the single tunnel out, the sole source of light. This was also intended to remind these sinners that God, in turn, was still watching them. As far as a prisoner in one of these cells could see, God—or the Church—was the *only* thing that still existed in the outside world.

In later prisons, a governor's house or some creepy all-seeing eye—a guard booth—was placed in the yard. This was both a security measure and a reminder to the inmate that a dread sovereign stood over him, that this ever-present ruler watched him, that he could be free if, and only if, he'd bend to the ruler's laws. These concrete symbols of God or the State and, in some cases, both, were placed directly at the focal point of the prison. These prisons had clearly delineated visual centers.

At the prison where I worked, which was typical of the modern American prison, the center of the yard was anchored neither by an altar, a governor's residence, or a guard booth. Instead, there was a basketball court.

It wasn't clear what this was supposed to symbolize. Or, in what direction it was meant to turn the mind of an inmate. Perhaps it was an example of moral neutrality: the prison's job is not to offer any object lesson nor to impose any sense of dread, but only to allow you to stay healthy while in custody. Or perhaps it was a sign of the modern prison's identity crisis—it doesn't know what its job is. It has no core. Or perhaps the basketball court was not intended to arouse any feeling, but the opposite: to lull, to distract.

The basketball court at the center of the prison yard struck me as a failure of imagination. But for some inmates, this wasn't so. These courts were, after all, their Nature. Their only earth and sky. The place where seasons were observed, if not quite experienced. By default, the prison basketball court figured into the imagination of some inmates, and often appeared in writings and drawings. For Ming, a recent addition to the inmate library staff, the court was a recurring image in his poetry. Most notably in his poem *Sightseeing*:

> *The sightseers in us like the way*
> *the rain or sun keeps coming down—*
> *outside the alarm-rigged windows, the pigeons*
> *will not fly, and without their uniforms on*
> *briefly my fellow convicts leap toward*
> *the hoop, crowned by rings of sweat,*
> *the heated plumes of youth unfurling*
> *at gunpoint.*

But it was Jessica, and her vivid godsent dreams, who had the most immediate stake in the imaginative properties of the prison basketball court. Her prison was built around a focal point; her prison yard had a definite center. From a window in the prison tower she beheld not a symbol of the Church, but a son. Her lost son. An altar would have been superfluous.

Sabbath Children

During my supper break, I take a walk outside. I brave the sallyport, the heavy security doors, and make my way to the front of the prison. It is a chilly Friday night. The sun, like all day-shifters, rushes toward night. Even though I don't observe the Sabbath, this remains a spiritually charged moment, when workaday concerns vanish, when the vicious voices and petty falsehoods of the week glide away, and a divine breath drifts over the world, caressing all of creation. If one is tranquil enough, one will feel it. Even in my skepticism I can't deny it. I still make a habit of being outside to receive it.

I cross the treacherous highway interchange. An ambulance wails helplessly in traffic — it is stuck behind a hearse. Some drivers think this is funny. Some don't. I walk past the Boston Medical Center and into the South End, a rough Boston neighborhood that continues to gentrify. By day, the park on Washington Street is full of nannies pushing fertility-treatment twins and triplets. In the evening, children are attended by parents. By night, the park is given over to fiends and hookers.

I arrive at dusk. The park is full of young families. A pack of neighborhood hipsters — whose clothing lends them the look of nineteenth century circus performers — loiter by the gate.

A thirtysomething man in a gray wool suit, a young attorney type, paces. His muscular greyhound, who appears to be wearing a sweater set, is leashed to a park bench.

"Honey," I hear him say into his cell, "we both know you weren't a good wife, but that's water under the bridge, okay? But please don't take this out on our son."

Later I see him blow up at his misbehaving dog and pull it violently into submission.

I see a mother speak to her early tween daughter as though they are competitive girlfriends. "Why were you shy when you were talking to that man?" asks the daughter. Her mother gets defensive: "*I* wasn't shy," she says, "why were *you* shy?"

A young yuppie family wheels by, a father, mother, and one-year-old in a thousand-dollar stroller that appears to have anti-lock brakes. I hear the mother say to the child, "We're going to make a *big* circle around the park—*Wow-wee!*" She claps ecstatically. I don't know whether this gesture is touching or unspeakably grim. I decide to call it even. On the other side of the park, a seven-year-old in a tutu is overtaken by a spirit: she runs full speed, leaps onto a park bench, howls mightily at the moon, and then rushes back to mommy. The young professionals take this as a sign. They relinquish the park to the fiends for the night.

Back at the prison, I stand at the top of the outdoor stairs, taking in a last fresh breath. A toddler comes over to inspect me. In his tiny one-piece winter suit, his giant eyes peering at me through a tightly pinched hood, he resembles a little space explorer, roving a strange and foreign territory. And so he is. He examines my shoelace for a bit, and perhaps likes what he sees, because he smiles broadly. He continues on his journey, and discovers a fascinating discarded lottery ticket.

The line in front of the prison has swelled considerably in the thirty minutes since I began my walk. A mass of worried people, like refugees trying to cross a border. For many, these visits are a complex ritual, often political in nature, a single mother's diplomatic mission to secure a reliable ally in her man. While children from my community sit in marble synagogues in other parts of the city, followed by a warm Shabbat dinner at home, these children wait in the cold to visit a mother or father, or both, in a steel and concrete prison.

About now in the synagogues, the congregations are singing.

L'kha dodi l'krat kallah . . .
Go my beloved, the Bride to meet, the face of Shabbat, let us
    greet . . .

Here the line moves forward a few inches.

Standing apart from the crowd, on the side of the steps toward the prison tower, is a young mother. It is unclear at first why she is standing there. Suddenly, she lifts a tightly swaddled infant over her head, as though presenting the child to the tower itself, offering her baby up to some remote mountain deity. The contrast is startling: the baby, limb-heavy and soft as wet cotton, hoisted up against the cold wind and a tower that bears down massively. It's almost as though she's trying to make a point about the overwhelming fragility of this creature in her hands. For a moment, I fear, irrationally, for the infant's life, as if it's about to be crushed by the tower.

It is now dark. Inmates are visible in the building, floor by floor, moving about, the fluorescence of their cells matches the frigid light of the moon. I notice an inmate near the top of the tower, stirring. He stands as a distant silhouette in his window, one arm up in a sort of salute, as though skywriting in slow motion. From this distance, he seems almost as small as the baby, and as helpless against the weight of the tower. The silhouette man lowers his arm, which is the woman's cue, I suppose, to lower their baby. She nestles the infant safely back into his warm nook. Covers him fussily. His kindergarten-aged sister leans, sleeping as she stands, wedged between her mother and the stroller.

There are children everywhere in prison. Even before my first day of work, when I sat guiltily in the lobby, waiting to take my drug test, I'd noticed them playing, unaware of the adult solemnity of the surroundings. The children that day had been busy devising games, sporting events, entire Olympiads designed especially for that space. I watched as a little girl—whom I took as a prison lobby veteran— took the hand of another and showed her the best places to hide, initiating her as a member of the prison lobby gang. By now, she herself was probably a veteran.

And since then, I'd seen hundreds more. And not just in the lobby, or waiting outside, but inside the prison itself. During my first month at work, a prison shrink cautioned me, casually over lunch in the staff cafeteria, to be aware of juvenile behavior among inmates. Regardless of their actual ages, she said, a surprising number of inmates were the emotional age of children. The result, she said, of a lifetime suffering abuse, physical, emotional, sexual—a profile that was so common among inmates, especially women, that it was almost the norm. I had been skeptical of the shrink's mass diagnosis.

But it was hard to ignore daily instances of stunted behavior. I learned that even a hardened criminal capable of murder was equally capable of dissolving into a terrified child under the slightest pressure. Although machismo veiled these impulses somewhat among the men, immature behaviors were present in a variety of small actions: childish pranks, fibbing, attention seeking, acting out. I recognized a childlike earnestness in the inmate, aged thirty-six, who pleaded with me to give him tape so that he could stick his name, which he had printed out in a colorful, calligraphic font, to his school folder.

Play took on many different forms. Through a hallway window I once witnessed male inmates clutching dolls during a class. After the lesson was over and the inmates had dispersed, I popped my head into the classroom and asked the teacher, "What was *that* all about?"

She'd borrowed the dolls from the prison's parenting class, where they're used for demonstrations. But in this class, the teacher told me, the dolls served no direct educational function.

"They're just there for the guys to play with," she said, as if this made perfect sense.

Apparently, some of the men simply liked holding the dolls, pretending to care for them, to change their diapers. They made a joke of it, used it as a way to flirt with her. But even after the joke was over, they'd keep the dolls in their laps as they worked on their school material. They handled the dolls with excessive care, she told me, and placed them gently onto the desk as though they were actual infants. The teacher believed that the inmates felt more comfortable engaging in this type of playacting around her, a woman.

"I have to laugh about it," said the teacher, shaking her head, "otherwise I'd definitely cry."

But with the women inmates, these kinds of revealing behaviors were not subtle at all. They were impossible to miss. Almost every night in the library, a woman inmate would demonstrate some variety of childlike behavior: crying helplessly when a problem with a simple solution arose; writing a note, riddled with misspellings, in big curly letters; talking in a toddler's voice when she wanted me to do her a favor; painful shyness; hyperactivity; clumsy lying; squabbling over whose turn it was to talk to me. In the library, I saw a murderer suck her thumb. I broke up games of tag. And this was all reinforced by the structure of prison, where inmates have about as much control over their lives as children. And yet, almost all are parents.

Many inmates, especially women, felt comfortable in the library, one of the least prison-like spaces in the facility—and, whether I liked it or not, their need for child play would manifest itself on my watch. This was yet another unexpected use of the library space.

O utside, during my dinner break that Friday night, the line of visitors is calm. The prison is about to change its visiting policy from an open first come, first served policy to a policy of advance reservations made only by certain designated people. Each inmate will be allowed visits from a list of three people, plus attorneys. This is to help curb long lines and to ensure that children aren't hanging around prison after bedtime, like tonight. But mostly it's aimed at ending the era of fistfights in the lobby between women visitors who hold conflicting claims of *wifey*-hood or *babymom*-dom to a particular man.

The service in the synagogues is wrapping up with the kiddush: *And on the seventh day He completed His work.* Somewhere in town, my friend Yoni is having a beer with friends, celebrating the completion of his contract working in prison. The woman in front of the tower with the stroller is gone. The toddler space explorer is asleep in his mother's arms, next in line to enter the prison.

That's where I am headed, too. Time to go back into the library and greet the women inmates from the tower. I pin my badge back to my shirt, cut the giant line of tired refugees, pass through the lobby, wink at Sully, the prison night guard, slip through the metal detector, and wait for the heavy door to roll open.

The Church

"It took me years to realize what I did to Chrissy."

Jessica leaned over the library counter and whispered to me. The escort officers had just arrived.

For some reason she always began major conversations with only minutes to go before the end of her library period. Perhaps this was a deliberate effort to unburden herself without having to go through with a conversation.

A week earlier she'd come to me with a minute left and told me about the first time she went to court. She'd been a precocious seventeen-year-old with a fake ID. She'd turned a few tricks to earn the two hundred bucks necessary to buy a certain dress. "Took me one night to get the money," she said. "I was a fucking retard, though, you know? I wanted to see if I had the guts to do it. It was in New York. Fleet Week. I figured, what the fuck, I'll probably end up with one of them guys anyways. That's why I was going down there. Might as well make a little on the side." Because it was Fleet Week, the police were cracking down.

In jail, she began perseverating, obsessing over the question of how to address the judge.

"So," she said, "I'm in this holding cell, right, going fuckin' nuts. I've never been in this much trouble. And for *soliciting*! Holy shit. I was a kid who hung out with the wrong people, mouthed off. Shoplifted a little. Was into some really bad drugs. But this was a new one for me. And so far away from home." She kept fixating on the question of what to call the judge.

Sir?

Judge?

Do I use his name?

Isn't there another one I'm not thinking of?

There is. Fuck.

She'd heard it on the *People's Court* once. She'd never watched that much TV. Television was corny, the street was much more entertaining. But now she couldn't remember what they called that old judge guy. She fell asleep and had anxiety dreams about her teeth getting yanked with a wrench. When she woke up she asked an older woman inmate what to call the judge. The other woman laughed at her. *Don't call him an asshole. They don't like it.* But when she saw the girl was distressed, she gave her a break.

"'Your Honor,' hon, call the judge, 'Your Honor.'"

"What if he's a chick," Jessica recalls asking.

"Whatever's up there, wearing a robe? You call, *Your Honor. Your Honor.* Just say that and you'll be fine."

When Jessica got into the court she was shaking so hard it was difficult to stand. She was asked to plead. This was the moment. She hesitated for a long painful second. And then another. Everyone stopped to stare. The court stenographer shot her a glance. She'd forgotten what to call the judge.

Wait, no. She remembered.

"Your Highness, I . . ."

The court erupted in laughter. She heard her court-appointed defender mutter, "He *wishes*." The judge's face softened into a sympathetic smile. She'd messed up—that was clear. But she was too distraught to stop. Again, she tried.

"Your Highness, I . . ."

That was more than anyone could handle. "The judge almost had to clear the court," recalls Jessica, "there was so much laughing. The cops, the lawyers, the typing lady, the tranny hookers, the fuckin' dopefiends, okay, all fuckin' laughing their asses off." Later, she'd slipped and called him "Your Highness" again. But that time, she'd quickly corrected herself.

"But, tell you what," Jessica said to me, "it was the best defense I ever had. I got off with a warning."

That had been the comic version of her experience with crime and punishment. That night, with two minutes to go in the library period, she wanted to tell the other version.

With Chris, there'd been warnings, she told me. One Friday night, when she was rolling on any pill she could get her hands on, plus some Jameson to make it interesting, she'd left the boy with a babysitter, a girl her age whom she had met in a court-mandated NA meeting. One problem: the babysitter herself was fucked up that night. So fucked up she didn't notice the toddler run out of the house. Didn't notice his absence until 3 a.m., when he'd already been gone hours. A neighbor found Chris crouching at the side of a street. The boy was mute. After he calmed down, Chris asked for "Mumum." Jessica returned at about 11 a.m. The neighbor didn't report her. But she'd got the message.

Then one morning Jessica woke up, unsure that she'd been asleep. Her consciousness was often so hazy it was hard to tell. She was still high from the night before, and the day before that, and the night before that. She didn't remember going to sleep. But she remembers waking up and knowing, *Today is the day*.

On the back of a used piece of gift-wrapping, she scrawled a note. Laid out the facts in brief, without dwelling on emotions. *I'm a junkie*, she wrote. *That's not going to change.* She was eighteen, barely in touch with her family. They didn't even know about the kid. She loved her son, but it wasn't enough for him. *He's a good boy*, she wrote, *Please give him a good home. God bless.* She didn't sign it in any form.

She and Chris took the T to a rich neighborhood on the other side of town. They went for a walk. Played on a jungle gym. Rode down the slide together. The boy got tired. And that was the idea. She slipped into a church and took a seat in the back. She laid the sleeping child on a pew, with the note slipped into his pocket.

Within half an hour, she was waiting to board a bus at South Station. She bought a Greyhound ticket with the little money she'd scraped together—she had been planning this for weeks. By nightfall, she was in New York. By daybreak, she was in Tallahassee. She wanted a whole new landscape, new trees, new architecture, new accents. Never wanted to see New England again, wanted to pretend it didn't exist, had never existed.

"I was so fucked up and confused," she told me, "I felt *I* was abandoned. I really did."

Months later, in a moment of lucidity, it finally sunk in: What happened in the church that day didn't happen to her, it happened to *him*. It wasn't she who was abandoned. When this finally occurred to her, she stopped feeling sorry and began instead to hate herself. She almost jumped off a bridge in Tampa. Her sense of victimhood had been the only thing keeping her alive. She'd committed many crimes already in her life. But abandoning her child was by far the worst—and it was the only one she hadn't been punished for. Of course, this itself was a form of punishment.

"There's no forgiveness for endangering a kid and then leaving him," she told me. "I kept thinking, *his skin, his skin, his skin.* His skin was so soft. I imagined, I imagined bad things happening to that soft skin, his chubby little hands, how I wasn't there to protect him. Nothing's gonna make that right."

The officer entered the library. "That's a wrap," he shouted. Our conversation was over. I watched Jessica get into line. As the officers started their count, the other inmates chatted loudly, joked, bawled each other out. On the concrete, steel, and linoleum of the hall outside of the library, the din of their voices was almost deafening.

Inmates are counted repeatedly throughout the day. Sometimes an officer does his count gently, almost tenderly. But some do their count with a frustration that verges on rage—not necessarily at the inmates, but at the interminable nature of the count itself.

On that night the officer counted the inmates with undisguised hostility. And while most inmates deflected it, tuned it out, Jessica stood in line, silently absorbing the hatred. She didn't speak to anybody, nobody spoke to her. She wouldn't have a relationship with anyone around her—this would require her to divert her focus from the past, and this was impossible. She would remain alone and unforgiven.

The closest she got to a friend was her cellmate, a tiny Vietnamese woman who spoke not a word of English. The inability to communicate was essential to their relationship. They'd play cards silently for hours, she told me. Occasionally, accidentally, they'd exchange a shy smile.

The officer finished his count. *Shut. Up.* I could hear him shout from behind the library door. The women fell silent. The train rolled down the hall, through the yard, back to the 1-Building, and then up to the tower.

The Flowers Bring the Dogs

I recognized Chris from the time Jessica had pointed him out. He was not a library regular. The one time he'd visited, to pick up a legal form, he'd been awkward, almost reverent. Like he was holding his breath the entire time. He was no prison nerd. The shelves of books spooked him. In the library, he was nothing like the guy's guy of the prison yard.

Occasionally I'd walk past him out there. From up close I could see certain details not evident from up on the eleventh floor. The pained concentration in his face when he played basketball, as though his life depended on how well he shot the ball. There was little enjoyment in it. He'd labor hard to run up and down the court. He'd get winded, rest his hands heavily on his hips during breaks. And was brutal with himself if he missed a play. He took the game more seriously, more personally, than most of the other inmates.

When he wasn't playing, he'd goof off aggressively, systematically, with whomever would tolerate him. A small gesture spoke volumes: two fellow inmates exchanged a knowing look after he'd left off chatting with them—one leaning in and whispering something to the other. Were Chris's efforts at socializing making him as many enemies as friends? He was trying too hard to fit in.

When I passed him in the yard, I instinctively glanced up at the prison tower. From down there, the dark window where Jessica watched him during my class was more than just nondescript. It seemed inconsequential. Remote. There was some part of me that wanted to walk up to Chris and point out the window, explain its significance. To bring the thing into focus. Wouldn't he want to know? Or perhaps he'd just be creeped out by the whole business. He was, after all, being watched by a near stranger. Two, as a matter of fact. I didn't know him, and had only a staff-inmate relationship with Jessica. It wasn't my place to meddle. And anyway I had other things on my mind, my own family drama.

My mother was about to fly to California to visit her mother on her deathbed—*for the fifth time.* Or maybe it was the sixth. I'd lost count. *When is she going to die already,* I thought. It was a cruel thought. I wasn't proud of it.

I'd seen my grandmother, Fay, only a few times in my life. My formative encounter came when I was eight years old. In my grade-school presumptuousness, I'd asked if I could take full possession of her silver dollar collection. She barely regarded the question and flicked me away like a gnat. *No.* Then I asked if I could have just one silver dollar. Again, *No.* Then I asked her if I could hold one coin for just a moment. Finally, she turned to me and gave me her full attention.

"When I die," she said in her thick Polish Yiddish accent, eyes bulging and finger wagging, "you can *dance* on my grave with them!"

It took me roughly a decade to see the humor in this comment. And then a few more years to sense the tragedy. At eight years old, however, it was much simpler: it filled me with horror. To me, a young American kid, my grandmother was a hideous demon who had emerged from the flames of the shtetl to curse our happy, safe lives in the New World. She'd survived death in all its European forms—typhus, pogroms, revolutions, world wars—for the sole purpose, it seemed to me, of blowing death's secondhand smoke into our faces. Why was this grown woman so protective of her silver dollars? What did my request for her coins have to do with her grave? And why did she command me to remove a Michael Jordan poster and call him *that schvartzer* when she knew he was my hero?

My mother's feelings toward my grandmother were, of course, much sharper, and complicated by feelings of a daughter's love and compassion. Fay had been a harsh and often unforgiving mother. She'd kept her house immaculately, terrifyingly clean and free of any ornamentation. Her food was bland. Her children called her

"Mother." She banned friends from the house and kicked out those who'd slipped in. My grandmother dished out the emotional abuse, which was constant, and delegated the physical abuse to my grandfather, a good-natured but passive man who obeyed his wife's orders to beat the children.

When I'd asked my mother to tell me about Fay's life, she'd take a deep breath and tell me what she knew. That Fay's mother, a saintly woman, had time for everyone but her daughter. What my mother knew, or cared to remember, often came in the form of isolated facts. Fay read the newspaper cover to cover, she told me. I always got the feeling that her internal world wasn't known to my mother, and that it was better left that way. Glimpses into Fay's soul mostly disturbed my mother. Why, for example, had she once advised my mother to not hug my sister, then a toddler, and wondered aloud why my mother verbally expressed love toward this child? For my mother, this was a shattering insight into her own unloved upbringing by this woman. And it wasn't just love that went unexpressed. There were other things that could not be discussed.

"I would have to beg her to tell me about her life in Poland," my mother once told me. "She would begin to tell a story, but as soon as she mentioned anyone's name, she would cut it off and say, 'But what does it matter? Hitler killed all of them.' Every story was like that."

For my grandmother, who escaped Poland as the clouds gathered on the Nazi invasion, storytelling was something worse than painful. It was a simple impossibility. As far as she was concerned, there were no stories. Stories develop, move in some direction. Stories have endings, *need* endings. Tragedies have a final act that implicitly allows the storyteller and the listener to believe that even cruel deaths retain some value—namely, their worth as a story for the living.

"I am dead, Horatio," says the tragic Hamlet. "Tell my story."

My grandmother did not believe in this. For her, murder ended more than life. It ended the possibility of telling the life's story. "He has my dying voice," says Hamlet, "the rest is silence." Even in life my grandmother didn't have a voice, just silence.

As a child my mother was not satisfied with this silence. She wanted to know. She'd sneak into her mother's room in search of clues. Hidden in her mother's drawers were photos full of mysterious people, mostly cheerful girls. My grandmother's girlfriends and cousins. When my mother asked Fay about the people in the photos, she would begin a story and then cut it off. *It doesn't matter, they were all murdered.* And that was it. When my mother persisted, Fay pointed to one of the smiling girls in the photos and told her young daughter that the Nazis had hanged this girl in a well by her pigtails. This was the only detail she would divulge. The only one that mattered.

A few years before she died, I visited my grandmother at her nursing home in Northern California. She was very frail and had mellowed considerably. But she never lost her edge. I asked her how she was enjoying the surroundings, the nicest weather in the known universe. She shrugged dismissively. I suggested she walk in a nearby garden, resplendent in gorgeous plants. She glanced skeptically at the garden and said, with her pitch-perfect comic timing, "The flowers bring the dogs." My grandmother was terrified of dogs.

It could have been the title of her autobiography: *The Flowers Bring the Dogs.* She was an alchemist of misery; she could turn anything, even tulips and lilies, into pure negativity.

I pressed on. I asked her to tell me about her past. She would speak only about her arrival in America and how displaced she'd felt. She told me she "used to be someone" in Poland. In America, she said, "I was nothing." I asked her who she used to be in Poland. She didn't answer. I asked about the photos. She denied knowledge of them. I asked about her friends. She ignored the question, pretended she didn't hear.

I had decided to tape our conversation. I wanted some documentary evidence of her life. Something, anything, to remember her by. I knew she'd never agree to speak into a recording device. This was a woman who, after all, distrusted flowers. As her grandson, though, I felt entitled to this small inheritance and decided to record her secretly.

But paranoids have sharp senses. And I'm not much of a secret agent. She detected my fidgeting with something under the table, and my guilty face gave me away. Now it was her turn to ask the questions, my turn to deny. So went our conversation. It was about as emotionally honest as a police interrogation, and ended with each of us staring at the other with guarded eyes.

Later, I listened to the recording and was struck by the textured sound of the empty air, a breeze interrupted only by the hum of a distant airplane, the creak of shifting chairs, the slight whistle of my grandmother's breathing. The microphone had captured the contours of her silence. That was the last conversation I had with her.

My mother took a morning flight to California to be with Fay at the end. I probably should have gone with her. Instead, I was standing in the prison yard—coming up for air—watching Chris struggle to run the length of the basketball court. Above us, the window, now dark, where Jessica watched him during my class. And above that, an airplane soared.

Blueberry Muffin Day

At long last it was my turn to attend the three-day prison orientation. One might think that orientation would, like orientations the world over, like orientations since the dawn of time, occur during the first few days on the job, or better yet, before work began. God knows I could have used some official training for dealing with the Coolidge-types, the Angry Seven, and various others. But, for reasons unstated, many months were allowed to pass before any official orienting would occur. But, even so, I was grateful. I still didn't have a grip on things.

I arrived fashionably late. But not too late to take in the sights. The sheriff's outpost in Chelsea was a low, cinderblock bunker wedged between a muffin factory and a methadone clinic. Muffin World, as the factory was called, emitted a constant, wonderful cakey aroma; Methadone World, as I called it, thankfully emitted no aroma. The sheriff's outpost was used to train new prison guards, but doubled as an orientation space for civilian prison workers like me. A man, clad in double denim—blue jeans and a blue jean jacket, mismatched—was splayed out unconscious on the wheelchair ramp of Methadone World. His long hair and arms dangled brutally over the railing. An obese, red-bearded trucker sat across the way, on the loading dock of Muffin World. Holding a steaming cup of coffee and a cigarette in one hand and a half-eaten muffin in the other, he was squinting at the passed-out man.

The outpost was chock-full of cop gear. Posters identifying various species of handgun. Badges from various brother cop outfits, many with curious cartoon insignia. Inspirational slogans about Courage and Fortitude. For three days we were to sit from 8 a.m. to

3 p.m. in marathon classes on topics that ranged from dealing with security threats to writing incident reports to ratting on our coworkers to recognizing contraband. And of course, lessons on why it's not wise to comment on your colleague's cleavage.

Any thought that this day would be productive was quickly dashed when I saw my union boss, Charlie, sitting at a desk with a big smile on his face.

"This is my favorite time of year," he whispered to me. "Total waste of time."

Charlie was a connoisseur of malingering. He enjoyed killing time the way some people savor aged gouda.

"Just sit back and relax," he said.

Relaxation, however, was not likely. The orientation, which was required of all staff once a year, had little to do with teaching us how to do our actual jobs. It was more of a guided tour through the nine levels of Dante's Inferno. Rapes, suicides, druggings, hypnosis, pistol-whippings, hangings. The sharpening of daggers. We explored every manner of villainy devised by man. But instead of Virgil as our guide, we had Sgt. Dan Hickey.

Actually, we had various officers, taking turns horrifying us. One officer went off on a half-hour tangent in praise of his favorite constitutional amendment.

"Fact," he said. Almost every thought began with this word. "None of you would be sitting here if it wasn't for the Second Amendment." Considering that we would have been happy to not be sitting in a cinderblock bunker in Chelsea at 8 a.m., his argument lost a good deal of its rhetorical force. Noting that some states allow off-duty prison guards to carry guns, he called on the Massachusetts legislature to change its laws so that he could carry his piece on the playground in case a child called his daughter a name. Charlie slipped me a note: "Fact. This guy is going to be in *jail* by the end of the year."

We spoke of stress. "Raise your hand if you have a second job," asked the officer. Almost every single hand went up. "We all know the middle class is dying in this country," the officer continued. This wasn't a theory or a seminar topic. It was a shared reality for everyone sitting in the room. Although everyone there worked a government job, complete with union benefits, almost no one was making enough to live and support families.

"If you're an officer, you probably got alimony," he smiled at his own joke, which actually is no joke. "The bottom line: You got to find healthy ways of dealing with that stress."

One healthy way, he noted, was giving yourself a little treat. When his marriage was on the rocks, he told us, he would allow himself a slice of cake before bed every night. Those still paying attention found this comment heartbreaking.

Another officer spent an entire ninety minutes on the subject of suicide. To be fair, suicide is truly an important subject in prison; inmates under extreme pressure may turn to suicide and it is the prison's responsibility to prevent it. But the level of detail on the issue and passion with which this session was taught seemed excessive. Halfway through, the truth came out. When someone subtly asked why we were studying the latest national statistics on suicide, stratified by region, age, and gender, the officer blew up.

"My brother, okay, didn't have the courage to face his problems, just like the rest of us do every day, so you know what he decided to do?"

Here the janitor, a friendly Albanian man, raised his hand; the officer ignored him and went on.

"He found the closest train tracks and threw himself in front of a commuter train. There were parts we never found."

An audible gasp went up in the class.

"And do you know *when* he did it?"

I looked at the janitor, but he wasn't raising his hand this time. I heard someone whisper, "Oh shit, *no . . . Christmas?*"

"On *Mother's* Day," said the officer, crossing his arms. "Do you have any idea what our Mother's Days are like now? Do you know what kind of hell my mother goes through every Mother's Day? Do you know what his wife and kids go through? He took the easy way out, left us to deal with life's problems. My brother was a coward."

The class sat in stunned silence. The janitor looked bored. When the officer returned to his slides and began a massively detailed description of the warning signs of suicidal ideation, everyone was able to relax a bit. After a short session on arson, we watched an unedited amateur video from the inside of the infamous Station nightclub fire, which killed a hundred people, one of the worst nightclub fires in American history. After watching the harrowing footage of people screaming and crying and pushing and burning to death, the officer flicked the lights back on.

"Lunch," he said.

The afternoon session picked up where we had left off. An officer walked in and, without saying a word, slammed a billy club really, really hard onto a desk. The whole class jumped. The desk almost buckled. The woman seated in front of me cried out, *Dear God!* The white-haired caseworker seated to my right clutched his chest. Charlie just leaned back and grinned. The janitor, I believe, was still in the john.

"Now, ladies and gentlemen, anyone wanna tell me what that

could do to your skull or to the skull of one of your coworkers?" said the officer.

It turns out that the billy club was actually not a billy club but five or six magazines curled up tightly and then duct-taped together. Apparently, this creates a rather devastating weapon. And a handy introduction to contraband. It was a session that touched upon my post in the prison.

"Any librarians here?" asked the officer. It sounded like, and was, an accusation.

Possibly because the officers spoke in a staccato of rhetorical cop questions or because we knew where this was going, Forest and I didn't answer. Finally, when it became clear that the officer actually wanted an answer to the question, Forest generated some form of pitiable squeak.

"Raise your hands," the officer commanded.

We complied.

"We rely on you, gentlemen. Contraband of all kinds, including weapons, often starts in the facility's library—why do you think inmates go there? It's not to read *Moby-Dick*, okay?"

Forest looked deflated and sunk into his chair.

We were presented with a sideshow of curious contraband objects, homemade weapons that bore an uncanny resemblance to a medieval armory. Homemade maces, spikes, mauls, flails. A battle ax–looking thing. Shanks of every size and shape. A homemade baseball bat. Nothing was as it seemed—every item looked vaguely familiar as something else. Scotch tape and chips of plaster could be squeezed into a tight ball, placed into a sock, swung at your head. This could also be accomplished by a bar of soap in a sock, or hardcover books in a laundry bag. The sock weapon could knock you unconscious. A fan in a computer needed little alteration—it was already a sharp blade. Magazines and hard covers from books could be used as body armor. An orange peel could be fermented into a nasty little batch of liquor, "homebrew." Once fermented, it could be used to burn through metal to help cast a knife. In other words, an inmate could get drunk and make a shank at the same time—a lovely combination.

A floppy disk? Easily outfitted into a switchblade. Chairs could become guillotines. Shoelaces might result in genocide. A pen? The officer just laughed.

"You kidding me? You could assassinate the president with a pen."

But before we could think about how that might work, the lights were off and the officer was setting up a video. "This oughta show you what a pen can do."

We were treated to another unedited security video. This one starred an inmate sneaking into a prison dayroom, barricading the door, and proceeding to beat another inmate senseless and then stab him repeatedly with a pen (which he lifted, to my relief, not from the library but from the infirmary). We were witnessing an actual murder. By the time the footage picked up, the victim had given up resistance. He just lay there. The murderer seemed bored. He stabbed his victim slowly and methodically. And repeatedly. But without a soundtrack or any contrived cinematic frenzy, murder turns out to be rather dull on film. It looked more like he was poking holes into a raw potato. The video ended, the lights went up, and we were given the end of the day quiz.

Waiting for the quizzes to be graded, we stood out on the front steps, staring out at nothing. Those who smoked, smoked. Those who'd quit smoking ate potato chips.

The folks at Methadone World must have been on break, too, or just had nowhere to go, because they stood on their steps, a mirror image of us, smoking and eating potato chips and staring. We were like two groups of weary sailors aboard dingy pontoon boats, floating past each other on a polluted river.

Out of boredom, I waved. A little papal motion. My gesture did not appear to register over in Methadone World. Then, oddly, about thirty seconds later, one of the more beat-up fellows, the double denim guy who'd been passed out over the railing in the morning, did finally lift his arm in unsmiling salute.

"You smell that sugar smell?" asked one of the training officers. Nobody replied.

"They make a different kind over there every day," he said, nodding toward Muffin World. He took an anguished drag of his cigarette. His mouth curdled.

"Today's blueberry muffin day."

He flicked his cigarette into the parking lot, and walked back into the bunker. A cloud of smoke lingered where he had stood, then faded. Everybody passed the quiz.

On Smash

After orientation things at work seemed different. I got the sneaking feeling that that had been the point: to bore and horrify you for three days until going in to work at the prison seemed, by comparison, a most wonderful treat. At the same time, the litany of contraband, the deeply disturbing scenario of fire in prison, the myriad ways of messing up, made me slightly uneasy about entering the building again.

This was normal, I was told. Union boss Charlie explained

that people typically return to work from orientation slightly disoriented. "Everyone comes back thinking everything's contraband," he said. "Like everyone's out to get you, you know? Like the cons are always trying to stab you and the guy who works down the hall is gonna write you up, and the girl over there wants to sue you for being a knucklehead." This paranoia soon fades, he assured me. And then you can return to "doin' nothing and seein' nothing." He winked.

Still, when I returned to work after orientation something really did seem different. People were rushing around all morning. Outside the library, officers sprinted down the hall. Then up the hall. Out into the prison yard and then back in. A few plainclothes officers, whom I'd never seen, snooped around. Later, a major strolled by, surveying the situation.

Within an hour the halls were clear of inmates. Silence, unusual for the middle of the day, prevailed. The library detail at that moment—Fat Kat, Pitts, Teddy, Dice, and Elia—tried to look busy and stay below the radar. The chessboard had already been folded up and put away. The banter ended. The last thing they wanted was to be sent back to their cells, where they'd be put on smash, locked down for hours, and possibly days, at a time. This was standard procedure when violence erupted.

I stuck my head out of the library and asked an officer what was going on. Without looking at me, he responded with one word.

"Beefs."

"More than one?" I asked.

He turned and regarded me with something strongly resembling suspicion.

"Yeah," he said, "3-3 and now 3-1. Some beef from the street."

Just then he noticed the inmates working in the library. He quickly averted his eyes and walked away. I recognized the gesture. This wasn't his post. If the inmates in the library were out of place, let someone else deal with it. He had other headaches.

When I got back into the library, Fat Kat smiled and said, "It's popping up there, right?"

"I'm guessing you know more about it than I do," I replied.

As usual, he did. Even though the action was not happening in his unit, he somehow was abreast of the particulars. Word spread quickly in prison. A beef in one unit could quickly spread to others and become a large-scale problem.

"Spanish dude just came into the unit. Black dude recognized him from the street. I heard it was a six on one beat down up in 3-1 . . ."

"Is this gang stuff?" I asked.

Fat Kat looked away and muttered, "Probably."

Teddy glared at him and said, "Don't say nothing, man."

"You mean, in front of me?" I asked Teddy.

"Yeah," he said, sheepishly. "You gotta understand how it works in here. It's not that I don't trust you . . ."

"Yes it is," I said. "But I understand. I'm not supposed to trust you either."

Fat Kat smiled congenially and turned to Teddy.

"It's a' ight, Akh," he said, using Teddy's street name. Short for the Arabic, *akhi*, my brother. "It's cool."

Teddy deferred to Fat Kat. He walked away. Like the officer, he wanted no part in this.

But before Fat Kat could go on, the officer on duty marched into the library. "Gentlemen! I don't know why you're still here, but it's time to go back."

The detail let out a collective sigh and shuffled out. Just then Miller opened the door and walked in.

"You gotta love lockdowns!" he said to me from across the room. The inmates exchanged a look. Miller headed straight for the magazines we kept behind the counter. He grabbed a *Sports Illustrated*.

Miller and I had never clicked. Hulking and spirited, a bit of a towel snapper, he was a young prison staff teacher whose cockiness seemed entirely unjustified.

"What can I do for you?" I asked.

"I need the DVD player."

He waited at the counter, reading his magazine. I wondered why he "needed" the DVD player, considering that his class was just canceled.

"It's in the back," I said.

He seemed annoyed that I wasn't getting it for him.

"So what do you *do* all day?" he asked. "Are you going to be, like, a prison librarian forever? Do you go to school for that?"

I changed my mind and decided to get the DVD player for him after all. I retrieved it from the back room, wheeled it out the door, and sent him on his way.

Later that morning, I made some copies in the main Education Department office area, down the hall from the library. My boss, Patti, had uncharacteristically closed the door to her office. Through her window, I could see her on the phone, taking notes. Union boss Charlie emerged from his office with purpose. Now I knew something was wrong. He seemed tense, not at all his usual good-humored self. I noticed Miller approaching.

Charlie stood in front of the main door to the office area, blocking Miller's entrance.

"Hey," Charlie said. "SID wants to see you. Right now."

Miller froze.

"SID?"

Charlie nodded slowly. "That's right, Scott."

"I don't know what that is."

Yes he did. Everyone did. I had worked at the prison considerably less time than Miller, but I knew SID. It stood for Sheriff's Investigative Division. They were the prison's internal detectives. Miller must have known as well, and yet he was playing dumb. Now I was absolutely certain: something was definitely very wrong. Charlie wasn't having it.

"They want to talk to you, Scott. I think you know what this is about."

Miller stared. His face had gone alarmingly, cadaverously pale.

"I don't know what you're talking about," he said.

"Just go to their office, kid. It's next to the shift commander's."

Miller closed his eyes, bit his lip, and departed. I turned to Charlie.

"What the hell was that?"

"Trouble."

"Is it about this lockdown?"

"I don't wanna know," he said as he retreated into his office. Once inside, he shouted out, "And neither do you, Avi."

Holla!

But knowledge in prison is recycled like air, and I was certain to find out about Miller. In the meantime, the library continued to play its part revealing prison secrets. The kite, and skywriting, it turned out, were not the only means of long-distance communication. Inmates also communicated through radio waves.

I'd learned of this during a lull in the women's library period. I'd been chatting with some inmates who lingered around the circulation counter, leaning against the Amato sign, which, in all its crusty resilience, continued to warn inmates against doing just that. The women tried in vain to shake me down for information about "the teacher guy," Miller, while I, behind my honest claims to ignorance, silently wondered what channel of information had relayed the news up to the Tower. Staff? A kite? A skywriter? A few more minutes of chitchat culminated in one of the women, a ringleader-type named Whiz—who claimed to be a "notorious female pimp"—smiling at me and saying:

"You know what, Av? You a' ight, dawg."

A few minutes later, after the women had conferred, a shy young inmate approached the counter and handed me a note. I noticed Jessica on the other side of the library, alone, pulling books off of the shelves, pretending not to pay attention to what the others were doing.

I unfolded the note. In razor-sharp cursive, in a script known as the "Felon's Claw"—which I suspect belonged to Whiz—I was instructed to listen to late-night 88.1 FM. This, it turned out, was an R&B call-in show on MIT campus radio. The inmates, led by Whiz, had decided to include my name in their weekly list of shout-outs. I felt honored. Why they had decided to tell me this by folded note, I couldn't say.

"What should we call him?" asked one, ignoring the fact that I was standing right there.

"How about *L-Boy*, or *LB*, for *Library Boy*?"

They all laughed. Jessica disappeared into the back stacks.

"How about, 'Avi,'" I said.

. . .

That Sunday I eagerly tuned in to "For Your Pleasure," with your host Ré Antoine. I turned the volume up so that I could hear it as I washed dishes. Ré Antoine, elongating each luscious vowel, described the show as a "comforter, keeping you and your partner warm with music that makes your body . . . *respond* to the rhythms . . ."

Respond? You and your partner?

I glanced over at Kayla, my girlfriend, to see if she'd caught this turn of phrase. She was busy checking her email. Across town, in a concrete cell block, a group of women inmates was also sitting next to the radio, all of us simultaneously keeping ourselves "warm with music." What exactly had I agreed to? Perhaps I shouldn't have let them use my real name on the show. My bosses certainly wouldn't have been thrilled to have my name included in a sexy late-night call-in show with a group of women inmates.

Still, it was a fairly upbeat program. The phrase "do the right thing" got used a lot. There was a vaguely positive, AA-type message. The show's music, incidentally, turned out to be a dud, as far as I was concerned. I sat through it, mostly bored. I'd hoped for R&B classics, or at least the best contemporary. Instead, they played one whiny, derivative pop ditty after another. It was a schmaltz-fest. I was beginning to look at the clock, suddenly feeling sleepy.

At long last, the hour for the "Roll Call" arrived. Kayla and I, and, across town, scores of inmates leaned in a bit closer to the radio to hear what would come next. In his cool cat, late-night voice, Mr. Antoine read what seemed like a full half hour of shout-outs, one-line messages addressed from one person or group to another. In many instances these messages were coded and identified only by initials or street names. *This one goes out to RJ and Mookie from L-Ray: we on that.* Most were messages of support, *Keep strong, my good brother.* Some vaguely romantic, *I wanna see that beautiful smile of yours soon.*

To my amazement, most, possibly all, of the messages contained prison lingo. The shout-outs, it seemed, were all from or to inmates. Many were both to *and* from inmates—an interesting method of intraprison communication. Almost all of the messages referenced the prison where I worked. *This one goes out to all those turtles in the Bay, up in 1-10-2: "stay strong," from T.R. trying to do the right thing out here.* One after the other, prison people got shout-outs.

I was confused—was everyone who listened to this show an inmate in prison? This was a new concept for me: a radio station, based in the free world, which catered to mostly inmates. Even some officers and other staff got shout-outs:

Thanks to Lieutenant G. for trying to do the right thing over in the 1-Building.

It occurred to me that sending a shout-out was a great way of buttering up a staff member. Clearly I had fallen for this. Finally, my shout-out came.

This one goes out to . . . (Ré Antoine paused as he struggled to read the note) *to . . . Avery . . . from the L-Crew.*

"Wait," said Kayla, detecting my irritation. "Was that *it*?"

"Yes," I said, miserably.

"I never thought I'd be with someone named 'Avery,'" she said, throwing her arms around me. "I'm so happy!"

That made one of us. Although I was usually amused by the never-ending corruption of my name, the use of *Avery* at that particular moment disappointed me. This was my big moment. I'd suffered through a good deal of third-rate pop for it—and it wasn't every day that I was mentioned on the radio. But I appreciated the coinage of *L-Crew,* "Library Crew." I liked that. I flipped the radio off.

The next day I thanked the L-Crew for their recognition—and I even hollered a thanks to Jessica, who was hiding somewhere in the back. But I also felt compelled to remind them, once again, that my name was pronounced *ah-vee*. Whizz looked deeply offended.

"You kiddin', me, dawg? I know your name is Avi!"

It's true, she did. It was an unfair charge.

"Okay, but Ré Antoine called me *Avery*. How'd that happen?"

Nobody knew.

As if on cue, a very large, very loud member of the L-Crew burst through the door. Brutish, of course.

"Hey *Avery*," she shouted, a triumphant smile on her face. "Did you hear the shout-out? I sent it myself."

"That sounds right," I said.

"Don't say we don't holla at you."

I'd said no such thing. On the contrary, I'd often mentioned that it seemed as though people were constantly hollering at me in the library. And it wasn't just the library. *Holla* was an apt description for prison communications generally. At any given moment, there was a great deal of hollering across the prison yard and in the blocks themselves. It was the best, and often the only, way to deliver messages. In prison, if you weren't whispering, you were hollering.

Of course, one of the few inmates who didn't holla, and who barely whispered, was Jessica. It wasn't an accident that I'd seen her sequestered among the library shelves while the other women—the L-Crew—sat together, composing their weekly shout-outs for Ré Antoine, or while they secretly stashed kites imploring male inmates to *holla back at yo girl*. Jessica was miles removed from all of this.

She was incommunicado. A part of me wanted to draw her out some-how. But I decided to give her space.

A week went by. And another. In the writing class, Brutish was still brutish, Nasty still curt like clockwork, Short continued to hold her ground. A new woman, Cheerful, turned out to be not so, after all. She'd been banished to the Hole. Meanwhile, solitary Jessica kept her vigil, and I kept mine. But her days of silent watching were winding down.

After class that Thursday, she lingered, waiting until the others had left.

"I'm leaving," she said.

"Where to?"

"Framingham [State Prison]."

"How soon?"

"You know how it is around here. Who knows? Probably next week sometime."

"What about Chris?"

The question of her life. She stiffened.

"What about him?"

I wasn't sure what I'd meant.

"I mean," I said, "are you going to try to, um, connect with him before you leave, or something?"

She gathered up her papers.

"No. Sorry," she said, and walked out.

After the next class she lingered again. And again, waited for the others to leave.

"I was thinking." She paused for a long minute, reluctant to con-tinue. Perhaps by habit, she gazed toward the window.

"Yes," I said, finally. The guard outside was beginning to get antsy. "You were thinking . . ."

"Yeah, so I want to give Chrissy a letter from me before I go."

"Okay."

"Will you give it to him?"

I sighed, but agreed to do it. I was officially breaking with prison protocol and sticking my neck out.

"And a little gift."

Again, I sighed. Passing notes between inmates was already pushing the boundaries, but passing "gifts" between inmates was courting serious problems.

"I can't do that," I said. Then hesitated. "What's the gift?"

"A drawing."

"Fine," I said. "Of what?"

"Of me."

Naming and Unnaming

I went into the staff cafeteria for an early supper. The caf was self-segregated between officers and civilian staff members. In the evening, when the shifts were smaller, the officers sat on one end of the room and civilians on the other, with four or five empty tables between. It was as if each group was trying to sit as far from the other as possible. On rare occasions, an officer and civilian staffer would sit together. Food was prepared and served by inmates. It was a strange and subtly charged setting.

That night, it was more so. I detected a feeling of hostility emanating from the officers' table. A few officers I didn't know gave me dirty looks. Others with whom I was friendly simply avoided eye contact.

I took out my sandwich and sat with a colleague of mine from the Education Department. She was friendly with people all over the prison and was a fount of juicy gossip.

"What's going on here?" I asked her.

She knew exactly what I was talking about, and leaned across the table.

"Miller was named," she whispered.

An inmate, she told me, was facing heat for something or had reason to believe his cell would be shaken down—a standard action against inmates for both official security reasons and officers' personal vendettas. This inmate, who was a student of Miller's, approached Miller with a shank, an improvised knife, asking him to dispose of it for him. Miller, probably thinking "no harm no foul," allegedly did exactly that, throwing the shank out in the trash bin of his classroom.

Miller had known the inmate a bit, and perhaps they'd become friendly. Perhaps he wanted to help the guy avoid further trouble and stay in class and earn a diploma. The inmate was, after all, one of his students. Or perhaps he was simply afraid to say no, fearing the possible repercussions of snitching on a violent criminal. Miller worked in prison. He knew the code: *snitches get stitches* (if they're lucky). He also knew that inmates have friends on the outside. Or perhaps the inmate blackmailed him.

Once the inmate had presented him with the shank, he couldn't pretend to not know about it: the choice was either to play along or to report the inmate. This itself was a form of blackmail. There could be no neutrality. Miller tried to compromise and deal with the situation quietly. This turned out to be a miscalculation.

When the inmate was brought in for questioning, he tried to curry favor with SID by offering them a juicy morsel: a staff member's name. Indeed that's likely why he'd strong-armed Miller into throwing out the weapon to begin with, something that he probably could have done himself: he needed some leverage for the interrogation he knew was coming. Miller's name was that leverage. And to make matters considerably worse for Miller, SID searched the trash bin. It was empty. The shank, it appeared, had been retrieved by another inmate and transferred back to the inmate population. The entire sequence may well have been orchestrated.

Soon thereafter, Miller had been summoned for questioning. That's when I'd witnessed Charlie telling him to go to SID. Word around the prison was that SID shook him down hard, reduced him to tears. But he repeatedly denied knowledge of the shank. Somehow—possibly by reminding him that he himself could do time for what he had done—SID had squeezed Miller hard enough that he confessed everything. Officers escorted Miller, red-faced and humiliated, from the facility. There is a protocol for officers' escorting staff out in this fashion. These incidents occasionally happen. A full investigation would follow.

I listened to the story with a sense of awe and dread. Poor Miller! His situation was a staff person's nightmare. A clear example of how being surrounded by criminals can easily turn you into one yourself, even with the best of intentions. And even if you typically made good decisions. What happened to him might have happened to any of us—who knows how we'd react if an inmate with a knife threatened us with blackmail or worse. My friend's phrase, *Miller was named*, made me shudder.

A few days later, I was waiting for the front door to roll open, en route to a mandatory meeting for all non-uniformed staff. We were going to be collectively chastised for the Miller affair and rallied to the mission at hand. Eddie Grimes, the officer stationed at the front gate—a student of Zen Buddhism who always kept a book of Eastern thought at his post—dropped a piece of wisdom on me. As I waited for the heavy prison door to roll open, I asked Eddie for some insight from his studies. He thought for a moment and dangled a pen vertically between two fingers.

"The master teaches," Eddie said, "hold the pen with great care but hold the weapon with even greater care, for the weapon protects the pen."

It was a statement that captured the essence of the officers' relationship to people like me. And it was a refutation of the cliché that the pen is mightier than the sword. Of course, in prison, where pens are turned into knives, this expression already holds a peculiar resonance.

At the meeting, we were told to, "Give the inmates nothing. *Nothing.*" Forest and I were depressed by this formulation of the policy. We were, after all, in the business of doing exactly that: giving the inmates stuff. We were also told that we had no confidentiality whatsoever with the inmates and that our loyalty was to the sheriff and the sheriff alone.

"Your ID card," said Quinn, the assistant deputy, "has two names on it, yours and the sheriff's. Those are your priorities here. Got it?"

Snitching was serious business. When you entered the prison, you would be asked to name people. How you named those people made you either a con or a cop. There was no third option, no neutrality.

Back in the library things were returning to normal. The inmates needled me for information. Among their population, rumors were rampant:

"I heard this wasn't the first time that teacher guy did this."

"I heard he knew the guy from the outs."

"I heard that the teacher guy was selling drugs to guys in 3-3 and was scared that dude was gonna rat him out."

Teddy, the ideologue, took a strong position on the issue.

"I respect that teacher," Teddy said, as he helped Fat Kat enter new books into the library's computer database.

"'Course you do!" said Pitts. "It takes a fool to respect a fool."

"Nah, man," Teddy said, "he was trying to help a friend. And even when the dude ratted him out, he kept strong, proud. Your *name*, man, that's all you got."

"That might be all *you* got," said Pitts, "but that teacher guy had a *job* until he decided to be a damn fool."

As usual, Pitts got the last word. The conversation died there. After a few minutes of quiet, Teddy spoke again. This time he addressed me.

"You're Jewish, right?" asked Teddy. "Is it okay if I ask?"

I was curious what line of thought had led Teddy here.

"Yeah," I responded. "I grew up Orthodox. Hard-core."

Fat Kat's eyes widened when he heard this; he looked up from the computer keyboard where he had been working. Like Teddy, Fat Kat was Muslim. He, however, was not a convert but a born Muslim, raised by back-to-Africa black activists. A week earlier Fat Kat had told me, with a big smile, about the time his mother dragged him and his siblings to a demonstration in Washington, D.C. Young Kat had stood in front of the White House waving his fist and chanting, "Reagan, Reagan's gotta go! We support the P-L-O!"

"I had *no* idea what I was saying," he told me. "I was just repeating what they said."

We had had a big laugh about it. Now Fat Kat looked at me.

"You was raised *Orthodox*? Like with the hats and the hair," he said pointing to his sideburns, indicating the traditional long side-locks of the Hasidic sects. I could see that he was trying to imagine me dressed in a black frock coat with matching black hat and curly sidelocks, stroking my beard and walking briskly down Lexington Avenue in New York City. I laughed.

"Not exactly," I said, "I was like a plainclothes Hasid."

"Yeah, yeah, *Hasids!*" said Fat Kat with a big smile and a clap. "I remember those guys from the Feds, man," he said, referring to Federal Prison. I later learned that Fat Kat also knew them well as reliable clients of a sex-for-hire business he once ran in Brooklyn.

"Those dudes don't fuck around, right?" Teddy, always the dili-gent disciple, asked Fat Kat. "Pardon my language," he said, turning to me.

"Yeah, they take care of they shit," replied Kat. "Man those dudes was funny, though. In the Feds, if the Hasids got upset with something, they'd swarm around the warden and start doing this . . ." He did an impression of a flock of nervous men chattering and furi-ously wagging index fingers. I recognized the gesture and laughed. Fat Kat was fascinated by Hasidim. I rarely saw him this animated.

"In the Feds," he went on, "there was this black dude—I'm talk-ing, straight up *black guy*—who dressed like them, the Hasids, and rolled with them. And we was just like, 'Okay, man, if that's how you gonna do it, that's cool.'"

Fascination with Hasidim, I understood. But, admiration? That struck me as strange. Blacks and Hasidim, as I understood it, had a relationship of mutual suspicion. And then there was the issue of style.

"Really?" I said. "*Cool?*" It wasn't a word I had ever associated with my Hasidic brethren.

"Yeah!" said Teddy, who had never met a Hasid in his life. "You ever see them dudes rolling, like four in car, matching beards, man, matching pimpin' hats, music bumpin' . . ."

Teddy, himself piously bearded, cocked an imaginary hat on his braided head and nodded rhythmically to a nonexistent bass beat. He dissolved into laughter.

"Yeah," I said, "when *you* do it, it's cool . . ."

"Nah, man, I'm serious. I respect those guys," Teddy said.

Pitts shook his head, "Here we go again . . ."

"They know what they about," said Teddy. "Isn't that true, Kat?"

Fat Kat nodded earnestly. "That's true," he said.

As Teddy began to chide me for neglecting my Orthodox practice and for not dressing proudly as the Hasid I was meant to be, it occurred to me that Hasidim were, in ways that I had never quite appreciated, the epitome of gangsta. The inmates on the detail respected the Hasidim because, in their minds, Hasidim embodied the ideals of the thug life. Hasidim had a reputation of viewing the world as us-versus-them, and running their businesses and community institutions without any regard for a system of law imposed by outsiders, persecutors of their community. And what's more, they did it in style. They dressed their own way, talked their own way, walked their own way; they wore distinctive, indeed, completely unique clothing, and they wore it with pride wherever they went.

But most of all, as Kat explained, based on his own experience in Brooklyn, "You did *not* fuck around in their neighborhood, unless you had the green light. If they caught you out of line, man, they'd fuck you up. Those dudes guarded their neighborhood by any means necessary."

"Yeah," said Teddy. "That's what I'm talking about."

That was the main job of a gang, after all. And that's what the

Hasidim were to these men: an exquisitely well-organized gang—a gang with a long and illustrious history, a proven track record.

Every gang ultimately strives to be a full-blooded tribe. Tribespeople share a common history and fate, expressed through religion. They are loyal to each other and to their families until death. And they would never, ever snitch. A gang wasn't just a group of guys roaming around wearing matching clothing; they were an attempt at a community. They shared a history, either real or imagined. It's not an accident that the Latin Kings gang attaches itself to ancient myths and observes their own holidays and fasts. Nor was it an accident that Teddy was attracted to Sunni Islam and to Hasidim.

I thought back to my Orthodox upbringing and how I was raised to say the line, part of the central prayer of Judaism, "And may the informers have no hope . . ." I had said this prayer every day, *three times a day*. When I said it, I meant it. I knew more about gang loyalty than I had realized. Apparently I'd been raised with it.

I still cringed when I saw someone graffiti "Stop Snitching" into a desk in the library or when Fat Kat went on a tirade against snitches. But I also understood it personally. I understood why Teddy wanted to respect Miller.

I wondered if, in some small way, I could help shape the library detail into a gang of sorts. In prison, where sharing is literally against the rules and community building is often seen as a threat to order, the library was a place built on the basic tenet of both a gang and of community: sharing resources. People share when they trust each other. And in respecting the library detail—by treating them like men and not prisoners—I hoped to earn their loyalty and to convert them to the cause of the library. And yet, Miller might well have thought the same thing about his students. I could respect the inmate library detail, but I couldn't let myself be deceived into thinking we were on the same team.

I never referred to an inmate by his nickname. I was a public servant; I was expected to use an inmate's official name, his gov. Still, it was hard to resist. The nicknames were so descriptive of personality. When a guy comes into the library every day and speaks in an incomprehensible Mississippi accent, it's hard not to call him "Country"—especially when that's what everyone calls him. If a name seemed appropriate for a person, it seemed inappropriate to ignore it. Months after an inmate left the prison, I often couldn't recall his gov. More often, I remembered his street name. But it was beside the point. In prison, when it came to naming, superior descriptiveness was irrelevant. Names expressed solidarity with a group; they were bound up in one's affiliation. I was on the sheriff's payroll and I had to show my solidarity with the law. If I used a street name both the officers and the cons would draw the same conclusion about my allegiances. There was no room for expressions of private relationships that were neutral to the cop-con division. One had to choose sides.

In a culture like prison, which is about honor and shame, how you use a name matters. Honor systems are obsessed with public appearances, public actions. If you use a nickname, you honor both the individual person and the group that named him. If you use the name, you're part of the gang.

And that's where snitching came in. Snitching was, essentially, an act of unnaming someone, an undoing of a person's street name. By naming another person to the authorities, one, in fact, reestab-

lished that person's official identity over and against his street identity. Miller had refused to name the inmate and the result was, as my
colleague had whispered to me that night in the cafeteria, he was
named. His name became another prison commodity to be traded
on the black market.

I decided to be more careful. It wasn't savvy to let inmates give
me a nickname, even a wonderful one like *Bookie*. Nor, for that matter, was it wise to have my actual name broadcast over the radio by
the L-Crew to all of Greater Boston. I had to avoid sending the message that I was somehow on the inmates' side in the prison war—
especially if I also did stupid things like mouth off to Officer De
Luca. Even if it wasn't my intention, I was misaligning myself by
doing these things. The next thing I knew, I'd end up like Miller,
a well-intentioned chump holding a shank for some inmate. If
I allowed inmates to name me, I might eventually allow them to
unname me. I couldn't get drawn in.

For example, with Jessica. By handing a "gift" from her to her
son, I wasn't really doing anything wrong. Or was I? Perhaps I was
even doing something right. It was hard to tell. But I was doing something . . . with an inmate. This, as I was told during orientation, was
how trouble started. The little transgression. I was moving into that
gray area, into what I'd been warned against repeatedly by my coworkers, and by many inmates themselves, and now formally by the deputy. I knew what pragmatic union boss Charlie would tell me: keep
your nose clean. Even if it goes your way this round, he'd say, next
time you'll get screwed; that's how it goes here. How many times had
I been told, "Keep your distance" and "Don't get involved"? With
Jessica, I was now involved. And every time I convinced myself that
it was fine, that I was doing something right, I remembered Miller's

mortified face, drained of all blood, lying to Charlie and probably in denial himself. If these hesitations hadn't entered my mind, I'd already be in denial.

The good news: people still had no idea what to make of my name, Avi, itself a nickname for Avraham. This name, which is as common as Tom in Israel and Orthodox enclaves, was exotic in prison. Many people still had trouble saying it. I got called everything: Ari, Javi, Ali, Artie, Avery, Arnie, Alley, Arlo, Albie, Harley, Halley, Arfi, Advil, Alvie, Audi (as in the car), Arby (as in the fast food chain), A.V., Harvey, Harvin, and my personal favorite, which I heard but once: Ally. That name got right to the point.

I heard many of these names on a daily basis. It got to the point where I was given an incorrect full name, Arvin, and then an incorrect nickname for that name, Arvi. After some annoyance at the constant mangling of my name I'd begun to embrace the situation. It was like having fifteen aliases. My mysterious, protean name gave me a cloak of anonymity in the prison. I couldn't be easily named nor easily placed. While it hadn't been wise to give inmates my name for a shout-out, it was after all my *Avery* persona who saved the day. I knew that at some point, perhaps, I'd have to choose sides. In the meantime, though, my name concealed more than it revealed. In prison, this comes in handy.

And there were other cloaks one could wear in prison. There were, for example, ways to diplomatically use an inmate's name without quite calling him by it. Buddha—whose actual name I've since forgotten—comes to mind. He and I hadn't gotten off on the right foot. In fact, we disliked each other immensely. One day, during a lull, I leaned over to Buddha in the library and said to him, "So why'd they call you 'Buddha'? Is it because you're a man of peace?"

Buddha, clearly approving of this riff on his pot-inspired name, smiled widely.

"Arlo, man, you're okay," he said. "You're an undercover *playa*— I like that."

Jessica's Portrait

It was in this undercover playa persona that I arranged Jessica's portrait. I didn't have to look far for an artist. Turned out Brutish's filthy hands were also quite nimble with the sketching pencil. The portrait session was set for a Wednesday night in the library. I brought in some supplies: cheap and expensive coarse grain paper, colored pencils, charcoal, one of those cool, triangular erasers that is in strict compliance with the standards set forth by the International Ergonomics Association. While we waited for Jessica, Brutish told me that her drawing experience consisted mostly of sketches for tattoos. She specialized in skulls, she said, and was eager to "draw one with skin on it." Everything was set.

There was only one problem: Jessica didn't show up. I began to wonder if she'd changed her mind. A few minutes into the period, I noticed the officer on duty motion to someone outside of the library. Jessica had been loitering in the hall, hiding, too nervous to enter.

When Jessica walked in, the inmates hanging around the counter, the usuals, gawked at her.

"Whadaya lookin' at?" she said, as she installed herself into a little niche at the end of the counter, between the wall and a shelf.

It was pretty obvious what they were looking at. If Jessica wasn't quite made over, which would be a rather difficult enterprise in prison, she was dramatically touched up—and in a delightful array of improvised contraband cosmetics. Her hair, which usually fell in sorry knots just past her shoulders, was freshly shampooed, combed up into a cheerfully messy little nest, tied in place by a torn ribbon that looked suspiciously like the material of a prison uniform. Her lips and cheeks were rouged, too heavily, with some blood (which I prayed was her own). The eyebrows were plucked. The eyes outlined and lids shadowed jet black with an unidentified substance, and to Evil Handmaiden proportions. A flower—which, on closer inspection was construction paper and shiny gum wrappers carefully folded, origami-style, into six wide petals, symmetrical as a dahlia—was tucked into her hair. She looked pretty, and a touch loony.

The pièce de résistance was her aroma. She was generously doused in some designer perfume clipped from a magazine. These were known around prison as "smellgoods," and prized by both male and female inmates for use during prison visits. Perhaps she hoped that some of that scent would come through in the drawing itself. She needed only a well-placed ostrich feather or two, and a crimson-dappled white rose, and she might have posed for Madame Vigée Le Brun in Versailles.

She didn't feel elegant, though.

"Quit starin'," she said.

Trying to keep things low key, I led her to a quiet spot in the book stacks—where I'd set out two facing seats—and produced the drawing materials for Brutish, who was thrilled to experiment with the new implements. There was a quick debate about the pose. The artist herself demonstrated one approach: chin down, eyes up, lids half-drawn, mouth slightly ajar. An alluring magazine cover shot.

"No fuckin' way," said Jessica.

She sat down and adjusted her makeup.

"I look okay, right?"

"You look beautiful, baby," Brutish replied.

"This is a pretty big deal, isn't it?" Jessica said to me.

"Definitely," I replied.

I suggested she turn to profile, as though gazing out of a window. This was dismissed as artsy. No, she insisted on staring forward and smiling. I told her that looking happy was invented for snap photography. But she insisted. After righting her posture, adjusting her makeup yet again, and folding her hands on her lap, she produced a wide Christmas-card smile. Ten minutes into the session, however, her lips were quivering, the tendons in her neck had begun to strain, and her smile turned ghoulish. But Brutish carried on with surprising deliberation.

Jessica said she hoped her son would keep the portrait. Maybe he'd hang it in his cell. Or, one day, in his home. Maybe he'd make a tattoo out of it. Brutish told her to stop talking.

A Letter from Torchin

It took two more sessions to complete Jessica's portrait. Then Brutish took it back to her cell and, with the use of a contraband sketching charcoal, touched it up. The next night she brought it to the library.

"Shit looks good, right?" she said, sliding it to me across the library counter.

I had to agree. The blend of features that made it unmistakably Jessica had been executed perfectly, and a tad favorably. The proud, firm tilt of chin; the premature jowls; the adult exhaustion under child eyes; the faint and not so faint scars; the subtle mischief implied in the eyebrows; the failed attempt to straighten the curl of sarcasm from the lips. The embellishments of makeup and hairdo.

She handed the portrait to Jessica, who winced at it, but said, "Looks great, hon, thanks," and gave Brutish a big hug.

"I guess I can't give you a hug," she said to me. She extended her hand with a smile.

Jessica wanted to hold on to the portrait while she finished writing her letter. The letter, she told me, was to include stories about her family. About her upbringing. Mostly the good stuff, she said. When she was done with that, she'd give the letter and portrait to me, to give to him.

I wondered how her son would receive these documents. What would he read in the haggard, prettified face gazing back earnestly at him? How would the voice in the letter sound to his ears? His mother, a complete stranger—a prison inmate, like him. It was impossible for me to understand.

My closest approximation was to imagine how a child of Chris's, Jessica's grandchild, might eventually look at this portrait. With the remove of a generation, the experience would inevitably be colored as much by detached curiosity as raw emotion. In a small way, I knew something about that. As my mother had flown to California to be with my dying grandmother I had made a small discovery.

From the back of a bookshelf in my parents' house, I found a one-hundred-page typed, bound volume titled Family History. For some reason this document had been collecting dust for decades without anyone bothering to read it. The document was a faithful transcript of interviews with the entire Eastern European generation of my mother's family, my grandmother and her generation. It had been compiled by an older cousin back in the 1970s. I opened it up and was immediately engrossed.

I learned of the great feud between the rabbi and the mohel

trader, the old world equivalent of a used-car salesman. Srachiel's descendants still credit the holy man's blessing for the triumph of their furniture store years later in St. Louis.

The stories in this little book were marvelous, full of adventure and details of home life, comedy and tragedy, narrated in a resonant immigrant English. My relatives spoke of their parents and grandparents, painting a vivid picture of family life stretching back into the nineteeth century. "He had big eyebrows and used to make bets with the grave-digger," went one description. And another: "She was a big woman with a big coat and a lot of pockets. During the World War I, she would go around the front selling things from her pockets to both sides." Everyone had a nickname. There was Yossel Angel of Death. Aharon Watch Out, who had a blind horse. When he rode the horse through town he'd yell, "Watch out, watch out!"

But most of all, this book gave me the singular opportunity to hear my grandmother talk openly. She spoke of her excitement and anxiety as a provincial girl going to the big city for market days. And of her love of weddings. She described in detail her sister's wedding: the weeklong cooking preparation, the singing, the comedian telling dirty jokes—which annoyed her sister—the local children throwing snowballs in front of the old wooden synagogue. She could still taste the delicious fluden, which had turned out better than the strudel that day. She could still hear the rabbi singing, she said. My grandmother was not given to sentiment, and certainly not shtetl sentimentality. I'd never heard anything close to this from her. I was in shock.

She still didn't talk directly about her experience of loss, about (the guy who does circumcisions) in Torchin, Poland, in the 1920s. For undisclosed reasons, these men hated each other. Their rivalry boiled over one day when the mohel, who also happened to be the town's butcher, was called in to circumcise the rabbi's grandson. He "accidentally" botched the procedure, setting off a small-scale civil war in the shtetl.

A generation earlier, my grandmother's grandfather—my great-great-grandfather, Srachiel—had decided to travel to a new town and become a Hasid in the court of the Great Rabbi of Karlin. Srachiel had conveniently embarked on this spiritual journey after he already was married with two young daughters. When it became clear that Srachiel had no intention of ever returning to his family, his young wife did something scandalous for a woman: she traveled, unaccompanied, to the town where her husband was laying low as a saint-in-training. She marched directly to the Karliner Rabbi's House of Study, a buzzing hive of busy Hasidim hunched over large volumes of the Talmud arguing with each other, and probably also occasionally playing footsie. This was not a place for a woman. The men stared as she pounded on the door. They told her to beat it. She pounded harder. They told her more forcefully to beat it. But she hadn't made this epic journey to be turned away at the door.

She did what any half-crazed, goal-oriented person might do in that situation. She ran around the building, smashing every single window of the House of Study. This apparently got the attention of the rabbi himself. He invited her in and let her plead her case. The rabbi turned to Srachiel, the young mysterious Hasid, and asked him if it was true that he'd abandoned his wife and children. He fessed. The rabbi commanded him to return home and gave a blessing that he'd succeed in business. Srachiel became a the photos in her drawer, or the family and close friends she'd lost in the war. But it was by far the most extensive version of her story that I'd ever heard—and in her own voice. For whatever reason, she had been more candid with a relative who was not linked to her children. Although my grandmother remained a mystery to me, I now had something tangible. This was the inheritance I'd wanted.

Now, after my mother had spent so much energy to forgive this complicated woman, and as she tried to let her go, my grandmother had given us something more. As she was dying, and her absence became literal—her silence absolute—her presence emerged, just a tiny bit more, in these few typed words.

Perhaps for Chris and his future children, Jessica's letter would be something like that: rare and valuable words from a silent person.

A Picture of a Mailman

The cynical officer at orientation had said: "The inmates don't go there to read *Moby-Dick*." In a way, he was right. Jessica certainly didn't visit the library to read *Moby-Dick*. But she also wasn't there to cause trouble, as the officer had been suggesting. So why was she now a regular?

Jessica had told me she "wasn't much of a reader." But I could tell by the way she handled books this wasn't quite true. Perhaps she had been a reader once and quit. Or had lost the ability to focus. She claimed to have read the back cover of almost every book in the library, but rarely checked anything out. And never, so she said, actually enjoyed the occasional book she did end up reading. She didn't come to the library to find a book, but to search for one. She was an infinite browser.

Sometimes I'd join her in the search. Nothing that she came

across, or that I could pull off the shelf, was quite right. I was drawn to inmates like Jessica because they were a challenge. I would try to find books for her everywhere I went, at bookstores, yard sales, on Amazon. I wanted to solve the puzzle. Where on earth was this unnamed book she was looking for?

Some books were close calls, but the one she sought remained elusive. Sometimes I wondered if maybe this book hadn't yet been written. I suggested to her that she write it—some people wrote, I said, because the book they'd most love to read, that they *need* to read, simply hadn't yet been written.

She just shot me a sidelong glance and said, "Yeah, right."

And so the search continued. A few minutes later she told me that any book she'd write would be "too fuckin' depressing for anyone to read."

"That's the American way," I replied. "You tell people your horribly depressing story, and you feel better about it—"

"And they feel worse," she said.

During one of these searches, I pulled a Sylvia Plath volume off the shelf. It was a book of Plath's letters. Jessica told me she'd read it. Twice. Coming from an infinite browser, who was "not much of reader," this was, of course, a significant comment. Plath was the only writer who held any interest for her. Apparently, Jessica, who trusted or distrusted authors based on their photos, had been willing to forgive Plath her 1950s Smith College cuteness. Perhaps this was because she wasn't interested in Plath, the writer, but in Plath, the person. She was more interested in the private writings, those not intended for publication. The journals, the letters.

She wasn't the only one. I had created a Plath shelf in the poetry section at the behest of Plath's ardent fans—mostly among the women inmates—and reluctantly on my part, given the suicidal tendencies of Plath's martyrdom-obsessed cultists, particularly those in prison.

I asked Jessica what she liked about the Plath letters and journals. She brightened up at the question.

"So much," she said. "Everything."

She began flipping through the book and for a full twenty minutes, read me favorite passages. She seemed particularly interested in Plath's mysticism. She was drawn to a comment in a letter to Plath's mother, dated June 10, 1958, that read, "had my fortune told by a subway gypsy whose card, ironically enough, showed a picture of a mailman and said I'd get a wonderful letter soon that would change my life for the better." Fifteen days letter, Jessica said, flipping a few pages ahead, Plath writes ecstatically of wonderful news that she got through the mail. She sold two poems to the *New Yorker* for a total of $350. This, as Plath herself noted, was surely the fulfillment of the subway gypsy's vision. As a Bostonian, Jessica was especially charmed by Plath's comment that the $350 would be enough for "three full months of Boston rent!"

Jessica was also interested by how often, and how thoroughly, Plath wrote to her mother with good news. Every last cent she or her husband, poet Ted Hughes, earned from their writing was touted with an exclamation point, every good tiding recounted with dramatic embellishment. And yet, as amateur Plath scholar Jessica noted, her journal entries from the same period—sometimes overlapping the very same days as letters to her mother—told a more nuanced story.

"That's always the way it is, right?" Jessica said.

One episode in Plath's life made a particular impression on her. Plath and Hughes had found a dying baby bird. They tried desperately to save the badly injured creature. Plath became enamored of the "plucky little thing." But in the end, they had decided to put the chick out of its misery. They gassed it in a box. The bird "went to sleep very quietly," wrote Plath, "but it was a shattering experience." Jessica shook her head when reading this.

"You know," she told me, "that's how Sylvia went, right? Gas."

I told her I did know—comments like these from Plath fans were the worrying kind. But she was right, it was an interesting connection.

Jessica also told me that Plath had worked in a mental hospital, which I hadn't known. "She was obsessed with this one patient," Jessica told me, "who was afraid she was gonna give birth to an animal—like an actual furry little rabbit! Sylvia was into some pretty messed up shit, right? But that's why I love her."

Jessica had clearly given these books a serious read. But she was done with them. Back to square one, she told me. Searching endlessly for a book.

We continued browsing quietly for a minute or two. I pulled out some candidates. She unequivocally rejected them. And the process continued.

"I remember the time I laughed the hardest," she said, for no particular reason, clearly absorbed in some private reverie. "Do you remember yours?"

"I don't think so," I said. "I'd have to think hard about it."

"I remember," she said. "It was when my friend Billy's casket was lowered into the ground."

She gave me another sidelong glance.

"Pretty fuckin' funny, right?" She said.

Billy, a friend from childhood, owed a lot of money to the mob.

It wasn't like in other neighborhoods, she told me, where they'd shoot you and leave you to rot like roadkill. In Whitey Bulger's Irish mob, they'd kidnap you and that was it. You'd never be seen again. In the case of Billy, his mother was told to pay a ransom for his body. This was an attempt to extort money from his rich uncle. The uncle had refused to pay the ransom and so the body was never returned. The uncle, however, paid for the casket, which was buried empty.

"It was a bad day," she recalled.

On that bad day, Jessica had started drinking again. She had been clean for almost two years, having weathered various storms of her recovery, including a friend's suicide and her sister's murder. But the pain was cumulative. At the wake, she got trashed on Jamesons and Long Island Iced Teas, and screwed a near stranger upstairs. Soon after that, she was using again.

Why did she laugh during the funeral?

First of all, she said, she was drunk off her ass. But it wasn't just that. "It's not that it was funny," she said. But something about it, something in the absurdity of watching everyone crying as a big empty box was put into the ground. She couldn't identify what it was, but something made her laugh.

"I dunno," she said, "I was thinking, *fuckin' Billy probably'll show up in back and say 'fuck is everyone crying about?'* That's something he'd totally do. We didn't even know if he was really dead. It was crazy."

As she was telling me this, and as we continued looking in vain for a book that probably didn't exist, I couldn't help but think of the absences in Jessica's life. Those, like Billy, who were not there, but there. And her son, in the same facility, visible, but impossibly far away—there, but not there.

A Ribbon to a Stranger

Jessica's portrait and letter. I was moved by this use of the library. So much of my job involved intercepting letters—a practice I hated—disrupting communications, trashing people's written words. But here was a chance to do the opposite. To create a conduit of words, to connect people through a letter. Who knew what it would mean to Chris and Jessica? Maybe it would begin a new chapter. If not, perhaps one day Chris's children would find the letter hidden in a drawer—as my mother had found her mother's photos—or collecting dust on a shelf, as I had found my grandmother's interviews on my parents' bookshelf. In this way, they'd gain a tiny view, for better or worse, of where they came from.

A week passed. Then another. She wanted the portrait touched up more, she said. She needed to rewrite the letter. She apologized. I told her not to; she wasn't doing this for me, she was doing it for herself.

Then she was gone, transferred to a different prison. She'd departed without saying goodbye, without leaving the letter or portrait. My first thought was of Chris. I'd told him—through a messenger; he never came himself—that I'd be giving him the gift from his mother. At first, his messenger had curtly informed me that Chris didn't want a fucking thing from her and seemed justifiably skeptical of me. But a week later the messenger had come in asking for the letter and portrait. I'd told him it was on the way. He had visited almost every day for a week. I'd see him waiting patiently behind a crowd of inmates who had stormed the library counter with their requests. He had come for this reason alone. And every time, I told him the same thing: *It's on the way. It's in the mail*. After a while, the messenger had stopped asking me about it. He stopped coming to the library altogether. But still, I had remained hopeful.

Now Jessica had left without giving Chris a thing. I sent him a note through another inmate. It said, "I tried, Chris. I'm really sorry." I felt bad for having raised his hopes. I shouldn't have been so optimistic, shouldn't have said, "it's in the mail."

I couldn't get Jessica's letters out of my mind. That horrible letter of abandonment that she had placed into toddler Chris's pocket at the church that day in 1987—and now this, the letter she did *not* put into his hands. The small thing that would have been the immeasurable difference between something and nothing. Still, I held out some hope that Jessica would send him something through the actual mail.

But then Martha the gossip approached me in the library. Jessica, she told me, had ripped up the portrait and a draft of her half-finished letter shortly before she was transferred. Martha saw the shreds in the garbage bin.

I thought about how isolated Jessica seemed that night when I saw her standing in line, as the prison commotion swelled around her, the laughing inmates, the shouting guards. Oblivious to her surroundings. She had just told me the story of abandoning her son. Her guilt and shame, her deep regret had sapped her senses. Just by looking at her that night, waiting for the officers to finish their count, waiting to march back to her prison cell, it was clear: Jessica was done. She hadn't been tuning out the noise around her. She wasn't ignoring the others. No, it was that she herself barely existed. Her presence then was papery and insubstantial. No wonder she'd ripped up the portrait. Ghosts cannot give gifts.

. . .

There had been one gift, though. Given to her cellmate, the Vietnamese woman who didn't speak any English, whose inability to communicate with Jessica had formed the basis of their relationship. The woman was acutely anxious and would stroke a tiny piece of fabric compulsively, day and night. I witnessed this myself in the library. After a couple of weeks, she'd stroked her worry-totem down to a pile of furry threads. From the prison black market, Jessica had procured a tiny black ribbon, the kind used by mourners. The deal was done in the library—and she gave her cellmate the gift on the spot. The exchange happened near the bookshelves closest to the counter, where the Vietnamese woman had been flipping through books in a language she couldn't read. The woman smiled at Jessica, and proceeded to stroke her new ribbon. Not a word was exchanged

A few months after she'd given this gift, after she'd ripped up Chris's letter, Jessica was dead. The news came by way of Martha the gossip. She had arrived red-eyed one night in the library. Standing a few feet from where Jessica had sat for the portrait, Martha leaned on the counter and told me what she knew. Less than a month out of prison Jessica had overdosed.

"I heard she died in a boarded-up building," Martha told me through her tears.

This apparently wasn't quite true. A more reliable source later told me she'd overdosed and died at home. But I suspect this detail—that Jessica died alone in an abandoned building—had somehow made sense to Martha. When she'd delivered the news to me, there certainly had been an awful kind of plausibility to it.

The other inmates gave Martha space to cry at the library counter that night, though a few came over occasionally to put an arm around her.

"She was my friend," was all Martha could say.

When she had calmed down a bit, she added, "Jessica thought of you as a friend, you know."

"I know," I said. "I considered her a friend too."

In prison this was a complicated, impolitic thing to say. I was surprised how easily it had slipped out of my mouth. But at that moment, the shock of the news had forced out the uncomplicated truth.

Was it a suicide? With addicts it is sometimes unclear. Often unanswerable. So indeed was the related question of why she'd turned her portrait, and the letter to her son, into a pile of ripped paper in a prison garbage can. I could speculate but I'd never really know. Even if I did, I probably wouldn't truly understand.

A ribbon to a stranger—this may have been the last gift she had in her. Perhaps it was as much as she had left to give. My mother once said that the one gift she'd received from her mother was her mother's long life. Time. A gift given accidentally, but no less precious. It had been the single factor that allowed my mother to forgive my grandmother. Jessica was not able to give even this passive gift to her son. An early death was the final affirmation of her belief that forgiveness was not possible for her in this world. She'd given birth alone at Boston City Hospital. She'd abandoned Chris alone in a church. And in prison, when she was so physically near to him, she may have finally realized, or perhaps decided, if she hadn't already, that she would remain alone. Perhaps it was precisely this proximity, the sight from that window in my class, and the unavoidable challenge it presented her, that finally brought this grim truth to her. That possibility weighed on me.

For days I kept imagining the fate of the world's misplaced letters. I started noticing them everywhere. All the right letters sitting on desks and dressers, slipped into purses, abandoned in email Draft folders, forever sealed and unsent. Shredded. Forgotten, sometimes intentionally. And the wrong letters, placed in someone's hands— which, once delivered, may never be taken back. Emailed and immediately regretted.

When I looked around the world, I couldn't see these letters. But I became aware of their indirect presence. They contained life's great subtexts, embedded between the lines of cell phone conversations of strangers on the bus, in the hazy motive of a coworker who told me she was taking a "mental health" day off after receiving a difficult email from her mother. These notes were virtual, folded up, hidden, like letters tucked into books of the prison library. A kite, barely visible in the sky, bound to a person by an almost invisible string. Even the unsent ones are very much present. Especially the unsent ones.

Man Down

I was stuck. It was a Friday afternoon. After finishing up an early shift, I found myself detained longer than usual in the sallyport, together with a group of officers and assorted staff. The doors rolled shut, locking us in with the loud metal-to-metal crash that alarms visitors, and which staff members don't even notice. It had been months since I'd passed into this second category. It was only after the second door—the one that would let us back out into freedom—had failed to open, that I realized we were locked in together. An emergency call went out. I heard it clearly from the radios strapped to the belts of the officers locked in the sallyport with me.

Man down in 3-3.

"Oh fuck," said an officer next to me. "Here we go."

"This could take awhile," a nurse said to me, on the presumption I was a volunteer.

Until things were settled in 3-3, we were locked in this little limbo between freedom and prison. Everyone was coming off of a long shift, some were coming off double shifts. It smelled like overworked officers: a combination of worn rubber, leather, stale coffee, and sweat-soaked polyester. Not even a nurse's overpowering perfume could mask it.

Through the dark, bulletproof glass that separated the sallyport from the central command center, I could see security cameras broadcasting the chaos in 3-3. I leaned in toward the thick glass to get a better view of the screen, which beamed a lurid light into the darkness of central control. I saw inmates in blue prison uniforms running in and out of the picture. Then an officer running. Then an inmate hop on a table and shout something. The wisdom of bolting prison tables to the floor suddenly dawned on me.

I was so absorbed in the scene broadcast live from the prison war zone that I almost missed the drama happening right there in the sallyport. As the group grumbled and sighed, and shifted uncomfortably inside our accidental prison cell, someone spoke. At least I thought he was speaking. A second later it was clear he wasn't speaking, but singing.

Everyone went quiet and turned to the source. The singer was a large, loping labrador retriever of a man, top-heavy, a shaggy officer's uniform, scraggly beard and stately belly, a big, nutty grin affixed to his face. He smiled as he sang.

"*My story is much too sad to be told—but practically everything leaves me totally cold . . .*"

An officer heckled him from the other side of the sallyport, "We're not gonna give ya dolla bills, ya fat bastard."

A few people, mostly officers, laughed. But he ignored the comment and pressed on. Though still barely audible, his singing gained in strength. It had a pleasant little swing to it. He was playing it up, cocking his fist like a microphone, and assuming various jazz singing poses, to the extent possible in a tight, locked space, packed with people.

"*The only exception I know is the case—when I'm out on a quiet spree—fighting vainly the old ennui—and I suddenly turn and see . . .*"

And with this, the big man made a surprisingly lithe full spin in his bulky officer's boots and, mischievous smile widening to capacity, swung around until he was in a face-to-face serenade with a short, plump contractor.

"*Your fa-bu-lous face . . .*"

She blushed, and everyone laughed.

I suddenly remembered the chaos in 3-3 and I turned my attention back to the closed-circuit security TV.

By the time the officer launched into the refrain, "*I get no kick from champagne—mere alcohol doesn't thrill me at all,*" every staff person locked in the sallyport, including me, was smiling. And not despite the violence up in 3-3 but because of it. You had to be open to humor in order to work in this place or you'd grow hopelessly bitter. Or simply numb.

Often the humor turned dark. During a recent staff holiday party I'd laughed with everyone else when, during a gift exchange, someone presented, as a gag gift, a "hooter kit"—the container of bathroom supplies, a tiny cheap toothbrush, toothpaste, and soap, given to inmates who were too poor to purchase these things from the prison canteen. The hooter kit is one of the bleaker, more poignant expressions of prison loneliness. The question I'd asked myself at the party, while twenty or so of us laughed as a coworker pulled the hooter kit out of a hat, was not whether the joke was witty (it was not) nor whether it was tasteless (it certainly was). The question was why was it funny anyway. Partly it was the surprise of seeing the kit appear out of place. But mostly it was because in prison you were often presented with the options of dark humor or no humor. And the former seemed like the better choice, the only way to feel that your strange place of employment was also just a human workplace, complete with awkward holiday parties and stupid gag gifts.

But my ability to cope through humor, my smile, was short-lived that day. I just wasn't feeling up to it. At that moment, stuck in the sallyport, I *felt* stuck. Crammed inside of a machine, I was given to the sudden awareness that this wasn't the mere sensation of feeling crammed, but the literal fact of it: I was crammed inside of a machine. A small system with two heavy doors rolling on tracks, controlled by a remote will, a situation not unlike that of a lab rat. It took only this small bit of pressure to puncture my equilibrium, letting in a torrent of emotions. Jessica's death. I wasn't doing well with it. It had shaken me personally.

I kept returning to what she'd said to me, her face and hair done up with such sincerity—it must have taken her hours to acquire all of the materials and to pull that off—she'd turned to me, smiled, and said, "This is a big deal, right?" What an understatement that had been. It was the first time in many years, maybe since she'd abandoned her son, that she was taking some major initiative, exerting her will. She was trying to push back against the immense machine of her fate, before it was too late. It had been a very big deal indeed.

Stuck in the sallyport and feeling stuck, my defenses breached, I was suddenly overcome by a wave of emotion. For Jessica: who, with the complicated staff-inmate relationship behind us, I could now call a friend—one who died broken and alone. And for her son, a kid with a rough future. And for me: a fool for using the library as anything else but a place for inmates to get silly thrillers. I felt deeply ashamed for telling Chris that his long-awaited letter was "in the mail." Books are not mailboxes, said Amato's sign. I hated that sign. To me, the library was at its best when creating the space for Jessica's letter to pass through, to be delivered. But perhaps the sign was right. My optimism amounted to a cruel joke played on a troubled eighteen-year-old orphan. I was overcome by a shrinking feeling. *Oh shit*, I thought, *I'm actually going to cry like a little girl in the sallyport.*

I stared at the one-ton steel door and willed it to open, so that I could spare myself this. I stared and willed it open, but the door remained locked. It wasn't working. I tried to divert my mind with something else.

I shifted my gaze to the dark figures moving around in the control room itself. Set against little flashing red and green lights, switches and levers, and various monitors beaming images from the violence in 3-3 and from all over the prison—and a monitor, set low and out of view, that beamed in daytime TV—these dark forms stood, sat, leaned, held paper cups of coffee to their shadow-darkened faces. From where I was standing in the sallyport, it was hard to make out anything in there. But I noticed two long, fine feminine hands, like a pianist's, working over a switchboard. I hadn't noticed it before: such brutal doors operated by such a pair of refined hands. While their

owner remained shrouded in darkness, those elegant fingers, illumi-
nated under a small lamp, tapped buttons, pulled switches. After a
few more painful moments, they hit a master stroke. The heavy steel
door rumbled open and we were set free until the next day.

The Automat

The next evening I spotted the prison shrink in the staff
cafeteria. I made a beeline for her. She was a tall, thin woman
with big clunky jewelry and poofy hair that hovered over her like a
fair-weather cumulus cloud. There was something comforting about
her professorial disarray. She pursed her lips, furrowed her brow, and
paused for long moments before answering serious questions. I had
one for her that day.

Before saying hello, before giving the woman an honest chance
to dig into the tofu salad she'd brought from home, I put my tray
down next to her and said, "So what's so bad about countertransference anyway?" She paused, and pursed her lips.

Countertransference was a concept I'd heard her mention once
before. The idea, as she had used it, was basically that people who
work with populations like psych patients or prison inmates might
identify a particular individual with someone important in their own
lives. And, as a result, regard this patient or inmate in a similar mode
as they would this person. For example, treating an inmate with a
strange, seemingly unwarranted blend of sympathy and jealousy
because he reminds you of your brother.

"Well," said the therapist, "a lot, potentially. Especially if you
aren't, for whatever reason, paying attention to it."

The practical dangers, she said, included inappropriate unpro-
fessional behaviors of all sorts, from bending rules to throwing all

propriety out the window. The feelings themselves are natural and inevitable. It's important to be aware of what is happening, to keep the situation in check by setting boundaries, and, in some cases— especially for a therapist—to ask yourself if the patient is eliciting these feelings in you because of *her* behavior toward you: that you see her like a daughter, for instance, because she views you as a mother. A therapist may have to carefully explore this patient-doctor relationship in the context of the session itself.

"Sounds like a headache," I said.

"It is," she laughed. "But I'm in the headache busines, and so are you, by the way."

She added, "Let me know if you ever want to talk about it."

I didn't. The talking cure doesn't do much for me. I tend more toward the brooding cure. In my brooding, I had decided that I was experiencing a reverse transference: not seeing an inmate as though she were a loved one, but rather seeing a loved one as though she were an inmate. I saw some of Jessica—her tortured solitude, the abyss of silence—in my mysterious grandmother. I had always judged my grandmother by her malicious words and actions, and never tried to understand her predicament. Never really appreciated that she was an intensely lonely person. A prisoner.

In my writing class I found myself distracted by the empty chair in which Jessica used to sit looking down at her son through a prison window. I had asked the women to write about Edward Hopper's 1927 painting *Automat*, to personify in words the lonely woman in the painting. The assignment was inspired by Jessica. But when I started to think about the woman in the painting, I found myself thinking of a certain portrait of my grandmother.

Once, in order to shake my grandmother out of despondency,

my aunt had forced her to buy a new dress, get a makeover, and sit for a photo portrait at a local mall. I knew this photo well. It was the one of my pale grandmother in a hideous blue suit, hair set like a trench helmet, wearing too much lipstick and looking as dour as ever. This was the photo I had long associated with the sneering portrait of Mussolini in my eighth-grade history textbook. The moment I'd turned to that page in the World War II chapter I'd thought, *Whoa, that looks* exactly *like grandma's picture!* I hadn't shaken that feeling since then.

But now I saw things more clearly. Like Jessica preparing for her portrait, my grandmother had been dressing up her vulnerability — one accessory, one stroke of makeup at a time — in order to sit defiantly in the presence of her loneliness. It was an act of self-preservation and quiet courage.

A small detail about Jessica returned to me. The day of her portrait, she had arrived with the bottom of her uniform pants cuffed, following a prison style popularized by the cool crowd of women inmates. She'd never cuffed her pants before. At the time, it seemed unremarkable.

But now, I got it. The cuffed pants — and for that matter, the perfume — were not meant to be depicted. They had nothing to do with the portrait itself. And that's not why she wore them. It was intended for her, to allow her to playact, to give her a way to imagine herself, for a moment, in a beautiful light. To be the person she'd wished she had been. I had to wonder if perhaps the entire portrait session was never really meant for her son. If it was, like her recurring dream of him, a fleeting moment of private grace.

I looked at Hopper's automat woman through the reflections of Jessica's portrait, and of my grandmother's. When I gave in-class writing assignments, I usually jotted down something myself. In the fifteen minutes remaining in the period I wrote the following notes into my wire-free, prison-issue notebook:

> *the privacy of droopy hats and thick lipstick*
> *to keep the darkness at bay*
>
> *clothed in brightness against the night*
> *to make it all go away*
>
> *but nothing can protect her from Nothing*
> *from the empty seat across the table*
> *the impossible window*
> *the overwhelming sense*
> *her tea has grown cold.*

In mourning Jessica this way, I'd found a means of mourning my difficult grandmother, an experience I'd been dreading for as long as I could remember. It clarified something else, as well. That I'd begun to need these writing classes as much as the prisoners who were my students.

After class I went down to my office in the library and did what any semi-repressed Midwest-raised kid would do with such a crush of emotions. I called my mother and provoked an argument about her parking ability. Which expanded into a commentary on her driving skills, before resolving into a critique of her commitment, or lack of, to a proper exercise regimen.

When I paused, she said, "Is that all?"

Could I admit the truth? That I was just calling to hear her voice, because I knew that, at some point in my life, this simple act would be impossible.

"No," I said instead, "that's *not* all. But I gotta get back to work now, 'bye."

Messiah by Kite

I reach into my pocket to fetch a coin for the vending machine in the officers' union clubhouse. I have my eye on a certain PayDay peanut caramel bar. Instead I pull out a note. I'd forgotten about it. Kites sometimes glide into my life like this, out of the blue. Sometimes wildly out of context. I'll be at home, at a movie or a restaurant, light years from prison, and one of these small, insistent voices brings me right back. I unfold the note.

Dear Messiah, it reads, *I know things is tough but you gotta hang in there brutha . . .*

I smile. One tiny ballot cast for theological optimism. I know the note refers to an inmate named Messiah, but one can't help but wonder. I take out my notebook, copy the words of the short note, and append a short gloss: "the Messiah's plight." I had never considered the unfortunate fate of the Messiah himself (perhaps Christians have a better sense of this). The Messiah has to suffer as long as the rest of us, forced to await his own long-overdue arrival. Poor guy. Maybe his fate is worse than ours.

This is the flip-side to the skeptical old Jewish joke:

A small town pays a ne'er-do-well to sit on a bench, wait for the Messiah, and to announce his arrival to the rest of the towns-people. For years, that's exactly what the man does: sits on the bench all day, every day, waiting. One day a man asks the ne'er-do-well why he took such a thankless, low-paying job.

"It's true, the pay is low," says the ne'er-do-well, "but it's a steady job."

In a world where nothing, not even God's promises, is reliable, at least one can rely on disappointment. And as the joke says, the doomed optimism business offers wonderful job security. It's a perfect summary of prison work.

At the moment, it is my work. When I return to my office, I draw up a propaganda poster to be placed in the prison blocks—it shows an image of the library and a child. *Use the Prison Library*, it reads, *So Your Children Won't Have To*. It's a bit pessimistic, perhaps, but also optimistic in a way. It turns out that even after I defected from yeshiva, I still abide by the medieval Jewish article of faith, which is itself full of doubts and subtle irony: *I believe with perfect faith in the coming of the Messiah, and even though he tarries, nevertheless I await his arrival every day.*

The Archive

Forest, my co-librarian, was beginning to wonder about me. In his abundant politeness, he'd kept mum. But one afternoon, shortly before taking off for the day, leaving the library in my hands, he finally turned around from his desk on the other side of our shared office and spoke up.

"So," he said, in his near whisper of a voice, "what are you doing over there?"

I'd been clearing precious shelf space for empty boxes and was now filling these boxes with piles of raggedy-looking sheets of paper.

"I'm making some storage area for kites and stuff found in the library."

"Oh," he said. "Okay."

He put his coat on, closed up a few Word documents he'd been working on. He stood watching me for a moment, wearing a pained expression.

"Like an archive?" he said.

"Yeah," I replied. "Exactly."

"I think you're more an archivist than a librarian," he said.

He told me that archivists and librarians were opposite personas. True librarians are unsentimental. They're pragmatic, concerned with the newest, cleanest, most popular books. Archivists, on the other hand, are only peripherally interested in what other people like, and much prefer the rare to the useful.

"They like everything," he said, "gum wrappers as much as books." He said this with a hint of disdain.

"Librarians like throwing away garbage to make space, but archivists," he said, "they're too crazy to throw anything out."

"You're right," I said. "I'm more of an archivist."

"And I'm more of a librarian," he said.

"Can we still be friends?"

He flashed me his shy smile and headed out the door.

I was rational enough to realize that refusing to throw out kites, and other such material, was a bit eccentric. But I couldn't help it. It seemed brutal to trash a letter that someone had taken the time to handwrite. And there was some part of me that thought, *Who knows, maybe these letters will be important to someone in the future*? I majored in history and literature, and wrote newspaper obituaries. I spent many hours looking at letters and artifacts that some oddball had decided not to throw out. There is no history, no memory, without this.

I couldn't bring myself to destroy records. When I thought about it, I could link this impulse to my emotional investment in Jessica and her letter: if not to reunite a family—a tall order under the circumstances—then at least to preserve a record, some scrap of family memory, for Chris and his children, if he has any.

For months, I had been vaguely conscious that the prison itself maintained an archive. But since it hadn't directly related to my work, I'd forgotten about it. Now, given that Forest had correctly diagnosed me as an archivist, I was curious what an actual prison archive looked like.

When I approached Patti with an awkward and vaguely phrased request to "see the archive," she said she'd see what could be done. That same day, Deputy Mullin, the warden, called me himself to tell me that he'd put me in touch with the prison archivist, Sergeant Gallo—whom the deputy accidentally, or possibly intentionally, referred to as Sergeant Gallows. Deputy Mullin had told Gallo/Gallows that I was a "history buff" and would "appreciate a tour." When he recounted this, he laughed faintly.

"Knock yourself out," he told me. "But watch out for Gallows. He's kind of a character."

In my imagination, an archivist—a real archivist, unlike me—is meticulous, pedantic, solemn, a person who doesn't let anything slip, neither a document nor a candid phrase. Sgt. Gallo was not this man. He was of another genus altogether. The sergeant was a charmingly unkempt fellow, quirky and freewheeling, a man who wore both his officer's stripes and his effusive emotions on his sleeve. Perhaps he preferred the solitude of the archive, or perhaps he'd been banished there—it wasn't clear. Gallo, who teetered as he walked, was a perfect square of a man, as though almost three decades toiling in a box-shaped cinderblock room, surrounded by boxes, had turned him into one himself. He grunted and snorted, boasted, told off-color jokes, and proudly subverted the ethos of his job: He told me that he'd been "itching" to destroy an entire wall's worth of boxes (once the court gave him permission, of course). He had no affection for history ("it's all bad news") and was much more concerned with making room for new documents. Apparently, he was more of a librarian.

"Empty space is gorgeous," he told me, "it's literally beautiful to me. But, as you can see, there ain't much beauty up here."

When I'd first arrived in the archive—riding on an elevator that started and stopped at the whim of a distracted officer in central control—I shook hands with Gallo and immediately marveled at the stunning view of Boston's skyline and at the luxuriant sunlight pouring in through giant skylights. He squinted in the direction of the grand windows, as though he had never noticed them. Perhaps he hadn't.

"It's all right I guess," he said, "if you're into that kind of thing."

He then harangued me for almost an hour about how nobody appreciates him or the work he does. Most of his fellow prison guards routinely implied that he spent his time "sitting around touching myself all day." Although the little square-shaped sergeant didn't find this amusing at all, he finally cracked a smile and conceded, "This is mostly not the case."

I asked him about the photos hanging over his desk. In the spot where most people might hang a family portrait or a pinup girl, he had photos of an old, decrepit brick fortress on a gray overcast day, the path leading to it marked by foot-deep tire tracks in fresh mud.

"That," he said, a smile suddenly brightening the thick creases of his face, "is Deer Island." The old prison facility. Everyone who'd spent time at Deer Island—inmates, officers, and civilian staff—all spoke of it as a depressing hellhole. But not Gallo. He became nostalgic when recalling the beach picnics and barbecues that officers had up there.

"There weren't so many *rules* at Deer Island. It was great. Nobody cared what went on."

For most people, that had been precisely the problem with the place. Gallo turned serious again and told me that nobody on the prison staff respects the archive space. When people hear of the existence of the archive, he said, "They think this means 'garbage dump.'" He'd been constantly turning away broken down prison fixtures and appliances.

Sometimes, however, he'd strip a fixture for parts. During his spare time in the archive, Gallo toyed with his "inventions." In a corner of the space, he'd set up a workshop where he built and tinkered with various devices he didn't care to discuss. Gallo was one of the more idiosyncratic people I'd met in prison. His hours in the archive ran from 4 a.m. to 1 p.m. every day. A singular shift indeed.

When Gallo had begun his tour, he had asked me, with bald incredulity—bordering on mockery—why I wanted to see the archive. I had no suitable response and relied on Deputy Mullin's excuse: I was a "history buff." Gallo had narrowed his eyes when I said that. But he executed the boss's order and showed me room after room of boxes containing incident reports, disciplinary write-ups, medical records, memos, inmate booking papers, and God only knows what else.

"Nobody really knows everything that's in here," he conceded.

He pulled out yellowed documents from the ancient prison at Deer Island.

"If you do time, your ugly file stays in here forever," he said, with a grin, "the prison archive doesn't ever forget."

But does it *remember*? And, what exactly does it choose to commit to memory? Would it tell a future historian that a man named Messiah once lived in a cell on the third floor? That the inmates named their basketball tournament the Summer Classic? Would it record the names of the prison's most watched TV show or most read book? Would it remember Jessica and her son?

The twenty-five-minute tour with Gallo had tantalized me. The space itself—its piles of papers representing decades of tangled history—reminded me of all that I didn't know and couldn't know. This itself is part of the wisdom of archives. By creating a finite space, where some things are included, some omitted, an archive challenges you to examine its dusty spaces, but more importantly, to search for what has been entirely left out. After Jessica's death, I felt an even greater need to preserve, to create a home for those things in danger of slipping into oblivion.

As I stood on the elevator, I made a decision to officially embrace my inner archivist. It would be another use of the library as a space—to amass the stuff of memory, artifacts, documents, fragments. By some neurotic compulsion I was undertaking this process anyway. I appreciated that Forest had been kind enough to dignify it with a name: a prison archive, a small collection that could fill in some memory gaps left by the official archive on the top floor. And even if I was a weirdo for doing it, I'd still be only the second strangest prison archivist in the building.

A Night Kite

As part of my self-appointed job as prison archivist, I decided to pay a visit to Deer Island and take stock of Boston's ancient prison. Although the facility was out of use, I hoped the structure might reveal something. More than most buildings, a prison *is* its architecture, an institution whose form is its meaning.

I knew the basic outlines of its story. In the 1840s, as property values rose in South Boston, the city relocated the prison from Southie to Boston Harbor. There it remained until 1991, a barely functional hulk, the longest continuously used prison facility in the United States. With the notable exception of Sergeant Gallo, and his wistfulness, there was a consensus of disdainful respect for Deer Island. For the prison guards, staff, and inmates, time served in Deer Island was worn as a badge of honor, proof that you were dangerous—nineteenth-century tough—that you had survived the primitive. The island prison was a notorious no-man's-land, a war of all against all, where electricity and plumbing rarely worked, wildlife roamed the halls, where inmates and guards settled disputes using the law of the jungle. One inmate told me that if you had been in Deer Island, you were "from a different era." On this point, all sides agreed. "Deer Island," went the refrain from both inmates and guards, "now *that* was prison."

Was, it turned out, was the key word. When I arrived at Deer Island I discovered nothing more than a pretty wasteland. There was nothing to see.

Today it serves two functions: the site of the country's second largest waste-treatment plant, a $6 billion complex, created by emergency federal decree to clean Boston's contaminated harbor—and an unmarked burial ground for nearly five thousand anonymous people. As a whole, Deer Island is a bulky 210 acres fortified by an elevated seawall built to global warming specifications. A few hills tumble abruptly into a lowland that is dominated by the sewage plant, a sprawling campus with no people, and large, prim, unidentified buildings of indefinite purpose. The air over the island is thick with a sweet putrid aroma, cut by an occasional salty breeze from the east. At the foot of the steep seawall is a modest sand and stone beach that seems to shrink with every black, foamy wave. From here, one stands flush against the vast blue-gray expanse of the Atlantic.

The story of the island's prison begins with a natural history, a buried record that must be observed today mostly in its absences. The first of which: there are no deer on Deer Island.

It wasn't always so. In deep history, the island served as a refuge for deer fleeing hungry mainland timberwolves. How they got there is a mystery. A nineteenth-century travel guide surmised that a few courageous deer swam the 325 feet that separated the island from the mainland, a saltwater channel known as Shirley Gut. Or perhaps they walked over ice. Free from predators, the deer flourished and grew into a colony, a merry cotton-tailed Eden. By dint of nature, therefore, Deer Island is primarily an asylum.

The island served as a wood commons for the residents of the Massachusetts Bay Colony. Men would row out to the island, collect wood, and hunt deer. Soon enough, there were no more trees to be had and the deer were hunted into oblivion. Thus began the human saga of the place.

Deer Island marked the area beyond the fringes of the new European inhabitation, the spot just on the other side of the social contract, the devil's ground on the outer reaches of the City on a

Hill—the domain of pirates, vigilantes, hangings, criminals, the stricken, and the dispossessed.

For the Natick tribe, Deer Island was a desperate exile, a seventeenth-century concentration camp. Having made the mistake of converting to Christianity—assuming the status of a "praying tribe"—the Natick were considered traitors by other natives and, at the same time, regarded with deep suspicion by the English. When King Philip's war broke out in 1675, frantic English colonists interned the Natick, along with other unwanteds, on Deer Island. Roughly five hundred people, men, women, and children, starved and died during the brutal winter.

In the nineteenth century, severely ill Irish immigrants who were discovered homeless in the overcrowded alleys of Boston's growing ghettos and on Boston Common were quarantined on Deer Island in order to prevent cholera and typhus epidemics. Some were transferred directly from their ships. Many never stepped foot on the mainland and were buried anonymously on the island. Their hope of starting again in America ended right on the cusp of the New World. Deer Island was also the plot where New Englanders with no family were given anonymous burial.

Throughout the nineteenth century Deer Island served as a refuge for the city's terminally ill, impoverished, abandoned, and insane—especially those of its ethnic minorities. Upon these fields of human suffering the prison sprouted in the 1840s, grew, and decayed deep into the twentieth century.

It was during the nascent years of the Deer Island prison that Hawthorne composed his retrospective sketch of Boston's first prison: "The founders of a new colony, whatever Utopia of human virtue and happiness they might originally project, have invariably

recognized it among their earliest practical necessities to allot a portion of the virgin soil as a cemetery, and another portion as the site
of a prison." Prisons and cemeteries give the lie to utopian dreams.
Deer Island was both.

From its earliest days, it was recognized as a beautiful, cursed
little plot of earth, nature's asylum turned into man's various prisons.
This tension between *asylum* and *prison* would persist throughout
its history. Was this a place dedicated to sheltering its inhabitants
from a dangerous world or to protecting the world from its dangerous
inhabitants?

In practice, it was a way station to oblivion, a purgatory for people
of no status, no future. Deer Island was like the medieval prisons discovered in ruins of gates, bridges, tollbooths—the in-between spaces
designed to lead somewhere but which themselves were nowhere
at all. For generations, Boston's outcasts lived in just such a limbo,
permitted a grand view of a city in which they were to have no place.

B ut the view went in both directions. It was in the shadow of
this doomed island—and possibly under the gravitational
pull of its eternal sadness—that Sylvia Plath grew up on Johnson
Avenue in Winthrop, the closest residential neighborhood to the
island, where her "landscape was not land but the end of the land—
the cold, salt, running hills of the Atlantic." Her view, her recurring metaphor, was Deer Island. In a poem, "Point Shirley," Plath
described the plight of her forlorn neighbor, the prison island, as it
was slowly, relentlessly gnawed away by the "sea's collapse," the "slut-
tish, rutted sea," the "squall waves." Her family home in ruin.

Plath wrote "Point Shirley" in 1959, the same year she and Ted

Hughes had visited her father's grave in Winthrop. Her father's sudden death, when she was eight years old, had been the central trauma of her life; she hadn't dared visit his grave until then. At the cemetery she had "felt cheated," she wrote in her journal. The tombstones were ugly, the graves too close together, "as if the dead were sleeping head to head in a poorhouse." She had been desperate to "dig him up. To prove he existed and really was dead." With her usual grotesque curiosity she wondered, "how far gone would he be?"

Plath had been so distraught that day, she and Hughes had to walk around town for hours as she struggled to regain her bearings. This effort ended at the gate of Deer Island, where a prison guard turned the poets away.

Four years later Plath gassed herself in her kitchen, the doors between her and her children sealed like the "planked-up windows" of her family's former kitchen in Winthrop, as described in "Point Shirley." The place where her grandmother used to "set / her wheat loaves / and apple cakes to cool."

In the early 1990s, the Deer Island prison was evacuated. A giant barrier was placed around the abandoned facility. The prison structure became the last to be quarantined, the last asylum-seeker, the final prisoner on the island. A team of exterminators finished off the massive rodent population that remained. The winter winds, gusting from the ocean, whipped right through its empty galleries. And then it was demolished. Its brick and steel ruins shored up into a massive heap, mixed with earth. The prison was also the last to receive an anonymous burial on Deer Island. Today, this steep man-made hill serves as the mainland's barrier, just barely, from the waste-treatment plant. The old prison is now nothing but a burial mound—in the technical, archaeological sense of this word: a tumulus, a *tell*.

This is one way to remember a prison.

The Liberty Hotel, across town, is another. Opened in 2007 with the ultra-now slogan, "Be Captivated," this four-star luxury hotel wears its sordid history with sordid elegance. From 1851 to 1991, the building served as the Charles Street Jail, a lock-up facility that housed detainees before they were sentenced to Deer Island or shipped off to another prison. The structure's "colorful past" and "commanding" architecture are selling points that the hotel's PR people have carefully crafted to suit current upper-middle-class taste for supposed local authenticity, the kind that prizes overpriced real estate with "exposed brick."

This is history as high kitsch, reflected proudly in the self-consciously urbane nomenclature of the hotel, from the name Liberty itself, to the hotel's four-star restaurant, Clink, and cocktail bar, Alibi—in which vestiges of original prison cells remain—and in luxurious extras such as the Key, a cocktail option so good that it merited its very own press release.

For the record, the Key, a $500 menu offering, gives the hotel's "refined" clientele the chance to "take romance from the bar directly to the bedroom" with such "romance-inducing amenities" as:

Candlelit room, mood music set
Booty Parlor Intimacy Kit (2 condoms, vibrating couples ring, massage oil and lubricant)
Silk blinders
Chipotle chocolate bar

Moulton Brown toothbrush kits
Late 1 p.m. checkout

This is exactly the kind of "classy" service that the pimps who patronized the prison library might have designed. Just as imprisoned criminals and the petty nobility shared castles in the fifteenth century, the nouveau riche of the Liberty share a space and a history with the city's most wretched. Eagerly, in fact: the better to make class distinction itself a high-end luxury item, to advertise their membership in a certain class (the stridently sophisticated) but also to clearly distance themselves from a class of which they are most decidedly *not* a part (the criminal underclass). To the patrons of the Liberty Hotel, the wood-paneled Clink is just a place to get a four-mushroom salade.

And to complete their all-inclusive experience, the Liberty offers noblesse oblige: a spokesperson for the hotel insisted that it would be "a tragic shame" to tear down a historic building, that they had a "responsibility to honor its history," and even noted that reusing a building was a "green solution."

If a building dedicated to misery, filth, and human failure remains in use long enough it can—and must!—be elevated to the status of quaintly historic, and if the structure is "commanding" enough, it is automatically beautiful. It's as easy as hiring boutique architecture and PR firms.

Refashioning suffering, violence, and heartbreak into high-end capitalist kitsch: this too is a way to remember a prison.

Prisons make fine ruins. Churches, civic spaces, theaters, all achieve a certain grandeur in their afterlives. But can they be said to have arrived at their *purpose* as a ruin? The telos of a prison, however, is precisely that, ruin and decrepitude. As it ages and the condition of a prison worsens, as the place falls into severe disrepair, overcrowding, and neglect—as prisons always do—the more truly prison-like it becomes. As the structural façades of reform and hospital efficiency peel, leak, rust, and rot away, a truer prison emerges. And when it arrives at the moment of actual ruin, it has ripened to its potential, the perfect prison: a dump. Perhaps it is more precise to say that ruins make fine prisons.

Or, as Bruce Wood, the project manager for the Deer Island prison demolition had told the *Boston Globe* in the final days of the facility's life, "It smells pretty bad in there, and it's dirty and grungy. It's a dungeon."

There was a time when people weren't shy about the relationship between rubbish and prison. First-century Romans built a prison underground, directly over the city's central sewer pipe. When a prisoner died, or was killed, the keepers simply unlatched a trap door and dropped the body into the sewer. Was it an accident that Deer Island was a site well-suited for both a prison and a waste-treatment plant? Was it a coincidence that the location of the current prison, South Bay—where I worked—was a garbage dump and incinerator site before it was a prison? The staff were certainly aware of the prison's relationship to garbage: to this day, they refuse to drink the tap water.

Despite this relationship to decay and refuse, the prison edifice itself is fundamentally designed to last. In any given society, prisons are some of the most solidly built structures. At archaeological sites they are sometimes the only extant structure, or the best preserved. In this sense, prisons possess the curse of self-memorial. Like the Greek myth of tragic Tithonus, they are their own memorial, destined to live forever and to decay forever.

But ambiguity is born of long life. Archaeologists are occasionally unsure whether an unidentified solidly built ancient structure is a prison or whether it is a treasury building. The polar ends of a society's assets—its wealth and its criminals—are guarded with equal vehemence. Both are of supreme concern and utmost value. Ultimately they are indistinguishable.

The other archaeological confusion of prison is with tombs. A ruin of a prison may just as easily be identified as a tomb. This ambiguity, too, is not a coincidence. It points to something beyond the structural similarity of prisons and tombs. A spiritual kinship. One of the legal foundations of incarceration is the theory of "civil death"—that a citizen convicted of a felony is considered dead as far as his full membership in society is concerned. His right to vote, to make contracts, for example, is dormant.

But even before civil death, before there was such a thing as a secular prison cell, the penitential cell was the place offending monks were sent for correction. In some instances, monks, noblewomen, or criminals seeking asylum from harsh corporeal punishment were voluntarily locked away in monasteries, then given a funeral ceremony. This wasn't mere rhetoric. These cells were living tombs from which these prisoners were never again to emerge. And they were to serve as a prototype for the modern prison cell.

Which is all to say that the dead body of a prison—even when it can be identified as such—doesn't yield many clear answers and only deepens the basic contradictions of its existence. The contemporary debate about prisons—whether their function is "retributive" or "restorative," designed for punishment or reform—is not current, but ancient, and not a debate but a riddle. Prison holds its contradictions in its body. Its dead cells, its inarticulate but well-wrought ruins tell opposing stories: a punishment and an asylum, home to both saints and criminals, a tollbooth to nowhere, a treasury and a sewer, a living tomb.

Almost nothing remains of Deer Island's sad human history. Aside from the few relics on display in the officers' current union clubhouse, the single remnant of the old prison is the Victorian guard booth at the front gate—the spot where a prison guard had turned Plath and Hughes away in 1959. The same guard booth that Esther, Plath's alter ego in *The Bell Jar*, had imagined as a cheerful "little home." In the book, Esther fantasizes that the prison guard who emerges from this unexpectedly domestic hut is the man she ought to have married. She visualizes an alternate existence living happily with this man, raising children with him.

Plath's Esther entertained other notions, as well. On the subway, she had told a stranger that she was on her way to visit her father, an inmate at Deer Island—even though her father, like Plath's, had been long dead. Perhaps this wasn't a lie but more of a fiction, a private truth. To Esther/Plath, perhaps it was plausible, even darkly comforting, to picture her father living as a ghost prisoner on the island. No wonder Plath described Esther playing a suicidal game in the waves. To her, Deer Island was a no-man's-land between the living and the dead.

Prison still inhabits this realm. Jessica wasn't the only ghost I'd encountered in prison. When the *Boston Globe* published its year-end list of homicides, I recognized seven names. I was only a degree or two removed from many of the others. Before I'd worked in prison, I hadn't known a single person from that grim annual catalog—nor had I known so many people who died of drug overdoses. But in prison I came into daily contact with a secret subset of the population: the marked. Those for whom prison was the last stop before the grave.

After spending a day inspecting prison ruins, I finally arrived at the living, breathing version of the thing. It was late, past eleven at night, a strange time to show up. But I figured that the place never closes and I had a key, so why not? I was in search of a certain book and the prison had the only library open to me at that hour.

The guard at the front gate is typically a personable fellow. A man who's "good with the public," in the parlance of prison administrators. He's also one of the only guards who carries a gun (no weapons are permitted in the prison itself). Grimes, the student of Zen Buddhism who kept an ancient wisdom tract at his guard post, handled the noisy day traffic of the prison. The night guard, however, embodied a different ethos, the attitude of the prison after dark. As Plath wrote, in "Night Shift," "Tending, without stop, the blunt / indefatigable fact."

For the blunt, indefatigable fact of tending the prison at night, Sully had his own approach. He was a humorist. Always had a "new one" for me. But when I arrived that night, Sully wasn't smiling.

"D'ya hear what happened?" he whispered as I approached.

This is not the greeting one wants from a prison guard.

"No. What happened?" I said.

"Someone was stabbed."

"Oh my God—who?"

"A famous actress. Reese . . . *something.*"

"Witherspoon?"

"No," he said, "with a knife."

A big twisted grin lit the guard's face. A wicked little laugh wheezed and rattled in his throat.

"Howd'ya like that one?" said Sully, giving me a firm slap on the back. "*No: with a knife!*"

After repeating the punchline a few more times, and laughing again with each retelling, he was through with me. I was permitted to enter.

The creepiness of prison at night was not diminished for being predictable. The halls were startlingly still, the yard thick in dysmorphic moon figures. Air shafts conveyed disquieting muffled squawks. But I'd anticipated something even more sinister and, after a few moments' adjustment, was actually somewhat relieved. When I arrived at my post in the 3-Building, the library, I flipped the light switch—the switch whereby I dispatched my minimal legal duty, in the suggestive words of the nineteenth-century prison by-laws: *such provision of light shall be made for all prisoners confined to labor during the day as shall enable them to read for at least one hour each evening*. The space was washed out in gray fluorescent shadows, quiet and uncanny. A library never feels empty, even when you want it to be. A few startled mice took cover. At that moment, I was content to share the space with them, deeply relieved they were not people.

I walked through the labyrinth of bookshelves, through Biography, Geography, Politics, History, Fiction. And, finally, arrived at my destination: Poetry.

Having spent a day exploring the dreary emptiness of Deer Island and the even drearier busyness of the Liberty Hotel I was grateful for this flesh-and-blood space. The old prisons didn't have libraries.

I turned to the Sylvia Plath section. In light of what happened to Jessica, I was seriously considering suspending it indefinitely. From my perspective, the shelf had served a simple practical function, making a popular writer more accessible. *More access, more access —*

this is the credo of a library. But maybe I was doing a disservice, contributing to the death-cult in elevating Plath to a special shelf. Perhaps as a prison librarian, who served a vulnerable population, I had a responsibility to not only connect people to books but also to protect them from some as well.

The idea bothered me: Who was I to decide what books another person should read? Censorship was not my job. And yet, how could I sleep at night knowing that I had a special section for *Ariel*, with these lines from the poem "Cut," "What a thrill— / My thumb instead of an onion. / The top quite gone / Except for a sort of a hinge / Of Skin . . . / I am ill. / I have taken a pill to kill / The thin / Papery feeling." From "Edge": "The woman is perfected. / Her dead / Body wears the smile of accomplishment." *Ariel* would never arouse the suspicions of myopic prison censors, who reserved the right to remove books of incitement and violence. But just because *Ariel* was art didn't make it less dangerous—in fact, it made it potentially far more so. I had women in my library who were borderline cases, cutters, suicide junkies, who might turn to Plath as an oracle of self-annihilation. Maybe I had a responsibility to shield them from this poem. Or perhaps reading the poem could help them in some way. Maybe I should teach the poem. Or maybe it wasn't my business, either way. None of this was obvious to me.

But I decided to put the questions off until work hours. I was off-duty, after all; the space was officially closed. At that moment, I was in the library as a visitor, a reader. I was there to seek, not give, direction.

I flipped through a Plath biography, hoping to learn something about her experience of the 1938 hurricane—alluded to in "Point Shirley"—when the Deer Island prison was still the view from her window. Sylvia and her parents had weathered the storm in the family home. The windows of her father's library had shattered. Entire homes had landed in the sea. Boats had floated to the other side of town. A shark lay in her grandmother's garden, as though it had simply sprouted there during the night.

As I closed the book, I was reminded why I had dragged myself out to the prison at this hour, to encounter a real library and not an online approximation. The book I was reading, like so many in the library, had a note left in it, a kite—a message for me, if I chose to see it that way. The moment I read it, I knew this document also had a place in my slowly growing prison archive. I folded it up and placed it on my archive shelf, next to the old government reports on prisons and newspaper articles about Deer Island, the nineteenth-century New England travelogues, the glossy brochure and press releases from the Liberty Hotel, random lists, a 1903 congressional report on prison archives, the ever-growing library of kites, the letter addressed to the Messiah, some information on contraband from my orientation class. The handmade wordfind game called "Things Found in Prison."

The note that came to me that night was an abandoned letter, a fragment from one of the prison library's tragic Plaths:

Dear Mother,
  My life is

Nothing more. An anonymous, half-finished sentence with no object and no conclusion. A *life* indefinite, unarticulated, open-ended. An unfinished, unsent letter. An infinity of white space. This too is a way to remember a prison.

DELIVERED

Part II

CHAPTER 3

Dandelion Polenta

Tousled and disheartened, tired as a fossil, the Messiah shuffled into the prison library at 3:26 p.m. on a partly cloudy Wednesday afternoon. Few noted his presence. Sitting behind the counter, Dice called out, "Hey, Messiah, how's it going, brother?" But the poor guy didn't seem to hear. Dice turned to me, shrugged, and resumed reading the paper. When the man reached the counter, he clutched it like a lifesaver, and rewarded himself with a quick, standing thirty-second nap. The Messiah, a.k.a. Chuck, an inmate in the 3-1 unit, was a dud. In retrospect, though, he was right about the one thing he told me before he shoved off back into the void.

"See that guy over there," he said, leaning on the counter. "You're gonna want to know that guy. C.C. Too Sweet."

I already did know a bit about this man, though only from afar. I saw how he rolled. He'd let the rabble shove in first: the users, gang-bangers, thieves, pushers, and bustas. These were not his people. Only then would he make his entrance. He'd glide into the library at a peripatetic pace, conducting an animated conversation with a young inmate or two. Disciples. Or he'd come in alone, his mind working through its own dialogue. You could see it in his face.

When he arrived at the front counter, he'd ask Dice, or Fat Kat, or me, to see a road atlas. It seemed odd, and somehow subversive, to hand out maps in a prison. None of these men was going anywhere. For them, there was only point A.

But C.C. had his reasons. Maps were crucial visual aids to the stories he told. C.C. favored the omniscient perspective. He liked to set his scene on a large scale, to claim large tracts of territory, to pinpoint the exact spot where his life intersected with the great big world.

"Right here," he once told me, pointing to Pennsylvania Avenue on a map of Washington, D.C. "That belonged to *me*. That's where you'd find Too Sweet, man. Right next to the White House. I ran the Black House."

When he saw a crowd gather for him, he'd take a little step back to give himself space to emote. He'd pause a moment to allow his audience to situate themselves. Then he'd smile.

"There's two things you need to know about C.C. Too Sweet," he'd begin, "he's *iniquitous* and he's *ubiquitous*."

Too Sweet had a million of these.

"Anyone here know what 'pimp' stands for?"

Nobody knew.

"Part pope, part chimp."

C.C. always put a special Southern emphasis on that word, *pimp*, like the way an Evangelical preacher says Jesus—*Geeee*-zus. C.C. said *pee*-yimp. I couldn't substantiate his claim to be a "famous *pee*-yimp, known around the nation," but he seemed fairly well known within the prison. He was a pal of Fat Kat, which meant that he was in deep. Prison elite.

A light-skinned black man of Cape Verdean descent, midthirties, slightly red-toned hair, balding and squat, with bricklayer forearms, Too Sweet was most proud of his "teddy bear" eyes, greenish yellow, small, perfectly round, and close set. His head seemed a bit too small for his body. On one forearm, a giant Playboy bunny tattoo encroached awkwardly on a tattoo of a thorny rose. It was as if he hadn't taken the ten seconds necessary to consider its placement. On his other arm, the name C.C. floated in pristine isolation—no other tats to cloud or complicate these letters.

You have to wonder about a person who etches his own name into his body. Usually one tattoos the name of the person one loves beyond all others. Or of one's God. Was this true also for those who tattoo their own name? Or perhaps they're simply uncreative. C.C. was certainly not in this latter category.

When he wasn't performing, C.C. kept apart from the crowd. Sometimes he appeared dejected, slumped in his seat like a ruined millionaire. But most of the time, there was something active brewing. I'd see him studying a map alone, lost in thought. Devising an escape, it seemed. And this wasn't so far from the truth. To C.C., maps were not a way of plotting a future route as much as returning to the past, to the lost places of his life—the list of which was ever mounting. He was a man whose life had been shaped primarily by streets, intersections, alleys, and highways. All of which had led him here. So he gravitated toward a book that laid these streets out before him once again, clean and blank and open to his interpretations. This was all he needed to begin his journey back.

It was in the midst of listening to one of these stories that I had asked him to join my creative writing course.

The Penguin Joint

I was in a recruiting phase for the class. Though pimps and hustlers were a natural—and, in the library, a most readily available—group from which to draw, I found students in all corners. C.C. was enlisted from the front. But I came across others in the back, on the periphery.

The back room, Coolidge's former office, had been liberated. It was now open to the general inmate public (though I did keep a few legal volumes there in his honor.) We occasionally used the room to screen movies—National Geographic nature films, PBS documentaries, and assorted features. The women favored *The Color Purple* or *Beloved*. *Roots* was a favorite among men and women alike.

But the most popular genre among the male inmates was nature documentaries about carnivorous animals. The men loved watching films with titles like *Cheetahs on the Prowl* or *Snake Safari*. When they grew bored of these, they'd play a film about tornadoes. But they preferred for the mayhem to have a face, and so predator flicks it was.

Some men would sit and watch the film, others would set up shop nearby—with a chessboard or a law book—and only give their full attention to the film during the good parts. Even from the other side of the library, I knew that the lioness had finally pounced when I'd hear inmates yelling at the screen, "Get 'em! Get 'em!"

Once, and only once, I heard an inmate take the gazelle's side and cry out, "*Run, run!*" You knew that the gazelle had succumbed and was being devoured when you heard inmates shouting, "You show 'em, lion!" or "That's what I'm talkin' 'bout!" I suggested *March of the Penguins*—a film that documents the struggle of penguins, who walk hundreds of miles to lay eggs, then spend an excruciating winter as the males shield the eggs while the females waddle, in epic fashion, to the sea to hunt before returning, again epically, to their starving kin with bellyfuls of food. The inmates scoffed.

"I'm a grown man," one inmate growled at me.

Another better-humored inmate tried to keep it simple for me: "Avi, man, that penguin shit is *whack*. Nobody wants to watch it."

I understood where he was coming from. The aesthetics of testosterone are clear on this one: lions make for better action than penguins. But still, I didn't relent. I forced the movie on them. Those bored enough to stay enjoyed the drama.

The next day a youngish inmate swaggered into the library in the exaggerated faux limp popular among my thug clientele.

"Yo," he said, as he approached the counter. I braced myself for his request. "You still got that penguin joint? We didn't finish it yesterday."

I smiled and handed him the DVD. After dispensing with the usual requests, I wandered to the back room, where *March of the Penguins* was wrapping up with the satisfying conclusion, the miraculous collective hatching of the eggs. The only person sitting there was the inmate who had requested the movie. He was watching the film intently and scribbling furiously in a prison-issue notebook.

"You like writing?" I asked, taking a seat next to him. Annoyed by my presence, he paused the movie and looked up.

"Just taking some notes."

"On the *penguins*?"

"Yeah. Listen, I'm trying to finish up here and I only got ten minutes."

I cut to the point.

"I run a creative writing class," I said. "You should join."

"Fine," he said, "sign me up."

He said this without so much as lifting his head from his scribbling. My eye picked off a phrase from his notebook, *It's about being a MAN*.

"What's your name?"

"Franklin," he said, "Chudney."

"Chutney?"

"Chu*d*ney. What's yours?"

"Avi."

"Javi?"

"No, *Avi*."

We shook hands and I expected to never see him again.

The Ides of January

Meanwhile, Shakespeare month was not going well.

I can't say I wasn't warned. There was plenty of Shakespearean foreshadowing. As usual, young Dumayne—recently back from yet another trip to the Hole—played the role of the truth-telling average Joe, the "saucy fellow" of Julius Caesar, whose streetwise cynicism portends problems in the universe.

Typically, when Dumayne came into the library his mouth was already in motion. He had little use for pauses between words. One afternoon he entered the library, mouth a-running.

"Yo-what-the-movie-this-week?"

"It's a Shakespeare play that was made into a movie," I said. Then added, with a touch of masochism, "*Macbeth*."

Dumayne flashed me a snapshot grin. He really looked like a larky kid when he smiled.

"You-kidding-right?"

"'Fraid not."

"Aw-man-that's-some-corny-ass-*shit*, man."

"Since when is murder and revenge corny? And it's got one of the great crazy bitches of all time. You'll love it, Dumayne."

"Shakespeare's-*old*!"

"You mean *old school*?" I said, fully aware of how lame I sounded.

"No-*old*, cuz. Like boring."

"Did you know that Shakespeare's characters call each other 'cuz'?"

"No-but-I-do-know-that-Shakespeare-is-whack."

This was, more or less, the consensus around the library. Unfortunately Shakespeare was the theme for January's film group, held each Friday morning. I wasn't surprised by the negative reaction. So I held my ground, hoping for at least some endorsements from certain key inmates. But nothing. I turned to Fat Kat. But the big man just sat there, arms crossed, shaking his head.

"Nah, man," he said. "Not this time. Nobody here wants to watch a bunch of British dudes waltzing around in pantyhose speaking old English. C'mon, Avi. Whaddayathinkin'?"

"It's Shakespeare," I reasoned. "Don't be afraid to admit that what's best is best. Every wannabe rapper in here wishes he had Shakespeare's skills."

But Fat Kat just waved me off. My teacher guy routine wasn't flying. He was right, of course. To make Shakespeare relevant to this crowd would require more time—and a group smaller than thirty. We were digging ourselves a hole.

The first week was a bust. Ignoring my pleas, Forest screened the 1940s Orson Welles *Macbeth*. The combination of British dudes waltzing around in pantyhose and ancient film production was a death knell. An audible groan went up as soon as the opening black and white credits appeared on the screen. We had done nothing but reinforce the notion of Shakespeare as outdated.

Dumayne approached me later that week. "You better have a good one next week, Harvey," he warned, "or there's gonna be trouble up in here."

The next film, *Shakespeare Behind Bars*, a 2005 documentary of a group of inmates putting on *The Tempest*, was slightly better received. This was the advantage of having set an astonishingly low bar. Even so, the abundance of sensitive/effeminate characters in the documentary put off most of my inmate audience. The fact that one of the strongest characters in the documentary was a sex offender was a major turnoff—particularly to a certain vocal inmate who just happened to be a sex offender. But at least the film was in full Technicolor. I could tell that some of the audience enjoyed the movie, but were too afraid to admit it.

Dumayne remained unmoved. His dark prophecies for what would happen if I showed another corny-ass Shakespeare movie had become distilled into a wordless shaking of his head and wagging of his index finger. His message was clear enough. Trouble was on the way.

But that Friday, we triumphed. *Othello*, starring Laurence Fishburne, had just the right combination of blackness, Laurence Fishburneness, Hollywood slickness, and raw sex appeal to go over well. Even Dumayne conceded that the library had finally done right. But his warnings remained in place. *Othello* would be long forgotten if we attempted another *Macbeth*.

But our final Shakespeare screening continued the hot streak. In retrospect, this should have been my warning. After screening the 1996 Baz Luhrmann film, *Romeo + Juliet*—starring Leonardo DiCaprio and Claire Danes as "contemporary inner-city gang rivals and star-crossed lovers"—the inmates kept to their seats. Usually they'd check out the moment a film was over, often sooner, and try to escape the library before the discussion of the film began. But not that day. Even Dumayne conquered his notorious ADD.

James, a young staff teacher and theology student, led the discussion. I took a perch in the back of the space, eager to hear the inmates' reactions. The film's themes of gang violence, love, and loyalty during conflict—and the urban, though somewhat unconvincing, American setting—resonated with the men. The conversation got off to a dizzying start. Hands were going up in every corner. Everyone had an opinion. Romantics lined up against cynics, young inmates united against old veterans. It was a rare occasion that one of these film discussions actually went well.

I asked the class how they thought costumes affected their experience of the play. I gave a quick crash course in theatrical costuming, in the construction of identity through clothing, of Shakespeare's affinity for identity confusion, the distinction between uniforms and costumes. For a group of men sitting in the shadow of uniformed officers, themselves in variously hued prison uniforms, this topic had a particular immediacy. Many of these men had traded gang colors for prison colors. Again, everyone had something to add. There were so many hands up and loud voices trying to talk over one another I hardly noticed a man walk past me.

This man was outfitted in the uniform of an officer. He was one of the many who routinely hung out at the post outside of the library, loitering in the hallway during the day shift.

Some of these officers were members of a SERT team—the Sheriff Escort and Response Team—a squad that could be dispatched quickly to prison trouble spots. When they weren't in action, they'd sit around gossiping, talking pussy and Patriots football and concocting union discord. SERT was a more desirable job than a harrowing post on a cell block—many of the SERT members were vets and saw SERT as their hard-earned right.

Though many officers were fit, some were simply fat fucks. Their years in the department could be measured in waist size, their fates on earth deduced from piles of prison cafeteria sausage on their lunch trays. Healthy young cadets sometimes grew into shuffling lardaceous blobs. The union ensured that the fitness test remained a onetime event, given as part of an entrance requirement and then never again. The sight of the SERT team mobilizing was sometimes a Keystone Kops affair. As a young cadet, a Marine, once noted to me, the SERT guys were "supposed to be a crack squad but are actually more of a butt crack squad."

The man who walked by me was a member of SERT. Or maybe a friend of the squad—I wasn't sure. What I did know, at a mere glance, was that he passed his misfortunes onto his hair and that his face, tormented by male pride, alternated three expressions: smug, constipated, and blank.

That day, he walked by me with purpose, without offering the slightest acknowledgment. It was strange that he was in the library. He wasn't a regular, as far as I knew. But random officers sometimes appeared like this, making rounds, sweeping for contraband, making their presence known. I noticed him as a shadow but quickly got distracted trying to help run the class.

The officer didn't look at or speak to any inmates, but instead disappeared into the library's book stacks. A moment later, he emerged. Retracing his steps, he walked right by me again, this time on his way to the door. Again, he ignored me.

And that's when it happened.

It started modestly enough, but grew with ferocious speed. Within seconds, there was no ignoring it. A foul, sulfuric smell overwhelmed the library space, no small feat. Inmates, who had their hands up to ask questions or to say their piece, instead covered their faces with uniform shirts. Some ducked their heads between their knees. Dumayne was jolted out of his seat, as if suddenly waking from a nightmare of attentiveness.

"It stinks like *shit* in here, dawg!" he announced, as if this wasn't completely obvious.

"Somebody farted," sighed an old-timer. "Bad."

The class devolved into pandemonium. The once orderly discussion, which had been contained to the main clearing, instantly disintegrated. A few inmates ducked out of the library. Those who remained took advantage of the chaos to do their dirty business: slipping notes and other contraband into favorite hiding spots. I stopped an inmate in the process of pocketing the library's newspaper, only to see another walk off with two magazines. At the other end of the library, an inmate quickly, surreptitiously, passed something to another. Another inmate who had been pestering me throughout the class to use a typewriter finally got his way. Inmates were streaming into the stacks, into the back computer room—doing everything but sitting and talking about *Romeo + Juliet*.

I was trying to understand what had happened. Did an officer just come into the library in the middle of a class and pass a massive gas bomb? Easily the worst and most tragic I'd ever encountered.

Had he, a grown man, actually come into the library during the class with the sole intention of doing this? It seemed too crazy to be true.

Meanwhile, the detail workers held court at the library's counter. A small group of library regulars had gathered around. These inmates were fuming. Some were clamoring for revenge.

"Motherfucker better *watch* his back."

"He better hope he don't run into me on the outs."

"That ain't *right!*" said a small man with a large 'fro. "Right in the middle of the fuckin' *class*, man!"

"That's how it goes around here," said Fat Kat, as he flipped through a *Car & Driver*. "Get used to it."

"That's fucking *dis*respect, right there," said another.

And Dice: "I'll tell you what that is: *demeaning*. Man shit on your fuckin' head and you expected to take it? Naw. Un-uh."

I looked out the library's large windows, out to the hall, where a group of officers were trying to contain their smiles, trying to stay casual. Strange that they weren't coming into the library to help restore order.

"Can someone explain what just happened?" I asked the inmates.

As usual, Fat Kat was completely in the know. Without looking up from his magazine, he said, "Dude came in with one of them fart sprays you can buy. And I think you know the rest."

"You saw this?" I asked.

"Yeah, man, they did it yesterday too. During Forest's shift, when 3-3 was in here. Cleared out the whole room, same as today."

On one side, there were gleeful officers; on the other, furious inmates. In between, me. I was responsible for this space and for the chaos it had become. Unless I implicated myself into this situation I was teetering on the verge of irrelevance. Somehow, I had to save face with both groups, inmates and officers. In a macho environment like prison, that meant one thing. Absurd as the circumstances were, the library, its mission, and its guardian (me) had been openly disrespected. If I couldn't restore some public dignity to the library and establish some deterrent power, the space would be undermined again and again. If the sheriff's officers weren't going to defend the space, I would. The spirit of Don Amato descended on me once again. The Sheriff Librarian persona bubbled up.

I marched into the hallway, trying to maintain my calm. The corridor was busy with inmates and staff. I spotted the offending officer. He and some of his crew were roosting on a bench next to the officer's post. When they saw me approach, they stopped talking, and again attempted to suppress their grins.

Trying hard not to accuse him—as I lacked evidence—I asked what he had been doing in the library. His face went through its various registers: blank to constipated to smug, and back again. He didn't make eye contact.

"I was getting a sports book," he said. "Forest lets us check them out."

The baldness of this claim, and the awkwardness of the officers' behavior, was all the evidence I needed. He hadn't gone into the sports section. Nor had he looked for anything. He had walked purposefully into the stacks, where he remained for less than ten seconds. And as Fat Kat had said, I knew the rest. Everybody did.

"Well," I said, "maybe you can explain this: there's a pretty nasty smell in the library and you were just in and out of there. Any connection between these two facts?"

"That smell's been there for days. It's got *nothing* to do with me, guy."

Now he was glaring at me. His lips fully retreated into his head. I just sighed.

"We both know that's not true," I said.

"Are *you* here every day?" he shouted.

The implication of his statement was that I was a college volunteer, a notion I never quite dispelled. Now he was standing. He walked toward me, chest puffed out.

"Yeah," I replied, also raising my voice—hoping it wouldn't crack—trying not to back down from a guy trained to tackle and subdue violent criminals.

"I work here full time," I said. "Every single day. Same department as you. Member of the union. I see you here every day, even if you don't see me. This," I said, indicating the library, "is *my* spot and *my* responsibility. The question here is why did you come into *my* space, in the middle of *my* class, and screw everything up?"

"You listen to me." He was bellowing. "Do you *fu*—," he caught himself before cursing. "Do you know where you *are*? This isn't the Quincy Public Library, okay? This is a *prison*. I got a badge. I do what I want. You don't tell me where I go."

He looked over to his buddies for support. They looked away. For a moment, all of us, it seemed, paused to solemnly honor the utter and transparent stupidity of what this man was saying. I racked my brain to identify which Steven Seagal movie he had poached the line about the badge. He spoke again, this man with no lips and a badge.

"You got absolutely no right to tell me where I go and when, you understand me?" he continued shouting. "Who's your supervisor?"

"Who's *my* supervisor?" I said, laughing. "Who's *your* supervisor? I don't have anything to explain."

I had accomplished my mission: to send a message to any bad

guy, inmate or officer, that I wasn't passive when affronted and to let them know that I would make their lives unpleasant if they messed with me or tried to undermine my mission. Maybe Officer Chuzzlewit would think twice before tangling with me and my library. Nobody wants to mess with a loose cannon. This was the credo of the Sheriff Librarian.

Within five minutes I was called into Patti's office. I knew that some of the hallway-loitering officers had been harassing the Education Department for years. Feeling smug, I dispensed some free advice.

"You got them right where you want them," I told Patti. "Now you have a good excuse to have these guys banned from the Ed Department."

She shot me a look from behind her computer monitor.

"Just write a report," she said.

I wrote up a quick account of what happened, and fact-checked it. My newspaper editors from the *Boston Globe* would have been proud. As I printed it up on the Education Department's shared printer, a veteran teacher summoned me into his office. The teacher was a Boston Irish, Dorchester-raised guy. Friends with a number of the officers. He later quit and joined the police force. He closed the door and seemed serious.

"This conversation is just between you and me," he told me.

"Of course," I said, still in newspaper reporter mode. "I won't quote you, I know you're trying to help me. I appreciate your advice: you think I overreacted—"

He cut me off. "Listen, you got every right to hand in that report. That guy was way out of line. But you should just be aware you're going to have a shitstorm on your hands if you do. These guys stick together, you know. They can make things very difficult for you."

He was kind to impart this advice, but none of this was news to me.

"I already have a shitstorm on my hands, quite literally; and these guys, for no reason, are already making things difficult for me. That was the problem to begin with."

I told him that I had no intention of bringing heat onto this guy and would gladly not submit a report—but I'd have no choice if the officer submitted one first. That was protocol.

"And anyway, the issue here," I said, grandly, "is *his* behavior and the collusion of his buddies."

The teacher laughed and put out his palm, making the stop gesture.

"Okay, okay," he said, smiling. "Easy, now. Just watch yourself."

Above Ground

Many people offered me their opinions on the Officer Chuzzlewit incident. The view submitted by a mysterious older inmate wasn't particularly memorable. It did however have the happy result of bringing this man into my consciousness.

I hadn't met him. But the day after the Chuzzlewit incident, I saw him leaning against the library counter, giving me a knowing look.

"Can I help you?" I asked.

This was apparently an uproariously funny thing to say. He slapped his hand on the counter, threw his head back, and howled.

"Can I *help* you?" he said joyously. "I gotta remember that one. Prison customer service! I should hire you."

I probably looked distressed because he added, "Oh, maestro, you're too serious. You a student?"

"No, I—"

"I am. I'm a student of *everything*. Macro, micro, the cosmos, botany, theology, you name it and I got my hands caught right up in it."

"Why don't I ever see you in the library?"

He snickered. "I'm a busy man," he said. "Besides, y'all don't have the books I need; I gotta buy them myself. Then I donate them to y'all. I don't take credit for it, now, but that's what's happening, right here, right under your nose. Believe me. A lot stuff goes on here you don't know about. You Irish?"

"No, Jewish."

"*Redstu Yiddish?*"

I tried not to act surprised. And replied in Hebrew.

"Okay," I said, switching back to our one common language, "now tell me how you know Yiddish."

"Ah man, I know the Jews," he told me, "I used to be in the above-ground swimming pool business. As you probably know, that business is run by the Jews."

I indicated that this was news to me.

"*Really?*" he said. "You really Jewish?"

He told me that the above-ground swimming pool business was run not by Jews but by *the* Jews. A cabal of Hebrews. Not that he minded. It was fine by him, he said, because he saw plenty of the action. They welcomed him in, invited him to their homes, to their Passover Seders. To prove this, he recited a bit of the Passover Haggadah, "*mah nishtanah ha-layla ha-zeh*, right?"

I asked him how he got into the above-ground swimming pool business.

"I'm not in the above-ground swimming pool business," he replied.

We stared at each other for a long moment.

"I'm also *not* in the carpet-cleaning business, the car scratch repair business, the star-selling business. I'm just in business. You dig? I'm an entrepreneur. I used to be a peteman. That's the old name for guys who hit up safes. I made friends with guys who worked in warehouses. They'd disarm the alarms of the warehouse, I'd come in at night, pick the safe, and walk out and we'd have a steak dinner and divide the cash. But then one day, I was scratching up this guy's car—long story—and I thought to myself, 'I bet I could sell something that would *repair* scratches in cars.' You see? I realized I was on the wrong side of things, man. That's why I was always so stressed out: I wasn't living up to my potential, I wasn't doing what I was supposed to be doing on this planet. I should be bringing joy to my brothers."

I had so many questions for this man, who now introduced himself as Alonzo. Or just Al. I wasn't certain where to begin. So I started with the obvious.

"The star-selling business?" I asked.

Selling stars is a lot like selling flowers, he told me. Similar business model. People buy them as gifts for special occasions, birthdays, anniversaries, etc. But it's mostly seasonal: Mother's Day, Valentine's Day, and whatnot. One major difference, of course, is that people generally won't buy stars more than once for the same person. This means slightly less volume. The good news, he assured me, was that there's almost no overhead, and it requires only a modest initial investment of capital—and certainly less capital than constantly buying imported flowers with a very limited shelf life. Stars, as he informed me, enjoy a shelf life in the billions of years and there's a virtual infinity of (free) supply. True, there's no way to adequately limit competition for the vast supplies; the field will eventually get crowded. But, while the idea is still relatively fresh, the competition is slight. He's been able to corner a niche in the market.

I interrupted to ask him what the hell he was talking about.

"I'm getting there, young man," he said. "You in a big rush?"

Actually, the officer on duty was beginning to fidget, indicating about five minutes remaining in the library period. But as I would find out, Al was never in a rush.

If you give Al twenty-five dollars, half the price his competitors ask, he'll sell you a star. You will be asked to name your star—usually something on the order of "Alison + Roger Forever" or "Johnny Gone But Not Forgotten" or "Baby Towanda." He enters the name into a log, which he then copyrights. The name is thereby "enshrined into law," as Al puts it. He sends you a certificate of authentication, an astral map that identifies which star is yours (with its new name appended, of course), and a packet of information regarding this star. When and where it might be found in the sky, when it was discovered, a bit about its natural history, what stage it's at in its life cycle, which planets orbit it. For forty-five bucks, he'll sell you a pair of binary stars, great for lovers, or twins, or best friends forever. He also sells planets and moons. Planets are great for kids, he told me; moons are for lovers looking for "something out of the box."

"Buying a star," he said, "it's like getting a tattoo but it's even more permanent. It's enshrined in law and heaven. And it's much cheaper. That's a good deal, brother. You're Jewish, you know a good deal when you see it."

I asked him if astronomers acknowledge these new names. It was intended as an innocent question.

"No," he sniffed, "they don't. But I ain't doing it for them. My customers don't care what a scientist calls it. He has just as much a right to name it as some dude with a damn Ph.D. The scientific community don't own the heavens, nobody does. Maybe, maybe, the United States owns the Earth's moon, because they *went* there and staked a damn flag *on* it. But that's it. Unless you go to an unexplored place, you don't have no claim to it. I've looked up the laws, man. Not that our laws have jurisdiction up there, anyway. I mean think about it, let's say an alien planet with a highly advanced civilization 'discovered' Earth—does that mean they *own* us?"

I figured it was a rhetorical question. It was not. He stared at me. "Would it?" he said.

"No," I said. "I guess not."

He went on for another minute or two about how real entrepreneurship is about democracy. The stars belong to everyone, to the people, not to governments. Above-ground pools, too: democracy, the American Dream. Every person has a *right* to a pool, not just rich people. Is it, he asked, strange to refer to a swimming pool as a right? *No*, he said, in response to his own question. It's about basic biology. We're part water creature. We're really amphibians. We *need* to be submerged in water for periods of the day. We're better, happier, healthier creatures when we "achieve this potential." He knows history, he told me. He knows that the theory of rights in America is based on nature, on science. Should the natural right to achieve our full amphibious potential be granted only to the rich, or should all people be able to afford a pool of water at a reasonable rate, with the option of paying on layaway (and no interest for thirteen months)? Isn't this the point of America?

This time I was ready with an answer.

"You're damn right it is," I said.

I was like the idiot in Plato's dialogues who constantly replies to Socrates' long, convoluted arguments with statements like "Why, yes," and "It is certainly so."

At this point, the officer outside was almost physically pulling Al out of the library. Alonzo turned to him and casually said, "I'll be with you in a moment, friend."

I told Alonzo that he should join my writing class. He winked at me and disappeared out the door.

The story of Alonzo in my writing class is brief. He didn't last long. He had no interest in my writing assignments. After a couple of halfhearted efforts, he showed up to class with a pretyped sheet. This was a prepared statement, an emphatic political manifesto, containing discourses on politics, economics, science, religion, and moral philosophy—most of which baffled or simply irritated the other people in the class.

Al was on a Marx kick, which I found odd given his romantic attachment to capitalism. After a few classes, and a few more keynote addresses, he'd either tapped his intellectual reserves or simply gotten the message that his audience was growing less tolerant. He stopped showing up and never visited the library again. But it wasn't the last I would see of Al, the entrepreneur.

Memoir of a P

Wordplay was C.C. Too Sweet's form of optimism. He came to the library to "chop it up," to "converse and conversate." A new turn of phrase meant a new world, new opportunities for self-invention. Since working at prison, I learned that a hustler's way with words was his one true possession and could never be taken away—but only if kept sharp. This is where the library came into play. If C.C. grew anxious, and this seemed often, he would make up puns and rhymes and try them out at the front counter.

During a debate with a fellow hustler, he scored major points when he said, "With all due, and undue, respect, the difference between me and you is the following: You are nonsensical while I, my brother, am ineffable. In case you ain't mastered your diction, I'll break that down for you — *ineffable*, meaning: *I can not, and will not, be effed with*."

Meanwhile, his legal troubles were mounting. But C.C. was more confident than ever.

"In the *new* millennium," he announced one day, "there's gonna be *plenty* of 'em!" He was referring to new opportunities to make some scratch. (I didn't have the heart to tell him that we were well into the new millennium.)

But it was with a hushed tone, and in regards to the new millennium, that C.C. first spoke to me. He was perplexed by the computer, and was shy about it.

"I'm a twentieth-century kind of guy," he confided, by way of explaining his preference for typewriters. I told him I was, at most, a nineteenth-century type myself. We started talking. He asked if I knew anything about writing or publishing. I revealed that indeed I knew a thing or two. He looked both ways, leaned in, and whispered, "I got something *hot* here."

"Great," I said. "Just what I need."

He had written the better part of a manuscript, a book. He said he'd received some positive letters from a publisher. I was intrigued. He had to get busy typing up this book, he said. He needed it formatted in accordance with submission guidelines. This meant undertaking the large task of transferring hundreds of handwritten pages into Word documents. He could type about eight and a half words a minute — he needed a lot of help. He'd probably need an editor, as well, he said. I offered my assistance.

"Maybe," he said.

I had just brought in an ancient floppy disk of mine as a donation to the library. I looped back into my office, located behind the counter space, and found it. I transferred out the old files, essays on Torah topics I'd written back in my yeshiva days, and made room for C.C.'s pimp memoir files. I wrote his gov on the disk—it would stay in my office for his use. I remembered my training during orientation: floppy disks could be easily refashioned into slender but terrifyingly effective blades, shanks, and were contraband of the first order.

"Kat said you was all right," C.C. said when I emerged and handed him the disk. He seemed to be trying to convince himself.

In prison these kinds of statements made me somewhat nervous. They could imply just about anything, from the willingness to help someone apply to college to helping them commit a double homicide. But I was happy to take a compliment. We shook hands. C.C. Too Sweet and I were now in cahoots. I noticed an officer standing by the door, taking note of this.

Too Sweet would show up in the library every day with a pile of handwritten pages popping out of the fraying, taped-up mailing envelope he'd converted into a folder. He had carefully written the words *Legal Material* on the envelope, in the hopes that this would protect his work from being confiscated during routine searches and shakedowns.

I discovered that he was already making money as a writer. He was one of a regular group of inmates who mined the resources of the library for material gain. Using our Microsoft Publishing program, these inmates would mass produce blank greeting cards with messages like, *Whatz Good Mommacita?* or *Holla Back!* The cards often turned up folded up and left in library books.

Or inmates would ask for multiple copies of the crosswords or wordfind games that we handed out and sell the extras. Or try to trick me into photocopying documents that looked exactly like legal forms, but turned out to be some variety of a "Warrant for the Court of Love," which stated, among other things, that "the defendant has the right to be caressed in a sexually explicit manner, until such time as she can no longer take it." These made a wonderful gift from prison for the holidays.

Other inmates would steal books, magazines, paper, markers, blade-sized splinters from the back of wooden chair—anything that wasn't tied down. Any of these items could then be sold on the extensive prison black market. I had to be especially vigilant about theft and hustles after big sporting events, when the prison was teeming with inmates desperate to pay up gambling debts. I usually closed down these illegal businesses. But I permitted C.C.'s venture.

When he was low on cash, he'd write poems and sell them to other inmates. I turned a blind eye and permitted him to make copies of these poems. C.C.'s freelance poetry business relied on some skill and creativity, not simple theft (not that theft was necessarily devoid of skill or creativity).

Some of his poems were holiday themed, particularly for Mother's Day. Others were just generic prison poems or love poems. Other inmates too lazy or unable to put their thoughts into words were always looking for poetry to mail to friends and foes alike. C.C. started a prison Hallmark company. For a dollar a pop, or its equivalent, C.C. would sell you this poem:

In Jail

Being in Jail is lonely at night,
It is waiting for letters that no one will write.
It is depending on people

You thought were your friends,
Waiting for letters no one will send.
It's sitting around with nothing to do,
Trying to figure out who is really who.
It is finding out hearts are made of stone,
And realizing that you are alone.
It is waiting for visits that never take place,
From so-called friends who've forgotten your face.
It's wondering why time moves so slow,
When prayers are answered but the answer is No.
I will do my time with my head held high,
Knowing that you ain't built to ride or die.
The day will come when I am free,
Then it will be my turn to forget when you need me.

C.C. also sold a version of this poem with a less threatening conclusion:

Then you'll see what I can be.

Other poems by C.C. were not for sale. These poems were more elliptical:

The eyes see absence
Musk that looms still
The breath that's close
Remembrance of times
Run as you can, hold strong
A flower sways willingly.

C.C.'s forays into poetry, commercial and artistic, were secondary, however, to his main project—*Memoir of a Pimp: The Real Life Story of C.C. Too Sweet*. I had suggested *From Rags to Bitches*, a title that, I later learned, had already been taken. But C.C. preferred the simple elegance of *Memoir of a Pimp*.

Almost every day C.C. would come to the library and we'd talk about his manuscript or just chat about life generally. We developed a rapport. During our first meetings, C.C. was struggling with how to begin his story. He decided on a teaser.

"I'm gonna hit 'em real hard with some heavy pimp shit, you know what I mean?—something real *greasy*," he told me, pronouncing it *greezy*, "and then, before they can say 'damn!,' I'm gonna back up and start from the beginning, when I was just a cute little kid."

It sounded like a good plan to me. I looked forward to seeing it. Until I did, I'd have to content myself with C.C.'s less ambitious efforts.

Warrant 69

ARREST WARRANT

A warrant for the arrest of _____'s heart has been issued, due to the fact that it belongs to me now. And you are no longer in control of it. I must inform you of your right to remain silent while I kiss you all over from head to toe. You also have the right, before sexual intercourse, to be presented a marriage license. Anything you say or scream during intercourse will be used against you in the court of "LOVE."

DEFAULT JUDGEMENT

Please be advised, once you sign this document, it will go into effect immediately without further notice. Your signature is required for this legal document. In the event of the loss of this document, NO other will be issued and you will be forced to plead this case as Total, Unrestricted, Unrestrained Devotion and Satisfaction, which will result in further obscene action against your sexual body. Which might include: Licking, Whipping and Kissing you until you pass out. I am forced to blow your mind in every sexual way imaginable for the rest of the years to come. If you don't go freely, I will have to take you by force.

SENTENCING

Your sentencing has already been decided for the best interest of all involved. You have been found guilty of "Love in the First Degree." The state of Love "demands" the maximum sentence. You are hereby sentenced to life with me, without possibility of bail, parole or good time. Your sentence is in a maximum security facility called "MY ARMS."

YOUR PLEA

Not Guilty _____ Date _____
Guilty _____ Date _____

Paul the Dog

Seven inmates showed up for the new cycle of my creative writing class. There was C.C. Too Sweet; young Dumayne; Jason who went by JizzB; Rob who went by Shizz; Frank who asked to be called Lefty, a request that was universally ignored; Fernando, a mysterious middle-aged Latino man; and, at the last moment, Chudney, the guy who took extensive notes on *March of the Penguins*.

From the moment I walked into the classroom, which was actually a large storage space in the back of the library, I could tell Frank was trouble. He was already mid-sentence, mid-paragraph, settling comfortably into the middle of an infinitely self-generating narrative. Within a second of conversation, he gave you the panic-inducing feeling that he could and very well might patter on forever. To speak to him was to interrupt him.

Nobody, however, was speaking to him. Nor were they listening. Even before the class started, there was already a distinct feeling of torpor in the room. Frank, eyes aquamarine, face boozed-out purple, resembled a hard-bitten Buzz Aldrin. An elderly boy, in high spirits.

"Do you believe in God?" he asked me as I walked in. Before I could answer or even sit down, he waved off his own question, "Aw, it don't matter if you or me believe, right? He *exists*, even if you or me or him or the other guy or Jason over here don't believe—not that you don't believe, Jason, I'm just making an example is all. I made a video for my church for Easter—actually, it was a bit after Easter—about why people should believe. I wish I could play it for you. It's basically just me sitting in my brother-in-law's shop talking to the camcorder about Jesus and how Grace saved my life and all that. I can't do it for you here, though, cause it's pretty long and I wrote it up and everything. You'd have to see it. My priest said it was pretty good. But of course he's gonna say that, right? My wife? She don't believe, though. Her brother committed suicide when she was just a kid, if you count seventeen as a kid, which I don't. I think kids should start working at fourteen. Anyway, she don't never use that word, *suicide*, but she ain't here, right? After he committed suicide she stopped believing. I feel her pain, you know, who wouldn't? But what I don't, can't and won't even try to understand is what God's gotta do with her brother's suicide. If he exists, he exists, right? Don't change if some guy, even your brother, blows their brains out. I don't want you to get the wrong idea about my wife, by the way. She's a good woman. Very loyal. Trust me, I *know*. She'll stick with you, thick and thin. We had this dog that got run over, he's a mutt, though I think he's mostly some kind of retriever, his name is Paul, after Paul Newman, who my wife has a thing for—honestly, I don't mind if she's, you know, attracted to other guys, that's normal, hell I'm attracted to *lotsa* other ladies, believe me, and some of them are attracted to me, including some good-looking ones. But I trust her, you know. And, God bless her, she trusts me. Anyway, Paul, the dog, he was hit by a SUV and now he's a paraplegic . . ."

"Man, you gotta be fuckin' *kidding* me," C.C. Too Sweet muttered, and threw his head back in exasperation.

"No, wait," said Frank, lost in thought, "that's right . . . he's a *quad*riplegic. You know, like paralyzed in *all* his body, except the head. Or wait, maybe in his head, too. Is that possible? I forget 'cause it's been so long, ya know, and my wife, she and I were already split right before I got pinched. Anyway, the dog don't move at all, he just lays there. Do they call you a 'quadriplegic' even if you're a dog?"

Frank had to be silenced or I risked losing the class, possibly for good.

Once I got Frank quiet and captured the attention of the other inmates, the class could start in earnest. I gave the guys my spiel about writing, and about how the class was meant as writing for the sake of writing and not, as prison writing classes tend to be, for any specific therapeutic goal. I wasn't trying to correct their morals nor was I interested in hearing how much they're improving. They could save it. I wanted to work on writing skills, period. I proved my point by giving them a neutral assignment to describe a place that everyone in the room had in common, Boston's South Station, and to write it for a reader who is not familiar with Boston.

"South Station!" said Frank. "That's where I first saw the light." But this time I preempted, "Don't talk, write."

The men got to work. Within ninety seconds, Dumayne threw down his pencil and declared, "This shits is boring, man."

I told him to write, not talk.

He wrote another word and then piped up again. "When do we learn how to write about *love*? I need to write my girly some poems. I don't wanna do this boring stuff."

Chudney spoke up, "It's *supposed* to be boring, man."

This was news to me.

"You're supposed to *make it* exciting," he explained.

"That's right," I said. "Thank you, Chudney."

"No problem," he said, with a satisfied smile.

Frank balled up his paper and threw it into the trash. "I didn't know you wanted it to be *exciting*," he said. "I got to start over."

Suddenly Chudney stood up and said, "And another thing—you gotta learn how to hold that pencil, man."

He walked over to Dumayne and was about to manually correct his writing grip.

"Um, Chudney," I said, "sit down. Right now. Don't touch him."

You didn't touch someone else in prison unless you were asking for trouble. This was a basic rule. I noticed Shizz, on the other side of the room, tighten his grip on his pencil. The last thing I needed in my classroom was a fight.

But Chudney ignored me. "Ain't no thing," he said, grabbing Dumayne's writing hand and pulling his fingers into the correct posture. "This little man here's a friend of mine growing up," said Chudney. "I call him my little cousin."

And indeed, as Chudney aggressively set his hand straight, Dumayne wore the proverbial sulk of a compliant younger brother.

"Now *that's* how it's done, son," Chudney said, patting him on the back.

The men returned to their silent work. I noticed Dumayne struggling, in vain, to hold the pencil as Chudney had instructed him. I noticed other things, too. You can tell a lot about a person by the way he sits and writes. Fernando, who hadn't uttered a word yet in this class, was a curious little man with an implausibly round head, an expressionless lampshade mustache, an autocratic pout. He sat with ironing-board-straight posture and scribbled decisively in florid Catholic-school penmanship, writing on his prison-issue loose-leaf paper as though he were drafting an armistice. He resembled a deposed but proud South American strongman. Perhaps he was.

I was pretty certain Shizz was not a strongman. His pleading eyes were the only steady feature on a face that was in a state of constant and rapid flux: a mask of worry morphed into despair morphed into a wicked private joke morphed into self-flagellation. The overall effect being a troubled, ambivalent soul. His pencil, too, was in constant motion and never left the page, though he employed the eraser end as much as the business end, and did so emphatically and with elaborate displays of emotion.

Frank was more sedate when writing than speaking. And certainly more punctuated. I sensed he was out of his element with the written word. This was probably a good thing for everyone.

Too Sweet seemed distracted and wrote a word or two every few minutes. This was a man who sat in his cell and wrote dozens of meticulously handprinted pages a day. He was tired out. I got the strong impression he didn't want to be here, that he had signed up out of politeness to me. When he did write, though, he did so in bursts, like a Richter scale registering a distant tremor.

And then there was Chudney. Chudney was, it seemed, a noticer. He stared at the heavens, waiting for the words to drop right out of the troposphere, poised, ready to catch them before they hit the ground and smashed to pieces. Since there was no window to the outdoors—or penguin movie to watch—he was stuck gazing at the ceiling. He assumed two distinct poses: sitting perfectly still, elbows on the table, fingers linked, head bowed as though in prayer, pencil, out of his hands, sitting on paper—and then, perhaps ready to receive his answer, he'd pick up the pencil and raise his head to gaze at the ceiling. He frowned often and occasionally copied some words down onto the page.

I gazed at the ceiling, too, to see if I could see what he saw. All I could make out, though, was an aged water stain with a dark, wet brown border that was slowly expanding.

After twenty minutes, an officer swung by, leaned against a bookcase, and pointed to his watch. I collected the papers, thank yous were muttered by all. I gathered up the pencils and counted them. Seven for seven. Every potential weapon was accounted for. This was the basic metric of a successful class in prison.

. . .

ater that night I read the short essays from the class. Shizz's was full of false starts, rhymes, plagiarized lyrics, extended metaphors, and other varieties of quasilyrical filler. It's hard to believe what a remarkable, tortured, smudgy mess a person can make of an innocent white sheet of paper in the span of twenty-five minutes. But there were some heartfelt and affecting moments in his account of a man trying, and failing, to catch a train. An appropriate subject for him, I thought.

Chudney's was a short and oddly compelling inventory of the strange people you see at the train station (himself included, he admitted). Dumayne offered a spare description of the physical space, floor to ceiling. Fernando's was incoherent; it was unclear whether he understood the assignment. Or English. Too Sweet sketched out a sad encounter he once had there. And Frank, in his frank attempt to be "exciting," wrote a fast-paced thriller about a train robber and a group of cops engaged in a shootout during rush hour (the upshot: there was blood). This, he said, was "based on real events," though he didn't specify which. Jason had given up, erased the sentence or two he had written, and filled the page with gang graffiti.

I was satisfied with this start.

To the Principal's Office

Word got back to me that Officer Chuzzlewit had submitted his incident report. He had, it turned out, conveniently omitted the detail about his chemical attack on the library. In turn, I submitted a report to my supervisor, Patti. She kicked it up to her supervisor. Within hours, I got a call informing me that the sheriff's deputies, Geoffrey Mullin and Jack Quinn, wanted a word with me.

Mullin and Quinn had different styles. There was a widely understood good cop/bad cop dynamic to their leadership team. Mullin, the senior deputy, was an attorney. Wry, judicious, above the fray: the good cop. Quinn, on the other hand, had a touch of upstart to him. Cocky, six-foot-something, shaved-head. The bald, virile type. A former college women's basketball coach and relative newcomer to the administration, he flipped between two modes: charming or confrontational.

I followed Quinn into Mullin's office. Something about it seemed strange to me. Then it hit me, literally. *Sunlight*. There was actual sunshine streaming into the office, which was on the first floor, on the edge of the yard. This was a courtside luxury box to inmate basketball games. As I entered the office, I heard the door close behind me and a languid voice, tinged with a mild case of Boston.

"Thanks for coming here, Avi."

It was Mullin. He'd materialized out of thin air.

"We're taking this matter very seriously," he said, gravely. I turned around to look at him.

He was standing behind his desk, wearing a New England Patriots jersey over his white dress shirt and tie. The Pats were set to play a big playoff game in two days. The absurd contrast between the football jersey and his grim police tone brought me perilously close to smiling. But I held it together, in deference to the sober subject of the meeting.

Quinn crossed his arms.

"There coulda been a riot," he said, abruptly.

I couldn't tell whether he was talking to me or to Mullin. But one thing was clear: he was outraged. For a second, it seemed he was blaming me.

"That's why we gotta look into this," replied Mullin, taking a seat behind his desk.

Both men were in war-room mode and didn't so much speak as debrief. I wondered if this was how they actually spoke to each other, or if it was some kind of act for my benefit. It was as though they wanted me to feel I was eavesdropping. I would have been perfectly happy to turn into vapor and slide out under the door.

Mullin looked at his watch, scribbled something down, and then looked at Quinn. "We should check his locker." This was part question, part statement.

Quinn, jaw clenching, didn't miss a beat. "We should check *all* of their lockers."

I turned back to Mullin to see how he'd react to this sudden descent into Stalinism. I'd always wondered how much these men acted in concert and how much they actually clashed. But Mullin gave no response, nor any indication he'd heard the statement. Was this a form of consent? He took a few more moments to scribble, then looked up again.

"There could have been a riot over there," he said finally, echoing Quinn's earlier statement. "And that's how we have to treat this." Mullin was clearly talking to me now. "Do you understand why that is?"

"Yes," I said. And I did: as preposterous as the incident was, the inmates were genuinely angry about it. And rightly so.

But still, I was a bit surprised that they were "taking this seriously." Mostly because it was a fart bomb. But also because as management, Mullin and Quinn had strategic alliances to maintain — why would they want to get embroiled in a petty squabble between union members?

"Okay," said Mullin, leaning back in his seat. "We read the report, but tell us again what happened."

Was this on the record or off? I wondered. I didn't want to ask, fearing that it would sound suspicious. But I had nothing to hide.

I told them all that had happened, including certain morsels that had been beyond the concern of my report. "And here's another piece," I added, leaning in. "This same thing, this business with the fart spray, apparently also happened the day before, on Forest's shift."

Mullin and Quinn exchanged a glance and a nod, a gesture familiar to me from cop shows. It said, *We got our guy.*

Feeling confident, I leaned back in my seat and offered up a modest proposal. "I think he should attend our class next week and apologize to the inmates."

The deputies exchanged another knowing look.

"Absolutely not," said Quinn, as Mullin muttered something about how this would endanger the officer.

I had figured I'd give my opinion even though I knew they wouldn't go for it. I knew the rules. Staff, especially officers, don't apologize to inmates. Such an action would undermine the power dynamic.

Quinn changed the subject. And he got to the point of why I was there. They wanted more names. As the deputies started flipping through officer photos—asking me, "Was this guy there? What about this guy . . . how about this guy?"—I got the sinking feeling that they were using this incident to settle some other scores. They seemed to have some people they wanted to nail.

Although other officers had been in on the mischief, I'd omitted their names from my report. I didn't want this to snowball. But when Quinn asked me point-blank if anyone else was there, I told the truth. I hadn't gone out of my way to indict any officer—not even Chuzzlewit himself—but I certainly wasn't going out of my way to cover for them. And some questions could not be avoided. For example, just where was the officer who was actually on duty at that post, whose job it was to *protect* the library? The answer: he had been standing right there, watching the incident unfold and smiling like a ninny.

I would have been happy to see this thing die. But the department actually seemed to be taking the incident seriously, as Mullin, in his football jersey, had promised. I was called in to speak with the prison's secret police, the SID. In a small windowless room, with a camcorder on a tripod staring me in the face, I answered minute questions for over an hour (with a break for water) from two investigators: a chatty, diminutive Italian American fellow and his unsmiling foxy partner, who said little but asked the tougher questions. Forest and an assortment of officers and inmates were likewise shaken down for answers.

During my water break, when the camera was off, the Italian American investigator confided in a near whisper that, "when I first saw these reports on my desk I thought, 'C'mon we're gonna spend our time solving the Case of the Fart Spray? We got better things to do.' But when I started reading through everything I thought, 'So these guys wanna bring in unauthorized HAZMAT into a correctional facility, which could be a felony, by the way, and then fudge the truth? These guys want to play it like that? Okay, fine, we can play like that, too.'

"Some officers think they can run around here doing whatever they want. Know what I mean?"

I got the feeling he was laying some bait for me, trying to catch me with my guard down, to coax more information out of me, or get me to reveal some personal bias against the officers. I just smiled and nodded politely. This whole thing was getting sillier by the moment.

Game Tight

The story begins in Manhattan. A harried and anxious wannabe young pimp named C.C. Too Sweet is driving a car full of prostitutes. The front seat is vacant, saved for the captain of his sex-for-hire squad. His most trusted ho. Although referred to by the title "bottom bitch," she is the top prostitute on this team, privileged to sit in the front.

After picking her up, he plays the women off of each other, making their night's earnings into a competition. Nothing is good enough. Each could do better. Predictably, the bottom bitch has brought in the biggest cash return and Too Sweet, after heaping abuse on the others, holds her up as a shining example. In so doing, he has proven that he's not all bad, that he appreciates and rewards good work. This gives the less experienced prostitutes something to strive for, while at the same time instilling in them a requisite sense of worthlessness.

C.C., the narrator of this story, now anticipates the sensitivities of his reader. A prostitute, he explains, expects abuse. If she doesn't get it, she won't respect you nor will she trust that you can protect her. Eventually she'll leave and find protection elsewhere. The women call him Daddy, and he has indeed become the abusive father figure they have come to expect. Through the abuse, Too Sweet has also formed a hierarchy that places the bottom bitch at the helm, a kind of middle manager, and makes her a crucial female ally.

C.C. emphasizes that a good pimp must know and understand

women in order to control them. This requires psychological astuteness, a finely calibrated intuition. He has to possess a natural understanding of the female mind. To be a sort of sensitive guy.

After reading this, I'd asked him to elaborate. He thought for a moment and then said, "You ever heard of 'emotional intelligence'?"

I nodded.

"The best pimp's got great emotional intelligence. No bullshit. And," he added, "C.C. Too Sweet's got some real skills in that department."

Too Sweet had a theory. When it comes to rhetoric, the pimp is king, Too Sweet claims. He asked me to consider Malcolm X. "Check it out," he said. "How does a man like Malcolm learn to move people, large crowds? He's got talent, right, and in prison, he gets knowledge from books. But where did he get the courage, the ability to stand up and chop it up like that? When I see old tapes of Malcolm speaking—and I'm talking about Malcolm with his clean-cut preacher's shirt and tie—when I see Malcolm talking, I say, damn, that man is a *pimp*."

This comment draws mixed reactions from some of the inmates in the vicinity.

Later he elaborated. "It's like this," he said. "I'm reading this book about jazz, right? Dude says that a lot of the best musicians, right, are classically trained. Like to play Mozart, right? That's how it was with Malcolm. That man was classically trained in the street swagger. And you gotta understand, man, this shit is ancient skills. There was mad pimps in ancient Egypt, wearing their togas and shit. It wasn't invented yesterday. Once he mastered it, got that classical training, see, then he picked up all that book knowledge and discipline, that man was ready to take over the world."

There was certainly something true in what Too Sweet said. Malcolm X's transformative experience occurred in prison, when his mentor, a fellow inmate, showed him, as he wrote in his autobiography, how to "command total respect . . . with words." Too Sweet abided by this. It was a belief that conferred some credibility to his behavior. He respected words because words bestowed respect onto him.

And this was where emotional intelligence—based on Too Sweet's extensive reading in pop psych—came into play. He had a theory that the most powerful men speak the language of women. It's much easier for a man to speak the language of men, he explained. But if he knows how to also move women, he is king. I noticed that Too Sweet's handwriting was curiously feminine. Or, to be more precise, its carefully wrought curly letters and circles over *i*'s resembled a seventh-grade girl's handwriting.

As a narrator, Too Sweet was good at anticipating his listeners' biases. Just as his unrelenting descriptions of a night in the life of a pimp were growing too malicious to keep me reading, he changed gears completely. As he'd promised: "before they can say 'damn,' I'm gonna back up and start from the beginning."

Until the age of ten, C.C. had had a happy childhood. His mother hailed from Tuskegee, Alabama; his father had been a U.S. paratrooper and ran a successful cleaning business. The family lived a happy middle-class existence in the Mattapan section of Boston. It was father, mother, C.C., his two older brothers, and the family dog. Family photos showed C.C. as a child, running around, playing, smiling, and hugging his mother.

One day C.C. came home to piles of shattered glass. His brothers were distressed. His mother, furious over his father's liaisons—or as C.C. put it, "his tricky dick for young pussy"—had smashed every window of the family home. These windows were never repaired. The family split. C.C.'s father, the family's provider, left.

At age ten, C.C. entered a universe of crime and violence from which he never returned. His mother relocated the family to Roxbury, to the projects right around the corner from where Malcolm Little had grown into a hustler and pimp before his rebirth as Malcolm X.

This move was more than geographic; it was a distinct and dramatic drop in economic class, C.C. wrote, a sudden fall from middle class stability into a chasm of poverty. It was the early 1980s. Young C.C. suddenly inhabited a world of urban decay: garbage-lined streets, empty lots, graffiti, rampant crime and homelessness, guns, gangs, junkies, rotting tenements, bombed-out neighborhoods. In order to get to school, he had to step over passed-out bodies lying in his building's hallway and in the streets.

A decade of race wars had left Boston as racially polarized as ever. Nobody—white or black—dared cross the clearly delineated borders into the Other's neighborhood. And if you did, you were, in C.C.'s words, "subject to a serious ass whipping." The worst—the crack and AIDS epidemics, the proliferation of automatic weapons—was right around the corner.

But the worst was what happened at home. C.C.'s mother, embittered by her husband's flight, by her heavy burden and her sudden poverty, struck out at her children in rage.

When his mother was at work cleaning homes C.C. was left alone to wander his new surroundings. He didn't have to go far to find trouble.

My first lesson in understanding the street swagger was when I would come home from school and spend the rest of my afternoon hanging out in the hallway listening to the local thugs talk about everything from pussy to robberies. My hallway was The Spot.

I used to sit in the hallway, listening to those exciting stories, watching the thugs roll their weed, load their pistols, grab their crotches, and flicking their noses in between sentences. All of it had me fascinated.

Unable to endure his mother's beatings and abuse, C.C. ran away again and again. His mother would hire local thugs to retrieve him and then she would beat him mercilessly. One of these beatings, a savage attack in which she used whatever she could find lying around—an extension cord, a chair, a lamp—left scars all over his body and turned C.C. to the street for good. He would squat in crack houses, stairwells, roofs, abandoned cars. He would lie on a cold floor staring at the ceiling, cursing his mother and wishing she would take him back with love.

He had a terrifying recurring dream: a rabid black dog chased him, but his legs were too heavy to move. He was never able to put any distance between him and it.

One day his luck changed:

I laid on the floor and fell asleep and started dreaming about the big black dog chasing me when suddenly I was awoken cold, sweating and trembling. When I looked up someone was standing over me. For a minute my eyes couldn't get focused because of the bright light that was in back of the person's head.

As soon as my eyes cleared all I could see was a tall pretty lady standing over me with a sparkling beautiful smile. I thought I was dreaming and she was an angel that came to take me away from the pain and misery of my life. I extended my arms so she could pick me up and fly off into the sky like in the movies.

She kneeled down, hugged me and said, "Hey little man, why you sleeping in the hallway?"

Once she spoke I realized she was a real person.

I softly responded, "'Cause if I go home, my mama gonna beat me."

"Why she gonna do that?"

"I don't know why, she mean, I hate her."

The lady sat on the grimy hallway floor with me and we talked for a while. She lived on the same floor where I was staying, she stumbled across me while taking out the trash through the back hallway. The lady took me inside her apartment and made me something warm to eat. Her name was Shirley and she lived in a very clean two-bedroom apartment with her man, Otis.

Shirley was 26 years old, tall, cinnamon brown skin, thin, with a beautiful Diana Ross mane that flowed past her shoulders to the middle of her back. She was a prostitute; Otis was her pimp. Both were heroin addicts.

Otis was a 260 lb. gorilla-looking nigga, but the slickest-talking, sharpest-dressing cat that I had ever met. Otis liked me right away and treated me like his son. He told me I could stay with them as long as I take the trash out and do chores around the house. I didn't mind because I didn't want to go home and get beaten. I stayed there and was happy. They made me feel appreciated.

Shirley would go out every night and work the street, come home every morning with big piles of money and toss it on the living room table before she went and took her morning shower. That was her routine every morning.

Otis would sometimes call me into the living room to help

him count the money and he would say, Lil nigga there ain't no money like ho money.

Otis owned two Cadillacs, a motorcycle—I never seen so much money before. I thought Otis was the richest nigga on the planet. I later learned that Otis was a minor player in the game and what he had was only scratching the surface of what a pimp could acquire by peddling pussy. I was only 12 years old then and I didn't understand anything about pimping, let alone sex. I thought that men would pick her up and give her money because she was so pretty.

Like so many subsequent father figures Otis was a mixed character: part role model, part cautionary tale. He was slick and successful—showing C.C. around the strip, showboating at the swanky Sugar Shack club in the South End—but he was also a miserable heroin addict who would leave C.C. in his Caddy while he went into a shooting gallery to get his fix. The presence of the child in the car, Otis believed, would deter potential thieves. He'd return two hours later smelling "as though he ate a bowl of shit, from vomiting, which happens when the dope enters the system." Cadillacs aside, Otis was a wretched mess.

C.C.'s narrative was a series of vignettes of such men: role models with deadly flaws. Men of talent and energy, and principle, who ended up broken, penniless, addicted. And worst of all, powerless and compromised. Pimps who had become the prostitutes of their own vices—and then of the system. He vowed never to be like that. But these were the people who had educated him, who loved and accepted him, who had taken him in when he was weak. To them he owed his allegiance. His fate was linked to theirs.

And then there were the women of his narrative. They ranged

from the abusive mother to the saintly prostitute Shirley. These two women were the poles of C.C.'s world.

It was no wonder that C.C.'s early career in boosting (shoplifting) and drug dealing didn't satisfy him. Or that he avoided drugs and guns. He had had a burning desire to be a pimp. It wasn't just a way to make money, but a way of seeing the world, a way of being seen in the world. Or as C.C. Too Sweet—steeped in pop psych jargon—might say: to be appreciated for *who he is*.

An Island of Deer

My attempts at teaching nature writing met with some resistance. I realized that some of the inmate students had barely any experience in backcountry woods, on desolate beaches, in deserts, in the middle of seas. Almost none had ever beheld the night sky in its full glory; to them, the Milky Way was nothing but a second-rate candy bar. Nature bored them because they couldn't relate. So I was told.

I decided to demonstrate that they actually had experienced nature and that, after all, they lived in nature, that the human city was as much a part of nature as an ant colony or a beehive. So I forced the class to write about their observations of nature in the city.

The responses to the assignment were interesting, as always.

True to his experiences on the mean streets, Too Sweet spoke of nature in the city in the starkest terms.

In the city nature is harsh.
    If you took a camera and made a National Geographic movie about the city it would look like a movie about life in the jungle, except with cars, lights, cigarettes and Armani suits. But

otherwise everything else would be the same. The strong kill the weak, the smart survive, and the smartest live like kings. But there time comes too cause theres always someone smarter and younger. Someone with a short fuse and nothin to lose. Don't get me wrong now. There are moments where things look beautiful. You'll see a bird fly way up the sky early in the morning after a long night and you weren't expecting it, or the snow fall really clean before people get it dirty.

But Nature in the city is not really beautiful. The beautiful things are only accidents. There mostly kids stuff. Truth is there is something wrong with humans. There different from other animals. It is there fatal flaw. That thing is vice. Let me give you an example. A mother bear protects her young, no matter what. She kills for her young. So does a human mother. Except sometimes. Sometimes a human mother puts her own desires before her children. She might even harm the child, beat him or leave him defenseless. This is called vice. Only humans do it.

But if you want to talk about nature in the city, think about this. Just like nature, the city don't never sleep. There are some animals that live by day and some that live by night. The more dangerous ones live at night. That's life in the city and the jungle. That's how it always was and always will be. The jungle is open 24/7 and so is the city.

Frank wrote an oddly touching description of his Christ-like dog, Paul. Justifying his interpretation on the topic of "nature in the city," Frank explained that "a lady giving birth is part of nature, even if it happens in a hospital. Well, my lady and I couldn't have a child so we adopted Paul. Paul was our dog but he was like our child."

The dog, as it turns out, had only three legs to begin with, so when the white SUV came gunning up the street, he had no chance to escape. He almost died. Indeed the people at the animal hospital said there was no hope, and that they should euthanize the dog. Frank's wife, Tracie, refused. After the dog was stabilized, it was determined that it was paralyzed. Again, the vets insisted on putting him down. And again, Tracie refused. She took the dog home.

Frank acknowledged that this was a strange thing to do, but insisted that this dog's survival had been a miracle. Tracie had lost too much in her life and wasn't ready to let the animal go. Frank fashioned a little bed, a converted coffee table, and attached wheels to it. They would wheel the wounded creature from room to room. When they cooked knocks and beans, he was there; when they watched *Everybody Loves Raymond*, he was there; and when they had friends over for poker, there he lay, on his makeshift gurney, always staring straight ahead.

Frank worried that the dog was suffering. He himself knew about trauma from Vietnam and hated to think that poor Paul was constantly reliving the accident. Tracie would sit next to the paralyzed dog for hours, petting him, and whispering secrets into his ear.

Frank concluded his touching, utterly bizarre story by saying that this was nature because a dog is part of nature and so are humans and so is a mother's love for her child, even if this mother is human and the child is a sick dog. It was a counterpoint to Too Sweet's cynical view of human motherhood.

There was only a minute or so left in the class. I decided to wrap things up and push off the remaining essays until the next session. Dumayne's hand shot up. It gave me boundless joy that he raised his hand in class. He was the only inmate in the class who did this, and he did it often, regardless of how many times I'd told him it wasn't necessary. But I would have been disappointed if he had stopped.

"Yes, Dumayne," I said.

"Chudney wants to read his joint. You should let him."

Chudney seemed a little annoyed that his young friend was speaking on his behalf, but didn't contradict him.

"Okay, fine," I said, "make it quick."

Chudney did exactly that; he read way too quickly. I couldn't really understand him and I was already distracted by the officer outside, pointing to his watch. I told him that it was good, even though I hadn't really heard it. And then I collected the notebooks and pencils.

Later, I had a chance to actually look at it. I read his essay on the elevator going up the prison tower to deliver books. It caused me to miss my floor.

One morning when I was ten I was up real early. I don't know why. Maybe I was just done sleeping for the night but I was up and atom right after the sun came up. I looked out my window and what did I see. A deer eating some grass in the lot across the way! Like it wasn't nothing at all. Then he got scared of a garbage truck. He ran up the street and stopped. After that he ran away just like that. I don't know about you but this don't happen to me everyday. I never seen a deer in my life and mos def not in the city with broken glass all over and cars parked all up on the side of the street. Even at the time I knew it was something special. Like a sign or something. I still wonder where it came from and where it went. I wonder if anyone else seen it.

Now I know your probably gonna ask me to DESCRIBE what I seen, cause you always do.

I smiled when I read that.

Not much tell you the truth. But I remember it like yesterday. The way it moved. Jumping and running like at the same time. I never seen that before. I also remember the sun coming up gold splitting through blue. I remember the deer's big black eyes. I remember his little white tail waving as he disappeared into the city.

C.C. the Author

C.C. dropped out of my class. He had other work to do. I didn't hold it against him. It's hard to hold a grudge against a macho guy who reads self-help books and talks earnestly about wanting to "boost my self-esteem." He wasn't ashamed to tell the story of the time a prison psychologist asked him to look in a mirror and describe what he saw. He had replied: "a balding guy who's too short."

He was working studiously to write his book. I encouraged him to read a passage of his book-in-progress at a poetry reading that I held in the library. He strutted up to the front of the room, full of bravado, and prefaced his reading by saying that he was "keepin' it *strictly street!*" He went on to boast that, "I am currently entertaining a few book offers." This latter claim was a complete lie, of course, and the former, about keepin' it street, was, as his audience was about to find out, highly debatable.

The passage that he read—a recollection of a childhood trauma, which he identified as his first encounter with violence—described his experience witnessing a cab driver being beaten and robbed. In a conversation with me afterward, he expressed regret and anxiety for having read the passage in front of the other inmates. It had revealed more vulnerability than he'd intended. And yet, it was interesting that of all the passages in his book, this was the one he had chosen to read.

He was so desperate to amount to something, to gain respect, that he felt he had to lie about fancy book deals. He was trying to figure out this new persona and it wasn't easy. He explained to me that a pimp is like a toddler: *always trying so damn hard to learn how to walk and talk right.* Obsessed with mastering the art of it. Now, it seemed he was trying to learn a new way to walk and talk.

And he was indeed working hard. Toiling over his manuscript, rewriting it, editing it, carefully piecing it together. And all in a harsh environment that conspires to make such efforts remarkably difficult. He was eager to learn the terminology and techniques of writing. We discussed approaches to editing and revising.

One day C.C. asked me, "What's the big thing missing from the book?" I thought for a moment and told him that he needed to draw his female characters more fully. Many of his descriptions only fed into his readers' assumptions of him as a user and abuser of women. I watched for his reaction to this comment; he was listening intently. The best way to speak to his readers, I suggested, was to show that he understood the prostitutes' perspective, that he viewed them as something other than prostitutes.

A few days later, he wordlessly dropped me a few revised chapters on the library counter. Instead of simply describing the physical attributes of each prostitute and where he met each one, he described the path each had taken. Their lives had been shaped by many of the same forces that had shaped his life.

C.C. had unwittingly changed the story. No longer was he simply the man in charge and they the female dupes. Instead, both he and his prostitutes came off as near equals in a shared and complex struggle for survival. Sometimes he exploited them, sometimes they exploited him — but most of the time, both worked together to simply stay alive and out of trouble.

Soon thereafter C.C. told me that he decided to stop referring to the women in his story as "bitches." I laughed when he told me this.

"Are you going soft?" I asked him.

But the switch made sense. After transforming the women in his story into three-dimensional characters, it was simply inaccurate to refer to them in this way. His characters were now complex human beings and the descriptive language had to follow suit. In his revised draft, the word *bitch* only came out of the mouths of his characters — including the C.C. Too Sweet character — but C.C. the narrator never used it. There was now a clear distinction between the voice of the author and the voice of the pimp. While the other inmates marveled at C.C. and me as we sat by the library's computer, discussing the literary merits of using the words *bitch* and *ho*, C.C. was making some progress. He seemed satisfied to have achieved this separation between his personas.

In developing a more honest storytelling voice, he had, literally, changed his life story. This narrator C.C. was just as real — or perhaps, just as put on — as the persona of pimp C.C. Which one was the real C.C.? I was never entirely certain. I doubt he himself knew.

As he often insisted, pimping was an identity, not simply a racket. If that were so, then disentangling who he was from what he did would be difficult indeed.

Sharing Books

Unlike Too Sweet, Fat Kat did not seem difficult to disentangle. He struck me as a mellow guy, not too concerned with proving himself. He loved kids and animals. My image of him was shaped by the time I saw him looking with pity at a pile of worn out and abused paperbacks that Forest was throwing out to make space for cleaner editions. When Forest invited him to join in this effort, Fat Kat shook his head and smiled.

"Nah, nah," he said. "I can't throw out no books, man."

"Why?" I asked.

"In my home growing up, you did *not* throw out books. No sir, never, um-mm."

He laughed and shook his head with this recollection of the past. At some level, perhaps, he recognized that he was being superstitious and yet he deeply abided by this mythos of his youth, the taboo of book disposal, the concept that books are sacred objects.

I knew exactly what he meant; I had also secretly excused myself from this exercise, recoiling at tossing books into the rubbish heap. And like Fat Kat, it had everything to do with my upbringing. For me, the seed of this feeling was planted in my parents' home—which is essentially a library with a kitchen and bedrooms—and later culti-vated in yeshiva. It bore some fruit in the summer of 1995.

I had recently become a religious nut—which is saying a lot, considering that my family was already Orthodox Jewish. My family's relocation from Cleveland to Boston had brought about this change. In the wasteland of Cleveland I had been a budding juvenile delin-quent. Although I'd attended a yeshiva day school, populated by wealthy Jewish kids, my neighborhood friends were anything but.

My buddies were young street punks and aspiring street punks. (I was in the latter category.) My ability to reliably shoot a basket-ball with both my right and left hands—coupled, I might add, with a wicked crossover dribble—helped me fit in despite being a yarmulke-wearing Orthodox Jew. At school, I studied the Torah and the Talmud; in my neighborhood, I shoplifted, rumbled, listened to hard-core rap, talked smack, and engaged in a variety of other activities that often don't end well.

When my father got a job as head of Harvard's Jewish community, my family moved to Boston. I landed in a quieter neighborhood and a more demanding school. My street-kid days were done. But, alienated from my new goody-goody classmates at my new yeshiva high school, the Maimonides School in Brookline, Massachusetts, I channeled my considerable adolescent hooligan rage into, of all things, intense Torah study.

It would probably take years of therapy to determine why I turned to the Talmud instead of, say, pyromania, at this point in my life. Perhaps I was attracted to the competitive, male-dominated world of the yeshiva. As Fat Kat himself had noted, the Orthodox exhibit some eerie resemblances to a well-organized gang—as an aspiring punk, I probably understood this unconsciously. Convinced that Maimonides School's daily 8 a.m. to 6 p.m. schedule was not rigorous enough for the serious scholar—i.e., me—I eagerly gave up my vacation and signed up to study Torah at a yeshiva in Efrat, an Israeli settlement in the West Bank. It was the summer after my sophomore year in high school.

My West Bank Torah summer camp was a fanatic's wonderland. It was perfect for me. Baruch Lanner, the rabbi who founded and ran the yeshiva, was a charismatic fat man who delivered brilliant, albeit maniacal, Talmudic discourses in the rasping style of an insult comedian. I appreciated the way he combined brash Brooklyn street talk with rabbinic erudition. The last I heard of Lanner, he was doing seven to nine years in the New Jersey system for abusing children; his crimes had apparently been an open secret in the Orthodox community for over thirty years. Rabbi Lanner liked to describe the yeshiva's schedule thus: "breakfast at 7, lunch at noon, dinner at 6. And when do you study? *Every moment that's not breakfast, lunch or dinner.*" Luxuries such as recreation, sleep, and basic hygiene were for the weak and the lily-livered. I was in holy-roller heaven.

I loved rocking the Torah texts. The exacting legal debates; the wild, provocative stories. I loved wrestling with the ancient books, having them speak to me in their original mysterious languages. Every morning, I'd wake up with Survivor's "Eye of the Tiger" playing in my head and strut to the House of Study—the *beit midrash*—like a prizefighter going to the ring for a title match. I was ready to kick some ass. Or get my ass kicked. Either way, I was content.

I camped out in the *beit midrash*, which was open 24/7. It was a giant room lined with bookshelves and rows of tables on the verge of collapse from the sheer quantity of books stacked on them. You were given a designated spot at a table. This is where you stacked your books, studied with your learning partner, prayed three times a day, and took power naps. Every student had a full tabletop set of the Talmud (six volumes), a complete Hebrew Bible, a complete set of Maimonides' Code (two fat volumes), Hebrew and Aramaic dictionaries. Then you had some of your other favorite medieval and modern commentators, and sundry tomes on Jewish law. If you were freaky, you had books on Hasidism or Kabbalah. If you were cheesy, you read contemporary "inspirational" texts. Whatever gave you your religious jollies.

I kept a five-subject three-ring notebook in which I had secretly begun work on my magnum opus: a verse-by-verse commentary on the Bible, from Genesis until Chronicles. In the great tradition of biblical commentators, I wrote my glosses in Hebrew, undeterred by the fact that my Hebrew writing skills were at a roughly sixth-grade level.

The windows in the *beit midrash* overlooked the terraced Judean Hills of the West Bank—the landscape Melville once described as "old cheese." The brilliant Middle Eastern sun poured in. Like a divine reward, the desert heat gave way every day at around 4 p.m. to a pleasant light breeze, which left a sandy deposit over all of the books. This was holy sand. Twenty minutes north was Jerusalem. Ten minutes north was Bethlehem, where the biblical matriarch Rachel was buried. Ten minutes south was Hebron, where Adam, Eve, Abraham, and Sarah were buried. On the next hill over, a three-minute drive from my yeshiva in Efrat, was the army base where my father had undergone his combat training for the IDF. This was where my ancestors had communed with God; now it was my turn.

The political situation was even more tumultuous than usual. The Oslo Peace Accords were going into effect. The Jewish settlers of Efrat, and their allies across Israel, were in a rage. Their target: Yitzhak Rabin. Just mentioning his name sent them into a foaming frenzy. Every day, there were demonstrations and confrontations with the army. From my seat in the *beit midrash*, I could hear throngs of people outside chanting, "Rabin is a traitor! The Land of Israel is in Peril! Rabin is a Nazi!" The entire town was awakened routinely at four in the morning by bullhorns: *Awake, awake, residents of Efrat! Go immediately to Rimon Hill for a demonstration!* In compliance with the peace accords, the army was trying to dismantle settler outposts, using the quiet of night to complete their mission. The settlers weren't having it.

When I'd first arrived at the yeshiva that summer, I was greeted with a gift left by the previous resident of my dorm room, an Israeli high school student who had studied at the yeshiva during the year. On my bed was a brand new copy of *Baruch Ha'Gever* (Baruch the hero, a pun on a biblical verse), a hagiography of Baruch Goldstein, the infamous settler who had opened fire on Muslim worshippers the previous year at the Abraham Mosque down the road in Hebron, killing 29 and wounding over 150. His actions had triggered a renewed round of riots and violence.

The debate in the yeshiva—mine and others around Israel—surrounded a cold analysis of the "theoretical" Talmudic legal basis for violently removing a leader who relinquishes Holy Land. Less than three months later, Yigal Amir, a yeshiva graduate, would gun down Prime Minister Rabin, then stand in court and proudly cite these very same arguments.

Although I found this talk morally reprehensible, I also owed an immense debt of gratitude to my yeshiva and its rabbis: they were my teachers, my spiritual guides.

My confusion reached a head one afternoon. Two friends and I had taken a lunch excursion to an amazing network of caves on the outskirts of the settlement. For thousands of years locals have enjoyed escaping the desert heat in these chilly, wet tunnels.

We emerged refreshed and in high spirits. Suddenly, out of nowhere, five Palestinian boys were standing in front of us. We froze. I looked at my friends, they looked at me. We stared at the Arab boys. They stared at us. They were wearing jeans and T-shirts, one of them wore an Adidas T-shirt. One of my friends was wearing a T-shirt that depicted a keffiyeh, or Arab headdress, superimposed onto Rabin's head. We had unwittingly trespassed right onto a Palestinian farmer's field. And these were the farmer's sons, who had been taking an afternoon nap in their field until it was invaded by a group of enemy boys with soup-bowl-sized yarmulkes on their heads and *tzitzis*, or ritual fringes, dangling out of offensive right-wing T-shirts.

We were scared shitless. These boys' reputation was well known to us. They were the kids who fearlessly faced off with armed Israeli soldiers, the child-soldiers of the intifada, the Palestinian uprising. They were tough and courageous. We, on the other hand, played adventure video games in air-conditioned suburban palaces.

"Tell them that we're American," whispered one of my friends, who must have thought that having been born in Jerusalem, I retained some secret powers of communicating with Arabs.

I gazed up the hill at the gleaming outdoor basketball courts of Efrat, tucked in safely behind a security fence and armed guard post.

Ever the courageous leader, I whispered, "Get ready to run, guys. On three . . ."

One of the boys, Moshe, stepped forward.

"Let me handle this," he said.

My heart sank. Dear God—handle it? What could that mean?

Before I could imagine the possibilities, Moshe, who was a few years older than I, approached the Arab boys. He did so slowly, with his palms up, to show that he came in peace. The Arab kids exchanged glances and stiffened up a bit.

Moshe removed his backpack and took out a worn volume of the Torah, the book of Numbers, complete with medieval commentaries. Like a good yeshiva boy he never left home without a book to study. He went up to the Arab boys' leader, opened the book and pointed to the text, and then pointed to the sky. He smiled and said, *Allah*. He pointed to the boy, himself, and the open book and again said, *Allah . . . Ibrahim*.

The Arab boy look confused. He wasn't the only one.

What the hell is he doing? I wondered. Couldn't he have mentioned Michael Jordan, or someone a bit more inspiring, a bit less divisive than *you-know-who*?

But he persisted. He closed the book and gave it to the boy. The boy took it. Moshe indicated that it was a gift. The boy smiled. Everybody relaxed. The Arab boys laughed. We laughed—and quickly shuffled on. As we made our way back to Efrat, to afternoon prayers at the yeshiva, we didn't dare utter a word to one another.

We never spoke about what had happened. Giving the book as a gift was a stroke of improvisational brilliance, but still, it was a remarkably taboo act for a pious Jew. Simply put, it was a sacrilege. The book itself, which contained the name of God, was a holy object: it was to be kissed every time you closed it, or if it fell to the ground, and buried once worn beyond repair. We had been taught that Jews had given their lives before desecrating it. And yet, here we had relinquished it to an enemy to save our hides. At the time, seeing the holy book in the hands of an Arab was more than we could handle. We were all a bit ashamed.

In later years, as I moved away from the Orthodox community, I looked back at that event with very different eyes. Moshe, I realized, was not only shrewd but wise. We should have been proud of what he did. There, on the same plot of land where Abraham himself had created a religion for all people, we, his warring descendants, had invoked his name and the name of his God in the cause of peacemaking. And next to a cave! It was all very biblical. This wasn't a sacrilege at all, but an act of holiness. (Ironically, it took my becoming irreligious to realize that.) We had been taught to place the Other on a narrow spectrum of pity, suspicion, and hate. We were taught to view boys our age as the enemy. But Moshe had found another way. He knew that holiness of the book was in physically sharing it.

In prison, like in the West Bank, book-sharing is taboo. Just as in the intolerant atmosphere of the West Bank there were people who said that it shouldn't happen at all: There were a few on staff who thought it was a bad idea. More often, however, I met people outside of the prison who made it clear they didn't want their tax dollars funding a pretty library for violent criminals.

I could understand that. Just as I understood the misery we had felt as kids in relinquishing our holy book to the enemy. It involved crossing a very real boundary. What did we accomplish by it, or by running a library for convicts? Perhaps nothing. But there was greater danger in not doing these things—or, at least, in not being willing to try.

Kat in the Hole

It was in the light of Fat Kat's shared reverence for books, and of his generally pacific attitude, that I tried to make sense of some news that came to me one afternoon: Fat Kat, I was told, had viciously attacked an inmate in the 3-2 unit. He was eventually subdued, handcuffed, and sent to the Hole. Solitary confinement. The news was gruesome. Kat and a younger cohort had severely beaten another inmate, had slammed his face against a railing, against the concrete floor.

I found this very hard to believe. This was a man who sat quietly reading his *National Geographic*, a man who could barely walk because of the pain in his legs. How, I wondered, was a person so concerned about hurting paperback books able to commit such violence to another human being? I personally didn't know too many vegetarians who were capable of that.

I knew that Kat was no stranger to violence. But that was theoretical. In the many hours I'd known him in the library, I hadn't seen a shred of evidence to that effect, and in fact had witnessed a good deal of counterevidence. He was done with "the game," he always insisted. He wanted a fresh start. I had believed him.

For days, I tried to imagine what had happened up there. I had trouble picturing this man going berserk. Had I been duped by him? Was I missing something important here? Was that calm just a front?

The library felt different without him. His role in the daily operation, his know-how, his sense of calm, were suddenly apparent in their absence.

I decided to visit him in the Hole. This was one of the privileges of my job: access to inmates in solitary. The officer on duty there seemed skeptical but quickly gave in to the more dominant impulse of apathy. I was let in. And I did actually have business up there. Fat Kat held a good deal of crucial information that library patrons needed: he had material on legal cases, various paperwork that he'd been helping certain inmates with. But of course I was mostly there to find out what the hell had happened.

Since he was in the Hole, in solitary confinement for twenty-three hours a day, his cell remained locked. I spoke to him through the steel door, through the deposit slot used for food trays. He smiled shyly when I showed up.

"So now you know what I look like locked up," he said.

We conducted our business quickly. He told me which case law, which forms, what information searches he had been working on and for whom. Then I wrote a note and pressed it to the brick-proof glass: *What happened?*

There was a pause. I gazed in. Kat is not a small man, but he somehow looked small in his dark isolation cell. Unshaven, tired. He was scratching his scruffy whiskers and looking around at the walls, the ceiling. He wasn't making eye contact. I gathered he was thinking of how to answer my question. This was the very image of acting cagey.

When he finally spoke, it was in a whisper. I couldn't hear him. I asked him to write it down. He shook his head no. He told me to put my ear to the door. I did. *The dude,* he whispered, and made the hand gesture of a gun shooting. *My sister, man.*

A month or so later, when Kat had somehow weaseled his way out of the Hole, he made a visit to the library, where he received a hero's welcome by the work detail and the regulars. The men actually clapped when he walked in. Some of them stood. Fat Kat beamed his big cherubic grin and waved to his public.

"What's good, Fat?" asked one of the inmates.

"I feel *great*, man," he announced, dropping a fist onto the library counter.

"I've been up to that mountain, son, and now I'm back. I lost twenty pounds. I'm down to 319. I had a lot time to think, to clear my head, you know? I got all my shit worked out."

He did look refreshed. It wasn't the first time I had seen this phenomenon. Solitary confinement is soul-crushing, life-alteringly horrible if it goes on for a long time. But in relatively small doses, it seemed to be cleansing for some inmates. It is the first time, sometimes in years, that these men have had privacy or quiet. Boat, who did time in a super-max prison, where he was locked up in his cell twenty-three hours a day, told me that he actually preferred solitary to being surrounded by incessant noise and petty violence.

Later, when we had a quiet moment, I asked Kat about the incident. I also told him in no uncertain terms that legit businesspeople might not want to do business with him if he continued to settle his disputes with violence. He had to remove this whiff of thugdom if he really wanted to go legit.

He didn't want to discuss the issue.

"Listen," he told me, "I'm serious about going in a new direction. I'm tired of all this shit," he said sweeping his hand behind him to indicate the prison, and the life that led him there. "But you got to understand something. This old hood shit, man, it *don't* go away. This motherfucker *shot* my sister. Shot her! Do you understand what that means? What would you do if someone like that shows up—"

"You can't get pulled into it. There's other ways of doing things," I protested, "it'll never end if . . ."

He shook his head. This was not debatable.

"No, man. You don't understand. You can change where you're going but not where you're from. I gotta protect my family."

We left it at that.

I thought about Fat Kat, the man who refused to desecrate a paperback, but willingly beat a man's face in. To him, there was no contradiction in this: the sacred must be defended. In my yeshiva upbringing, books were not considered mere objects but beloved living things, treated with honor and affection. When you finished studying a volume of Talmud, you recited a public prayer, which was actually a direct and personal vow addressed to the book itself: *We will return to you and you shall return to us; we are not finished with you and you are not finished with us; we will not forsake you and you shall not forsake us.*

To Fat Kat, loyalty was everything: loyalty to books, to his family. He would not forsake it. Especially when it was under attack.

The Return of Chuzzlewit

The next week I saw Officer Chuzzlewit loitering in front of the library. I'd been told that he was transferred to a posting on a cell block. But for some reason, he had been reinstated near my turf.

Apparently, he hadn't faced any discipline, which was fine with me. From the outset, I hadn't wanted any heat—and I certainly didn't want any escalation. But I was curious what had happened, given that the administration had made a show of "taking this seriously."

"What happened with the whole library incident?" I asked Deputy Quinn, when I ran into him in the prison yard. "I was kind of surprised to see you-know-who right back there."

Quinn's shoulders tensed. He looked as though he were about to grab me by the lapels.

"I wanted to fire him, and not just him," Quinn said. "But the testimonies didn't square."

"I don't get that," I said. "I mean, something clearly *happened*, because Brad"—the officer who'd been on duty at the library that day—"got punished. And you-know-who himself never denied going into the library, even though he lied about what he did in there. He basically confessed to being at the scene of the incident when it happened. How hard is it to connect these dots?"

"The inmates' testimony was muddled," Quinn told me. "They all ID'ed Flaherty as the person."

Flaherty?

I was speechless and could feel myself sink into a gloomy comprehension. This smelled worse than the initial fart bomb and was even less amusing. Three separate inmates each incorrectly identified the same officer—this was a remarkable coincidence. Though these inmates knew precisely who was responsible, each had pointed to a second officer, a man who hadn't even entered the library that day. What had persuaded the inmates to make these identical false statements? This was left to the imagination. Less murky was the result: The reports contradicted one another and so the whole case had been thrown out.

And then there was the union. I'd heard of an officer still on staff who'd been a lookout for another officer convicted of raping and impregnating women inmates. The union took seriously its job of protecting members from being fired.

But what protected me from retaliation? What would prevent an angry officer from filing a report that I sold OxyContin to inmates from my desk in the library? There was little, it seemed, to prevent such an officer from suggesting that I'd helped an inmate dispose of a weapon, as that teacher, Miller, had done (or did he?). Evidence could be planted in my desk. And my fact-checked, term-paper-style incident reports weren't worth the price of the paper of my college diploma.

All of this worried me, especially since Chuzzlewit now had an actual motive. I had, after all, embarrassed him in public and apparently almost gotten him fired. I had a feeling I hadn't seen the last of Monsieur Chuzzlewit.

Thug Sizzle

I went into the backroom of the library to set up my class and was startled to find Dumayne already there, seated with his notebook open, prison-issue safety bendy pen in hand and two spares lined up carefully at the edge of his desk, ready, as never before, to begin class.

Dumayne had somehow managed to slip out during lockdown,

through the Trap—the loving nickname given to the guard post next to his building—and get to class early. In prison terms, this was on the order of a minor escape.

He was motivated as I'd never seen him. This week's theme, love, was, after all, his motivation for joining the class, and he'd been waiting patiently, or mostly patiently, for two months now.

If he were as charming in his love writing as he was persistent about getting to this room today, he would do just fine. Though, from my perspective, it was almost cheating to teach a guy whose idea of a love poem was "I wanna make love to you nice in your heart." Nearly any string of vowels and consonants would sing compared to that. But he was trying.

Today he was a laser of mindfulness. When I walked in, his hand went up. I couldn't help but laugh.

"Really, Dumayne," I said, "you don't have to raise your hand. Class hasn't even started."

"Oh," he said.

"Was there something you wanted to say?"

"Yeah," he said. "We're doing love shits today, right?"

"Yes, love shits, and related topics."

Dumayne brightened up and said, "I'm gonna get started right away."

He began writing furiously. The combination of his hastiness and his continued inability to properly grip writing implements sent his bendy pen catapulting onto the floor. Without missing a beat, he picked up a spare and continued the effort.

The other inmates began to file in. As usual, Chudney arrived last. His fake limp was even more pronounced today. He strutted directly to the front of the class, picked up a marker, and wrote *Today's Lesson. LOVE. With the Master, Dr. Chudney Franklin.*

I took a seat and said, "Okay, professor, let's see what you got."

Ever the extrovert, he launched into a tirade, "Okay, it's like this, y'know what'm sayin', chicks be coming in all shapes and sizes, so you got to be able to bend and twist yourself into all kinds of shapes in order to, um, *fill that space*, ya know what I'm sayin . . ." And in case we didn't know what he was saying, he began gyrating and grinding.

"Thank you, Chudney," I said. "Have a seat."

Chudney collapsed into a chair, and said, "Seriously, fellas, I'm gonna hit y'all real hard on my opinions and views on love. You'll see."

"We all look forward to that," I said.

But, I had to admit, Chudney's love poem was probably the best thing that came of the next twenty minutes. At his turn to read, he stood up and dramatically recited a recipe for chocolate chip cookies. He had memorized it from the back of a bag of Nestlé's chocolate chips.

"*What?*" Dumayne laughed in disbelief. "What the fuck *was* that?"

"Man," said Chudney, taking his seat, "you don't know *nothing* about love, do you?"

Dumayne looked mortified, suddenly conscious of his ignorance.

"Just trust me, lil' cuz," said Chudney. "You make wifey a little card that says, *This is how much I love you*, then you put that recipe in there, and when she's reading it, right, you pull out some cookies that you made for her, on a nice plate with flowers and shit. You'll see what happens."

Dumayne nodded solemnly.

Since he had the floor, and confident that his love poem was the best in class, Chudney announced that his life's goal was to be the host of a TV cooking show. He even had a name for it: *Thug Sizzle, with your host Chudney Franklin.* He promised that one day, he would host all of us in his restaurant and that Chef Chudney — wearing a "big ass chef hat" — would serve us a feast on the house.

Frank, appropriately, asked if even he would be invited.

"Yeah," said Chudney, "you *and* your wife. Not the dog, though."

The Plan

A few days later, on a bleak winter afternoon both outside and in the prison, after I weathered a particularly gruesome wave of inmate demands, I spied Chudney waiting patiently at the end of the library counter. A *Boston Herald* was spread before him, which he glanced at absently. A younger inmate suddenly appeared behind him, leaned in very close, and whispered something into his ear. Chudney nodded slightly, but neither said a word nor changed his expression. The younger inmate vanished.

There was something in that small interaction that left me with the distinct feeling that I didn't know Chudney. And probably never would.

He had come to see me, which was obvious from the distracted way he had been reading the paper. As soon as I was free to talk, I motioned him over.

"I was serious about what I said the other day," he said.

I didn't know what he was talking about.

"I want to be a . . ." he looked around and lowered his voice to a whisper, "I want to be a *chef*, man. I want to have my own TV program. I'm serious about this shit."

And he was. He stared at me — almost imploring me, it seemed, to take him seriously. But he didn't need to implore. Sure, it was slightly ambitious, but not unfeasible. And kind of clever. He'd create a niche and then fill it: a hood cooking show. He was just the guy for the job. He was charismatic, smart, funny, loved food. He could have a show, why not? He could brand himself on marinara sauces and stuff. *Thug Sizzle*, sure. (Name should probably change, but who knows, maybe not?) And if Plan A didn't pan out, he could at least be a chef or something. It was probably a better career plan than selling cocaine.

On the library counter, he laid out a sheet of paper with the words *The Plan* written carefully at the top, and a frightening number of handwritten boxes each containing a word or two, *parole, construction halfway house, business degree, culinary school, TV internship, moms, son, bank, loan, brothers* . . . and on they went. There were probably thirty boxes connected through a battle plan of looping arrows. An even more complicated color-coded legend at the bottom explained this dizzying flowchart.

"Okay," he said, sensing my confusion, "forget that for now."

There was a strange desperation in his actions. He spoke in haste. Folded the sheet in a quick, rapid action, almost ripping it. It was as though he had to finalize and execute *The Plan* before daybreak.

When he got out of prison in a few months he wanted to work in construction for a while, make some money, pay some debts, some child support, and generally get on his feet. He had his high school equivalency wrapped up. Soon, he would start taking some business and culinary classes. He would intern or work in the mailroom or do whatever he could to get his foot in the door in TV. He would take acting classes. He would continue to rise through the ranks in the culinary field. He would do everything he needed to do to achieve his goal: To star in his own cooking show.

"Five to ten years," he said. It sounded like a prison sentence.

He had a lot of questions and wondered if I might answer them or help him find the answers. I agreed. This seemed like a worthy project for the library.

He fired off his first question: *How is that final step achieved?* Meaning: How does one go from having all the right degrees and experience to actually having a show? This was an answer I could give him on the spot.

"That's simple," I said, "you can't know right now."

He did not like this answer. It didn't jibe with *The Plan.* I explained that he must use his imagination to see how it *might* happen—and talk to people who have done it. I told him to use the same imagination he used in class to picture a scene: he's working as a TV intern, with a culinary certificate. He's a rookie gofer, but a trusted, hardworking part of the team. When the timing is right, he pitches something to the producer. If it's of value to the producer, the producer will use it. (*This is not a favor he's doing for you*, I pointed out, *he's doing it because it's in his interest. Don't forget that.*) If that segment airs, it goes into his résumé as a TV writing credit. It has begun.

"My point," I concluded, "is you can't know for certain now. But put yourself into the scene. You'll be front and center when an opening happens, and you'll seize it. And if it doesn't work out, it's okay. You'll have good experience and can work as a chef or have your own place or something. Always have to have a good Plan B, right?"

"Yes," he said. He was taking notes. "That's good, that's good."

I told him to hold on to *The Plan* and to make me a list of what the library could provide him to help prepare this effort. He said he'd get started on it immediately. He'd have me a list within ten minutes.

There was one more thing, Chudney said. "Don't tell *nobody*."

I promised him my silence—always a dangerous proposition in prison.

"I'm telling you about *The Plan* cause I trust you, man," he said. "There's a lot a fuckin' haters around here, Avi."

I gave him my word.

And so he sat down and composed a long list. His writing posture was exactly as I had remembered from the first day in the writing class: meditating—pen lying flat on the table—then staring at the ceiling, waiting for the words to precipitate down. It wasn't long before they did. In a flurry, he wrote:

1. degree programs (business, culinary)
2. CORI [Criminal Offender Record Information] issues
3. TV jobs, how do you get them?
4. recipes
5. more recipes
6. information on how to write a résumé and a business plan
7. loan info
8. recipes!!!!

When the officer arrived to end the library period, Chudney folded up the paper and whispered, "we'll call this thing TS—for Thug Sizzle."

As the officer ushered him out, I shook my head.

"No," I said, "let's not call it that."

I was sticking to my policy of no nicknames.

Dandelion Polenta

I created a hardcopy file for Chudney. In it I placed a growing stack of information. Applications for business and culinary
classes, financial aid and loan papers, information about business
plans, licensing for starting a business, tax forms, materials from the
Culinary Institute of America (CIA) and other culinary schools, with
special regard given to schools that didn't exclude ex-cons. It was
always in these types of efforts—in the attempt to help an inmate
figure out a legitimate life path—that I learned about the obstacles
facing people with criminal records. Chudney, for example, was
excluded from getting a federal loan for college.

I also threw in reviews of TV shows, bios, Wikipedia entries, and
interviews of TV culinary personalities. And of course, I included
some recipes. I knew that he liked Italian food, so I put in some recipes from Chef Giovanni Scappin, a teacher at CIA. I also enlisted
the inmate librarians to scour the library for cookbooks.

"You having a chick over, Avi?" Fat Kat asked.

"You know it," I said.

It was a harmless lie. The guys would work harder to find the
books if they were aiding in a sexual conquest. And I'd need all the
help I could get. It would be strange to find a cookbook in a prison
library—but, of course, it was a strange place. After an intrepid
search, the inmate library detail turned up two books. One in the Art
section and another in Fiction.

"Make something with a good sauce," Pitts advised me, handing
me a Southwestern cookbook.

"Why?"

He grinned. "So you can feed it directly to her in a spoon at the
end of the meal. Drives 'em crazy."

He moaned and pantomimed this, making me deeply regret having asked the question. He also advised me to wear a "really soft shirt, makes them want to touch you."

When Chudney showed up in the library the next day, I slid him the cookbooks and the file of documents. His face brightened up. He grabbed my hand and shook it.

"Thank you, man," he said. "This really means a lot to me. I'm gonna pray for you."

He seemed genuinely moved, which caught me by surprise. He flipped through the information, occasionally reading a passage aloud. He was in high spirits.

"'Dress Code,'" he read from the information I gave him from Chef Scappin's Italian restaurant, "'Business or country club casual (collared shirt and dress or chino-style slacks) attire is preferred. No jeans or sneakers, please.' I like that, man! You can tell people what they allowed to wear in your restaurant. 'No jeans or sneakers, please,'" he said, affecting an English accent. "That's some good shit, cuz."

He grabbed my hand again, enacting upon it a handshake of Rube Goldberg complexity. Again, he thanked me.

I asked him how he first got into cooking. He told me he used to cook for his mother; she relied on him to cook for his siblings. He also told me that when "working at home"—a subtle way of telling me he was selling drugs, or some such—he would sit in front of the TV watching hours of cooking shows (I imagined him measuring out baggies of cocaine, loaded gun resting on the table, waiting for his hooker to call—all the while, watching the Barefoot Contessa). Even in prison, he was sometimes able to watch some cooking shows, especially when a certain officer, a fellow closet foodie, happened to be on duty.

A few days later, Chudney reappeared in the library, speaking in semimysterious, musical phrases, some of which strained his mouth. *Steelhead trout with asparagus, aged balsamic vinegar and radicchio. Roasted Moulard duck leg with thyme and dandelion polenta.* He especially liked saying that phrase: *Dandelion Polenta.* Chudney was committing menus to memory, sorting out the different courses in a traditional Italian meal, learning how to pair spices.

I told him that I had a good recipe for a chicken with lemon. He noted, proudly, that this dish would go nicely with fresh basil or rosemary, sun-dried tomatoes, and olive oil. I agreed. I asked if he had ever tasted fresh basil, rosemary, sun-dried tomatoes, or olive oil. He had not. Nor, for that matter, had he ever tasted asparagus, aged balsamic vinegar, or radicchio. As for dandelion polenta, most people are in the dark on that front.

In his eagerness to advance onto this new path, he was training himself to cook by simply pairing words. From his reading, he knew that the words *balsamic vinegar* went with the word *asparagus* even though he had never tasted either. He knew that *rosemary* went with chicken and with lemon, even though he confessed that he wouldn't recognize rosemary if he fell into a bush of it.

I began finding recipes and fragments of recipes left around the library. I knew where they had come from. Chudney was pursuing *The Plan* zealously. He was even "experimenting" with composing his own recipes. Again, this was a process of mixing and matching words and phrases without really even knowing what they referred to. Ingredients made of sound and syllables, not taste or smell. It was a poetic way to learn the culinary arts. And it was a start.

Feeders

I considered bringing in some basic herbs and spices for Chudney. Kick things off with some fresh basil, rosemary, thyme. But I quickly nixed the idea. I could already see Officer Chuzzlewit's report: *Sir, today at 1450, I did see the facility's librarian hand inmate Franklin 0506891 an unmarked plastic baggie full of a green, leafy substance. They did proceed to exchange a handshake usually used by gangs.* He'd buy off three inmates to testify that I'd sold them Oxy-Contin in the library, that I'd delivered it in a hollowed-out James Patterson novel. I'd be in handcuffs before supper.

Caution was advisable here. According to Mike Russo, a coworker of mine, there were two kinds of prison workers: those who were feeders, and those who weren't. And Russo knew. Back in the days when he was an officer, before he became a prison computer teacher, he himself was a feeder.

Feeders were a secret subculture of prison workers who engaged in the illicit practice of bringing food in for inmates. Some did it routinely; some did it once in thirty years. There were as many motivations for breaking the rule as there were people who did it.

Russo had transgressed for pragmatic reasons. As an officer, he hadn't given stuff to inmates because he was a nice guy, he did it because it made his job easier. If you could buy some peace for the small price of a cigarette, then why the hell not? Back in the days when he was an officer, he told me, rules were considered more of a suggestion.

"It's not like today, when they'll bust your fuckin' balls for sneezing the wrong way."

But while Russo's willingness to give food to inmates may have been prompted by pragmatism, and spurred on by laxness, there was something else at play. He *identified*. As he told me, most of the inmates were "just regular guys." Russo, a navy vet, always referred to the inmates as "the guys." The inmates in his class were "my guys." He had nothing against the guys, he told me.

"I don't know their stories," he said. "I'm not gonna judge."

Russo also didn't judge feeders: "When you see a man grubbing you just kind of feel bad for him, you know?"

I did know. And I also knew that it wasn't just about feeling bad for the inmate, it was about feeling bad about yourself. An officer on an elevator in the Tower once told me he was proud of his job keeping bad guys out of society. "Someone's gotta do it, right?"—but that didn't stop him from going to church every week, for almost twenty years now, kneeling and confessing to what he called "the sin of locking a human being in a cage."

For those who didn't have the rite of confession—and perhaps even for some who did—feeding was a small, mostly symbolic, token of penance. A minor act of disobedience that helped you maintain a conscience, allowed you an identity apart from, and against, being a jailer.

In prison kindness was literally outlawed. Written policies not only precluded staff from selling, but even from *sharing* any item, no matter how small, with an inmate. This was part of what made the prison library—a *lending* library after all—such a radical concept. Resources were so limited, the rules so stringent, that whatever goods or services existed were sold at high prices. It was exceedingly rare to find an item that wasn't also a commodity. Everything was a quid pro quo. The idea that a valuable item like a library book or magazine, or one of the many services provided in the library, could actually exchange hands free of charge was anomalous in prison. To cynics, it was laughable. And sometimes they were right: it wasn't uncommon for free library services to be abused for financial gain. I heard reports of inmates checking out popular books like *The Da Vinci Code*, then auctioning off reading rights to fellow inmates.

Even gifts given from sheer kindness were illegal. That ribbon Jessica had given her cellmate to calm her nerves, was, from the prison's perspective, technically contraband. And it was part of what gave meaning to that small act. Jessica had actually taken a small risk in doing it.

In this environment of scarcity and distrust, a feeder was wading into trouble. If you pitched in some item, anything, you immediately became part of the black market. There wasn't much middle ground. Most contraband—including drugs—was brought into prison by staff. As a feeder, you entered the gray area between law-abiding and crooked government employee. You may have only given an inmate a sandwich, but the real problem was you knowingly breached the code of your job as a government employee. You compromised your credibility as a loyal, honest public servant. And the worst sin of all: you may have set your boss up to be embarrassed in front of his boss.

Feeders existed on the periphery. I mostly heard of them through gossip. A teacher who was a former monk, who did it out of charity. A bawdy older prison teacher with strong maternal impulses, who was constitutionally incapable of denying a person food. There were whispers of some who did it just for the thrill of breaking the rules.

I did it for Elia's birthday. He'd been an integral member of my inmate library staff since my first day there. I'd recently noticed that he seemed deeply depressed. He would mope around the library, organizing books in silence for hours on end. Just opening his mouth to talk seemed to pain him. In conversations, he'd trail off and say, "I don't know, man, I just don't know." He told me he felt eighty years old, even though he was in his early forties. He was lonely.

Elia had mentioned to me how, when he was living on the streets, he used to buy a chocolate cupcake at a certain café and sit on a park bench. For a moment, he'd escape his troubles. For his birthday, I bought him the chocolate cupcake. I invested far too much neurotic energy into this gesture. At ten different moments from when I bought the damn cupcake to when Elia showed up to work, I considered just eating it myself and forgetting about the whole thing. But, in the end, I decided to do it.

I approached him in the back storage room, after the other inmates had left. I told him, with evident anxiety, that I'd got him a little something for his birthday. I took out the cupcake and handed it to him quickly. I was officially giving contraband to an inmate— contraband that could be sold in prison at three times the amount I'd paid for it. Immediately I felt nervous. Then I felt guilty for feeling nervous. Then I felt stupid for making such a dramatic show of anxiety over a pastry.

He looked me in the eyes and thanked me, in that painfully sincere manner of taciturn people. Then he sat down, laid a napkin on the table, and began to eat. I stood by. This was a lonely man's birthday party, after all, the least I could do was keep him company. I also had a more self-interested motive: I didn't want him to take it out of the library and incriminate me. Though, of course, standing next to him while he ate was arguably more damning.

The way he feasted on this treat was oddly intimate, almost sensual. For a deprived inmate, a chocolate cupcake from the outside is more than just a chocolate cupcake. He was satisfying his hunger.

Actually, that wasn't quite accurate: *I* was satisfying his hunger. And now, like a voyeur, I watched. It occurred to me that there could be another, murkier motivation for a prison worker to become a feeder: to thrill themselves with exactly this dynamic, to enact a carnal powerplay with a prisoner. There could be something almost kinky in gratifying a helpless inmate's creaturely appetite. In prison, where power inequalities are extreme and absolute, where inmates have virtually no privacy, there exists a very real danger of relationships taking on an S&M quality. It really was hard to be simply kind.

S&M fantasies are an architectural feature of prison. In a kite I once read, a woman inmate narrated this fantasy to a male inmate: that he would show up in her cell wearing a prison guard's uniform—she fixated on the boots—and issue her a stern warning to get on her knees. At first, she'd be defiant and wouldn't comply. He would get a bit more forceful with her, etc.

In real life, prison affairs took on a whole new meaning when the risk of getting caught involved inmates and prison guards and security cameras. One staffer indeed did get caught, which turned out to be significantly less sexy than the proverbial workplace fantasy. The woman, a civilian worker who was married with children, was caught screwing a young male inmate in a maintenance closet. Another woman, an officer, was fired for becoming too friendly with the male inmates. And these were only the people who were busted.

I'd tiptoed into something here in the backroom with Elia. My real offense hadn't been giving him the contraband food but not giving him the space to enjoy it on his own.

Halfway through his treat, I wished Elia a happy birthday and told him I hoped this year would be better than last. Then I walked out, slid the glass door shut, and gave him some approximation of privacy.

In the Free World

It had been a long, late shift and it was almost 10 p.m. when I finally emerged in the free world. As I walked down Mass Ave., on my way to the bus, I heard, then saw, a man banging on the plate-glass window from inside a Dunkin' Donuts, trying to get my attention. I drew a blank. But when he lifted his sunglasses, I recognized the eyes, small and sleepy, almost swollen shut—they belonged to an old library visitor, a pimp named Anthony, or Ant. He liked to read Spanish royal history and *Car & Driver* magazine.

It was difficult to recognize a former inmate on the street. While I looked exactly as I did in prison, an ex-con looked like a completely different person in his street clothes and jewelry, under new lights, in a new setting. Often he'd possess a different affect, a different attitude. Sometimes he'd be drunk and/or high (not that I didn't encounter inebriated inmates). The free person would bear an only abstract resemblance to the inmate you knew. As if he were the brother of that person. In most cases, the evil twin.

Especially when he was elaborately arrayed, covered, as Ant was, head to toe in the brightest of whites: a rakish pink-trimmed sweatband with matching belt, a giant fake diamond stud earring, thick-rimmed DKNY women's sunglasses, a button-down Lacoste short-sleeve shirt, with the top two buttons generously unlatched, matching knee-length dress shorts, and spotless white penny loafers (with a quarter, not a penny in the lip). No socks. On Ant's hands, bright red and yellow baseball batters' gloves; a Bulgari watch, or a quality knockoff, loosely fastened. A cheap, unlit Phillies Blunt, stuffed into a cigarette holder, dangled expertly from the side of his mouth, under a wisp of a degenerate's mustache.

In short, he was a model of the ghetto/prep school look favored by the contemporary American pimp, which Too Sweet chalked up to the pimp's tendency toward all things classic.

These run-ins had been happening more often. I could almost measure my time working in prison by the number of inmates—former inmates—I encountered on the streets. Before I worked in prison, there were none. After a few months, I would occasionally run into an ex-con. After a year it was a steady flow. There were days it seemed I couldn't take a step without seeing one. This sometimes amazed my friends. I'd be at a movie downtown, or on the subway, and a rough-looking thug would come up to me with a big smile and we'd catch up like old pals.

Holding one glove folded in his palm, like an equestrian, Ant gestured for me to join him in Dunkin' Donuts. This would break an unstated rule of prison work—my boss, Patti, had told me that she'd worked out an entire spiel for politely saying hello to an ex-con and moving on. She would never have sat down with this man. But I figured, *What the hell, I could use a doughnut. I'm not breaking any laws.*

"What's good?" Ant said, giving me an earnest thug hug. I gave a quick look around to make sure there weren't any prison colleagues around. Always a bad sign when you're on the lookout for snitches. The other few people in the Dunkin' Donuts shot us leery looks.

"What's up, pimpin'?" I replied. I couldn't help myself. He was wearing designer women's sunglasses in the middle of the night—a man's fashion decisions should be honored.

"Just keeping my P poppin', y' know whadImean?" he said, the cigarette holder dancing between his lips. We sat down at his table. He took out a napkin, wiped away some crumbs. I noticed two large cups of coffee. Long night ahead, I supposed.

"I know *exactly* what you mean," I said, confident in my pimp training, courtesy of C.C. Too Sweet. "Poppin', never stoppin'."

"That's what I'm fuckin' *talkin' 'bout*, book man," he said, leaning across the table and giving me some dap. Again, I couldn't help myself. It had been a long day and pimp banter was really the only perk of my job. I never indulged myself during work—but I have a general rule: in Dunkin' Donuts, all bets are off.

Just then, I discovered who'd been drinking the second cup of coffee. Exiting the bathroom was a slim, heavily made-up young woman tottering toward us on stilettos. She wore a complex updo, and a cross-cut polyester royal purple minidress. Through some concealed hardware, her small breasts were given a mighty boost.

"Avi?" she said, stopping short, almost toppling over.

Oh crap, I thought. *Who is this?*

This was a whole new kind of awkward. I tried to play it cool, to study her face without looking like I was studying her face. This likely amounted to a dumb grin.

"Do you remember me?" she said, giving Ant a quick look. Through a fake smile, he dug his teeth into the cigarette holder.

"Of course I remember you," I said. And, at just that moment, I did. "From the library."

I could picture her in the library, not quite twenty years old, undersized in her uniform. She was fond of art books. Deep in the stacks of the library she'd retreat with one of these volumes. She'd been an eager participant in the Frida Kahlo fad that had gripped the library months earlier. When I'd asked which Kahlo painting was her favorite, she'd immediately flipped to *What the Water Gave Me*, a bather's-eye perspective of a full tub—framed by two nail-polished feet—in which assorted toy-sized images hovered over the bathwater: two women floating on a sponge, the Empire State Building erupting from a volcano, a tightrope, various flora and fauna.

What did she like about it?

"No idea," she'd said. "But I love it."

This was one of perhaps two short conversations we'd had in the library.

"Oh *shit*, Avi," she was saying now at Dunkin' Donuts, collapsing into her seat, sinking her face into her palm. "You're not supposed to be here. What are you *doing* here?"

"Don't talk to the man that way," Ant said, quietly.

I gave him a dirty look.

"I'm trying, I swear I'm *trying*," she said to me, "I was in a program, I'm gonna do the right thing."

I didn't know how to respond. But Ant did.

"Bitch, shut the *fuck* up."

He said this in a near whisper, with such muted affect, that the meaning of his words almost slid right past me. A pimp knows how to be abusive in public without causing a scene, without creating even a ripple. It's part of his professional expertise.

"Hey, easy there," I said.

It took some restraint not to give him a piece of my mind. Or to tell her that she could still make things right, that there was help, that she was still a kid and shouldn't give up on school, that there were people who believed in her. Et cetera. In short, all the things she needed to hear from someone she trusted.

But I decided it would be counterproductive to speak. She would be blamed for his loss of face and later would bear the brunt of his anger. Anything I wanted to say to either of them would only further provoke and undermine Ant and endanger her—and possibly me. This wasn't prison. It was real life. Ant was her pimp and I was just some bony guy in khakis. Out here there wasn't much I could do. Getting involved would be, at best, pointless; at worst, dangerous.

Ant played it cool and ordered his bitch to buy me a doughnut, which she did, before I could object. He inquired after certain other inmates. *Fine*, I answered to almost every question. This whole situation was depressing me in a major way. What did he want from me? Why had he invited me in?

The answer depressed me even more: Why *wouldn't* he invite me in? I'd played along with his act, respected him with that title, *Pimpin'*, and generally honored his street persona. And now I was suddenly angry with him? Was I upset simply because I knew the girl? And if I hadn't, would it be okay?

I knew men and women like this. I'd heard their stories. But it wasn't until I actually witnessed them together, dressed in their street clothes, and until I myself was implicated in the situation, that I got it. The pimp talk, like the nicknames, identified me with the wrong side. In this case, with the abuse and exploitation of a young drug-addicted woman. If I indulged it, I was, in some way, complicit.

And if I had any doubt about this, I needed only recall her words. *I'm trying*, she'd said, almost in tears. Her desperate excuses to me that she'd been in a program, that she was trying to "do the right thing." Why had she been so defensive around me? She and I had never remotely spoken of a program or of her doing the right thing, or any of that. At least not that I could remember; many inmates asked me to help them find programs, to write application letters. Too many to remember.

But it didn't matter whether I remembered—she did. In my role at the prison, this woman had clearly identified me as a person involved in her rehab process, whatever that entailed. Now here I was kicking it with her pimp. Had she seen me call him *Pimpin'*? Had she heard me banter with him?

Even after working in prison, I hadn't shaken American culture's casual use of *pimp* and *ho*. But there was no ironic detachment with the real version of it, no dabbling.

You're not supposed to be here, she'd said when she saw me. She was right.

Too Too

My encounter at Dunkin' Donuts left me with some serious second thoughts about C.C. Too Sweet. Had I been turning a blind eye to this troubling character? In theory, I knew what he was about; he had told me. But did I really comprehend it?

Too Sweet's argument about pimping, that it was an art form—indeed the great male art form, the art form to which all others aspired—had been borne out by his writing talent. His verbal enticements, his ability to self-reflect and verbalize, proved his point: he was a good seducer and could shape the world through words.

He had no use for guns—these were for people who didn't know how to use words. Or, to quote him, "I don't need no Smith and Wesson, man, I got Merriam and Webster." It hadn't been obvious how to take such comments. But the truth was I hadn't given it much thought. They were amusing. That was all.

When he wasn't talking to me, though, I saw him overdoing it, boasting. I witnessed him indulge in the very "slick dialogue," the trappings of hustlerdom, that he himself had identified in his memoir as the telltale sign of a fraud. His wit, when it was working too hard, mostly betrayed his intentions.

"A real pimp always keeps it *low down* and *down low*," I once heard him say. And it was precisely in the act of enunciating this principle that he was in violation of it.

I was getting a sinking feeling about all of this. Was I being taken in by C.C.'s words, willingly hypnotized into buying his story and, by extension, him?

When I didn't return a revision in a timely manner—I did, after all, have a job—he let his rage show. He pounded his fist on the library's front counter and started pacing, restraining himself, it seemed, from putting his fist through a wall, or a person. My reaction to his anger startled me: I felt vaguely guilty, as though I had let him down, even though I was helping him free of charge and stretching, possibly violating, my work duties for him. For a fleeting moment, I could relate to those prostitutes sitting in the backseat, how they had felt bad for not bringing back enough money to satisfy him. This thought jarred me. I had to ask the unfortunate question: Was C.C. treating me like a ho?

I saw him in the library counseling young pimps, encouraging them, guiding them, teaching them the tricks of the mind control game—just as old heads had done for him when he was a young upstart.

I wondered about that musical name of his. *C.C. Too Sweet.* His friends often shortened it to just "Sweet" or "Sweets," which was apt; there was an undeniable charm about him. But lingering in the middle, that small but suggestive word: *Too.* Perhaps in its connotations of *overly* and *excessive*, that word revealed more than intended.

Until I met C.C. Too Sweet and the library regulars, I hadn't spent any time with pimps. My association with pimps was limited to what I saw in movies. Or to the zoot suited, fedora- and long-feather-wearing persona I'd encountered at collegiate pimp and ho parties, those get-togethers that gave elite kids permission to dress tough and, it was hoped, get drunk enough to get laid. But C.C. Too Sweet's life was far from a party.

As I considered this question—whether I had allowed myself to be blinded by C.C.'s enticements—I decided to Google the man. I didn't have any policy about Googling inmates; typically, I only did it if there was a specific reason. When, for example, hiring a particular inmate, I might want to Google him to make sure he didn't have a record of cannibalizing prison librarians. But the fact that I hadn't searched C.C. earlier, after I'd spent so much time working with him, may have indicated that I didn't really want to know. The morning after my encounter at Dunkin' Donuts, I did a quick search.

The *Boston Globe* reported: "Three Boston men were charged with kidnapping yesterday after they allegedly abducted two young women in Worcester and tried to force them to work as prostitutes in Boston's Combat Zone and turn over their proceeds."

Another, more recent, newspaper report: "Charles Jarvis, 35, of Roxbury, was arrested in a Super 8 motel in Quincy, Mass., with a girl, aged 14. She had run away from home the day before. He stood accused of three counts of rape, kidnapping, and attempting to sell the girl's body for sex."

Kidnapping, raping, and pimping a minor! A ninth grader! I almost fell off my seat. The image of him with this girl in a motel sickened me. This was so much worse than what I'd encountered the night before at Dunkin' Donuts. This was among the worst kinds of crime, the kind that even hardened criminals find reprehensible.

Perhaps more nauseating was how easily, how readily, I'd embraced him. For months he'd told me he was a pimp, had boasted of it. And now I was going to get angry and accuse him of . . . *being a pimp*?

What had I taken that to mean? I had to own up to my willful ignorance of what being a pimp actually entailed.

Still, he had glossed over certain crucial details. There were chapters of his book he'd conveniently neglected to show me. He told me they weren't ready. Perhaps that was true. Or perhaps he didn't want me to know the whole story. But of course, the responsibility was mine. I had allowed myself to get taken in.

My bosses would not be pleased with me, nor would they want to stand by me if I were placed under scrutiny. They certainly weren't going to risk their jobs on it and would advise me to do likewise.

I was a paid public servant, after all, part of a governmental agency that was under constant media scrutiny. The story of a naïve Harvard grad and former *Boston Globe* reporter, using public time and taxpayer money to help a career felon/pimp sex offender publish a tell-all book—which would be how a muckraking reporter would characterize C.C.'s work—this was certainly the kind of story the tabloid *Boston Herald* would relish. More importantly, though, perhaps they'd be right: why should a public servant help this guy? Maybe he should just rot in his cell.

I was also vaguely worried that C.C. could compromise me by spinning my bosses—or the paper—a salacious version of what was going on. In our editorial collaboration I was compromising myself and giving him leverage over me. He had little to lose at this point (except, of course, his manuscript). I, on the other hand, had my job, my reputation, my pride. If he felt pinched in some way, he might decide to humiliate me or to blackmail me with this. I kept imagining the tabloid headline, *Outraged Parents: Our Tax Dollars Helped Our Teenaged Daughter's Rapist Write His Tell-All!* The article would be accompanied by my prison ID photo, with my crew cut and my bewildered grin, bearing the caption "I thought it was a good read." These paranoid scenarios kept me up at night.

I backed away from C.C., without giving him an explanation. What was I supposed to tell him? *Sorry, it just occurred to me that you're a sack of shit?* Should I write a letter to Miss Manners: *What's the etiquette for breaking up with a pimp friend?*

After my initial disappointment and anger with him, and with myself, I settled into a more neutral position: simple self-protection. I took the road of avoidance. He was too sweet and I was too busy. I suddenly became too busy to sit and talk with him, too busy to edit or type his work. I needed some distance. He quickly grew guarded with me, barely containing his resentment in formal gestures of politeness. He knew that I knew.

The Season of the Hawk

It was the season of the hawk. High on the roof ledge, overlooking the prison yard, it sat, watching. Around prison, there had been much speculation about this bird. Many people, inmates and staff, were terrified of it. Some saw it as a good omen, a "spirit animal," possibly even the soul of a prisoner, flying around its cage.

As usual in the library, theories abounded. Some believed the red-tailed hawk favored the prison for its alarmingly large population of mice. Some claimed it made its nest here, though no one had seen it. Others said the government couldn't legally exterminate a protected species, and so had conveniently relocated the nest to prison, as a sort of cruel joke on the inmates. Naysayers dismissed it as a plastic decoy, designed to scare away pigeons (a mission that was very much accomplished). But the majority of eyewitnesses had noticed it move. Including those who had observed the bird soaring, larger than a man.

But most of the time, the hawk just sat up there, squatting and watching the human dramas below.

Copyrighted

One afternoon, during the season of the hawk, Chudney and I sat in the back room of the library, working on his cover letter for culinary school. He threw down his bendy pen in disgust. He couldn't concentrate, too much on his mind. When I asked him what was going on, he sighed.

"Dude walks into 3-1," he told me, "I know this guy from the street. He did some pretty bad shit to my mans not too long ago."

It was getting harder for me to decide what I wanted to know and what I didn't. In this case, I didn't want to know and didn't ask.

"And this motherfucker, who's also a motherfuckin' snitch, by the way—and I know this for a fact—he walks into 3-1, a big mutherfuckin' smile on his face, and you can be sure some shit's gonna pop. That's just how it goes, you know? And he knows it too: he wasn't smiling when he saw me standing there, that's for damn sure."

"So what happened?"

"Nothing," Chudney said, picking up his prison-proof bendy pen again, and scanning his application.

Chudney told me that he was "holding his fire," and wouldn't take any action against this man. He was itching to take revenge, though, and indeed felt a responsibility to avenge his friend. But he didn't want to go to the Hole or the hospital or catch another case, because he didn't want to get sidetracked from his work, from doing the applications and learning the recipes or preparing for his long-term goal of hosting a TV show. Getting involved in a gang war was not part of *The Plan*.

I commended him for his prudence.

"It ain't like that," he assured me. "The fight *will* happen. Unresolved shit, man, resolves itself eventually. That's how it goes. There's an enemy in the house."

It sounded eerily similar to what Kat had told me when he got back from the Hole. Chudney said that violence was inevitable in this situation. He wanted to avoid it, but was convinced it would happen. And possibly when he wasn't expecting it. The longer he delayed a response, the more opportunity he'd be giving his enemy to preempt. His restraint would be interpreted as weakness—or worse, smugness, indicating perhaps that he'd been talking to the cops. And asking the prison authorities to be separated from this man would also brand him a snitch. Every scenario led to some kind of escalation.

He was thinking of doing something stupid to get "lugged," to be placed in the Hole. But he was avoiding that approach, as well. For one, his enemy would see right through it. And, again, he wouldn't be able to work on his applications.

"So what are you going to do," I asked.

Again, he replied, "Nothing."

He returned to revising his cover letter. A few moments later, his mood lightened. He had written his first recipe. He pulled out a sheet of paper and showed me the recipe, with the caveat that I wasn't allowed to write it down or photocopy it. He needed to be protective of his stuff. I noted his name and a copyright symbol at the lower right-hand corner of the sheet.

"I'm thinking of getting this tattooed onto my chest," he said, pointing to the copyright logo. "I'm all about the copyright from now on. I gotta stay focused."

Later I walked through the yard en route to the staff cafeteria. I stopped to look at the notorious red-tailed hawk. Camouflaged brown-white and rust, the raptor sat perfectly motionless. So still I lost view of it momentarily, high in its perch above the prison yard, watching, watching, watching, with roughly eight times the visual strength of a human. It was not alone in its vigil. On the edge of the yard, officers stood gabbing with each other, watching the male inmates, and the women inmates sat up in the Tower, also gabbing, also watching the male inmates.

The hawk sat, eyes wide and unblinking, a minor deity sitting in a tightly coiled pose of meditation—a world of dramatic motion, implied in this exquisite stillness. I wondered if perhaps the decoy theory was correct, that this hawk was nothing more than a plastic effigy meant to scare away pigeons. But then it moved, lifting a wide, kingly wing, a formal unfurling, flexing the feathers along the edge of its wing, then drawing it back ever so gently, like a magician taking a bow. In a quick flash of white, it had revealed its underbelly. Even from down in the yard I could see it: a sturdy, hydraulic cylinder of a leg, and, in the curvature of those heavy yellow talons, almost useless for walking, a dreadful singularity of purpose. This was what caused me to shudder.

Stopping the Waves

Theme music goes up. Something slow and sublime by Gladys Knight and the Pips. Old school. Something that makes the older crowd feel at home and gives the youngsters a sense of tradition. The mood is relaxed. Chudney, wearing crisp tailored pinstriped dress slacks and shirt—or country club casual—comes onto the set, smiles, waves to his cheering live audience. The set is a sunny city condo, a view of the skyline.

Welcome to Urban Cooking, with your host, Chudney Franklin. *(He's nixed Thug Sizzle).*

As he puts on his apron, and rolls up his sleeves, he shoots the shit with his lovely assistant. She tells funny stories about her tyrannical two-year-old daughter who's just like her. The crowd loves it. The assistant is a black woman. Girl-next-door type. Maybe a stand-up comedian. She's got a little spunk. She chides Chudney.

"Look at the famous chef," she says to audience. "And he still doesn't know how to put on an apron."

Chudney opens his mouth to respond, but is speechless. He smiles and pleads guilty. The crowd chuckles.

After a casual chat with the assistant about the day's dish, he looks directly into the camera, rubs his hands together, and says, "Okay, let's get started . . ."

C hudney tells me that what he really loves about this fantasy is the idea that his son, who will be somewhere between ten and fifteen years old when this comes to fruition, will be watching from the wings.

"Can you imagine that, man," Chudney says, "growing up, watching your pops in front of the TV cameras? That'd be some pretty cool shit."

He tells me a bit about his son. Once, he was at the Connecticut waterfront with his son, age four. The boy would slowly approach the water, curious to get a closer look. When a wave would roll gently up the sand, the boy would scream in terror, turn, and run for his life.

But then he stopped suddenly and turned back to the water, crouched, and sort of threw his body backwards. It soon became clear to Chudney that the boy was trying to prevent the wave from sliding up the beach.

Chudney tried to explain to him that it was okay for the wave to roll up the beach. That's what waves are supposed to do. The little boy was not happy with the answer. Sitting in his father's arms, he scowled at the sea. Chudney still doesn't know why he was trying to stop the waves. Were they threatening to hurt him? His parents? Something about it had unsettled him. Perhaps, in the noise of the sea he heard the waves swallowing up the earth, could sense that they were a force of erosion and change. It wasn't clear. But what was clear, Chudney told me, was that he was brave enough to throw his body into harm's way.

"Courage, man," Chudney told me with a big smile. "You can't teach that shit."

The Plow Pose

I'd already assumed a particularly compromising yoga position when the officer walked into the weight room. The Plow pose basically has you on your back, balancing on your shoulders, with your legs straight and together, swung up and over, straight past your face—that is, when you're doing it correctly.

When you're not doing it correctly, and I wasn't even close, your legs are splayed. To most, this looks both comical and slightly painful. To some, it looks like something much more specific. The look on the officer's face indicated clearly that he was among this latter category.

How does one explain oneself in such a situation? Do I mention that this is a standard practice of yoga? Should I explain that the Hindu *Shakti*, or divine libidinal flow, is, according to that guru, Wikipedia, "conceived as a goddess which rises to the head, until it is united with the Supreme Being (Lord Shiva) and the aspirant [in this case, me] becomes engrossed in deep meditation and infinite bliss"? Is there any way for that *not* to be interpreted as an elaborate euphemism for giving yourself a blow job? I myself am not certain it doesn't mean just that.

This unfortunate scenario, inauspicious in any season, was particularly ill-timed. I had a PR problem. I had provoked a group of officers and had apparently almost gotten one, Chuzzlewit, fired. And, as luck would have it, one of those officers had to show up for a weight-lifting session, only to find me, still wearing my office clothes, my dress shirt unbuttoned, in *his* weight room, inflicting my homo/autoerotic Hindu exercise regimen upon him.

It was actually ironic. I was in the weight room partly because of my conflict with the officers. Their dirty looks were unnerving me; I was getting stress backaches. Someone had suggested yoga. I hadn't ever taken yoga seriously; it sounded like a hybrid between yogurt and Fonda—not the kind of thing a self-respecting American guy should get mixed up in. But I was desperate. And now here I was in the prison staff weight room, alone with an officer who had only contempt for me. And with my face squarely in my crotch.

Try as I might, I couldn't untangle myself. It turns out to be rather difficult, once committed, to shake oneself out of the Plow. Especially without first digging your face a bit further into your crotch. Finally I wiggled out and jumped to my feet.

"Just doing some stretches," I announced, pulling my arm behind my head.

This comment was ignored. So indeed was my very existence. The officer set up his barbells in silence. He was benching 175. I wondered how much I could do these days. It had been a while since I pumped iron.

Feeling confident, I made my way over to the bench press. I put on 100 pounds. Then I put on 20 more. Then 20 more, 10 more. I sat down, ready to bench a respectable 150. A man should be able to lift his own weight.

I wrapped my hands around the cold metal bar and fixed my eyes on the wall, at pinups of steroid-inflated men. My gaze was met by their bulging, bloodshot eyes. Even from fifteen feet away I could see every vein in their immense glistening bodies. These were not portraits but landscapes. Were these giant men happy? And what about the guy who'd posted the photos? What did he dream about? Did the officers who used this space enjoy beholding guys flexing in skimpy bikini bottoms?

I inhaled deeply and then exhaled just enough to budge the bar. I held the weight aloft, over my body. My back protested fiercely. My arms began to wobble involuntarily. This was not a good idea. I was in the gym, after all, because my back had gone out. If it failed me again, at that moment, I'd be in serious trouble. And all because I had to compete with this officer.

I sighed and dropped the bar back into place with a loud crash.

In the mirrored wall, I spied the officer throw me a smug little grin. I buttoned up my shirt and called it a day.

The Flip-Out

I was feeling as though I had to keep as close an eye on officers as on inmates. I'd become the target, or at least the pretext, for a subtle campaign of harassment. It came in various forms. First, I heard that officers were confiscating inmate library books more frequently than usual during searches, throwing them into the trash. Members of the library detail were being routinely detained and sent back at their checkpoint, leaving me shorthanded.

Then, for two straight days, no students showed up to my writing classes. When I approached the officer on duty about the problem, he showed me a note that stated my classes had been canceled. Who sent it? He didn't know. The note was conveniently unsigned.

The next week, when my classes finally resumed, an officer who I'd never seen swung by and stood by the door, staring in the entire time, casting a pall. Similar behavior was reported by other teachers. Everyone was whispering that these officers were looking for any excuse to point a finger at the Education Department. In the meantime, they were going to put everyone on edge.

The officers' keenness to incriminate me bore some fruit. One afternoon, the library screened *Da Ali G Show*, which featured a clownish hip-hop interviewer satirizing deadly serious guests. A three-second cut of Ali G—played by Sacha Baron Cohen—simulating a sex act with a tree became the subject of a report against the library: we were cited for our use of "inappropriate" content. Although the report wasn't taken too seriously by the administration, I was warned and told to monitor the library's content more closely. When I argued that Ali G was a *satire*, I was flatly told, "don't do it." Again, the officers had found a way to compromise my programming, to put me on notice.

All of this was beginning to destabilize my equilibrium. Twice in one week I found myself stuck in an elevator—not unheard of—the second time forcing me to miss a class. I couldn't help but wonder if an officer in Central Control was squeezing me, especially as these holdups extended almost twenty minutes each, far past the usual delay. Every time an officer or group of officers came into the library for routine contraband searches, I watched them with mute paranoia, fearing they might plant something or do something to embarrass me. I didn't know whom to trust.

But the petty claims weren't the real problem. It was the fear that these were a prelude to much more serious meddling. That one day I'd find myself sitting in the SID's interrogation room trying to explain why an officer found drugs in my desk and why three inmates claimed to have bought heroin or OxyContin from me. My recent stress-related back problems were preventing me from getting sleep. I was beginning to crack.

The final provocation greeted me upon my arrival for a Friday morning shift. Sitting on my desk was a freshly printed report. Written by none other than Officer Chuzzlewit himself, the document claimed I'd freely and knowingly given an inmate contraband including pens, pencils, and markers, tools that could be refashioned into knives or tattoo-making implements or sold for these purposes. In the report, I was indentified as "the short, thin blondish guy in the library."

Although relieved that the charge was relatively minor—that is, compared to the accusation of selling drugs—I was still unnerved. Was he signaling a warning? Was he demonstrating his ability to get away with any charge against me? Was I paranoid? Mostly, though, I resented the subtle suggestion that I was some sort of malnourished leprechaun who dwelled between the bookshelves. The short, thin blondish guy in the library, indeed. I'd had enough of this. I officially flipped my lid.

. . .

Because of my bad back, I hadn't slept the night before and was already in a state. It was 7:40 a.m. Twenty minutes until the day's first inmates were due in the library. Not enough time to get my cereal: looked like I'd be having revenge for breakfast.

Slightly deranged, I rifled through my desk in search of a Post-It note. They were all hot pink. No good. I needed something staid. *Yellow!* Yes, a nice, professional yellow note would be perfect. My mind was racing. I searched more. Still, all I could find were pads of hot pink. Half a dozen of them. *Fuck it*, I thought. *As Don Rumsfeld once said, "You go to war with the army you have, not the army you wish you had."* I scrawled my name on the hot pink adhesive note. And then, like a psychotic, I traced over my name a second time. A third. I underlined it three times, then peeled the note from the pad. I could feel myself smiling like a goblin. I threw open the library door. Chuzzlewit! Standing right there in the hall, holding his morning cup of coffee. Perfect. I walked up to him.

"Next time you wanna write a report on me," I said, "don't forget to include my name."

As I spoke, I placed the Post-It note with my name on his forearm. Unfortunately, my gesture lost a good deal of its dramatic flair: the note didn't stick. Not even close. With awkwardly intimate care, like a mother putting a bandage on a child, I reapplied the Post-It to his plastic coffee cup.

"*What?*" he said. He seemed genuinely confused.

I have a slight tendency to mumble, especially early in the morning (and especially, though I don't have much experience, when I'm slightly deranged). It occurred to me that I should have warmed up first. I'd flubbed my line. Regaining my composure, I repeated, this time enunciating like a freshman theater major.

"I said: 'Next time you write a report on me at least get my name right.'"

I pointed to the hot pink note with my name printed maniacally on it, hanging precariously from his coffee cup. He glared at me.

Feeling confident, I added, "And by the way, I'm not 'short,' I'm your height."

Chuzzlewit took my advice. Within thirty seconds, he'd written a report. Once again, I was summoned to the Deputy's Office. This time, however, to the windowless office of bad cop Deputy Quinn. And instead of Deputy Mullin, the good cop, Quinn was accompanied by svelte Major Morrison.

Was Morrison, this lissome, handsomely groomed gentleman, ever *not* a senior officer? His long face and sad eyes, his debonair mustache and crisp officer whites, demanded the accompaniment of a noble cavalry horse. He was present ostensibly in his role as shift commander, and probably as witness, but I got the strong impression he was actually there to amuse himself. The major crossed his legs, sipped tea like a diplomat, and did not bother to suppress a large grin. Quinn, as usual, put on the tough guy routine.

"Read this," he said, as I sat down.

It was Chuzzlewit's report about the Post-It note. The document, scripted in a bulky but supple hand, gave an oddly gripping fictional account of the incident. As per my demented provocation, Chuzzlewit had indeed used my Post-It note and referred to me by my full name. He claimed I shoved him. Twice. (He was good with details.) I'd also threatened him in a barrage of expletives, which he'd spun into full quotations that bore an uncanny resemblance to his own speech patterns. In the climactic moment of this tale, I had vowed bloody vengeance. According to this fanciful version of our encounter—which, despite myself, I found enormously entertaining—my attempted witty remark about our shared height was imagined as a dark threat: *And don't think that I won't do it*, I had allegedly said, *we're the same size you know.*

As usual, he named inmates who had witnessed the brutal attack—none of whom, to my knowledge, were actually there.

"Did you threaten him?" Quinn asked me.

"No," I said, trying desperately to restrain a smile. "Look at me, Jack. I haven't been to the gym in months, I've got a bum back. And you *know* me: Do you think I go around threatening people, especially a CO? He's lying and he'll continue lying until he's exposed."

Major Morrison, no longer amused, cut in.

"We could have had a serious problem over there, you know," he said, "You're lucky he didn't take a swing at you."

"*He's* lucky he didn't take a swing at me," I said.

This restored Morrison's cheer. He smiled again and sipped his tea.

"Did you assault him?" Quinn asked.

"Yeah, assault with a deadly Post-It note."

"Did you lay hands on him?"

"What does that mean?" I asked.

"Did you touch him?"

"Okay, yes," I conceded, "I put the note on him. Did I sprain his arm? I didn't realize he was so delicate. First I'm a short, skinny nothing and now I'm a guy who's intimidating him?"

"So you admit that you laid hands on him."

"I admit exactly what I said in my report: I touched him gently with a Post-It note, and not at all in the context of a physical threat. I think the issue here is—"

"I can't have staff members laying hands on other staff members inside this facility."

I looked at Quinn; he looked at me. Major Morrison drained his tea. And I knew that Officer Chuzzlewit, with his constipated face, had me in checkmate.

Within the week I was served with notice of my suspension without pay. Chuzzlewit's allies were impatient to hear word of my punishment. They asked my union boss Charlie to spill the beans. He refused, and in fact gallantly offered to pick up the notice from the Deputy's Office himself, so as to deprive the officers the pleasure of witnessing my walk of shame. Less than a month and a half after a released inmate had mugged me for $43, an officer mugged me for a good deal more than that. And this time, I had only myself to blame.

The Knowledge of the Knife

When I got home the night I was mugged in the park, I'd called my girlfriend, Kayla, to tell her the story. It's not every day you get mugged by someone who knows you. As I took off my coat and fetched the cell phone deep in my pocket, I composed the story in my head, organizing the comic elements. I would tell her that the mugging was my just punishment for paying money to see *Jackass 2*. I'd gotten what I deserved. The comedy of the event itself needed little embellishment. And that punch line, *I still owe you guys two books*, was funny stuff.

After a few rings, Kayla answered. She sounded tired. Her first year of medical school had thoroughly exhausted her.

"I've got a hilarious story to tell you," I said. "I got mugged, I'm fine, but here's the thing—"

"*What!*"

There was a dreadful pitch of desperation, of genuine fear, in her voice. This should have been my cue to stop.

"I know it sounds bad," I said, "but, trust me, it's funny."

But before I got to the part where the mugger recognized me as "the book guy," I could hear her getting upset. The sound was of choking.

"Wait, seriously," I said, "this is a funny story."

By the time I reached the part about the knife, she was crying.

"I guess that part's not so funny," I said.

Sitting alone in her room three hundred miles away, she was now sobbing miserably. It was past midnight. It had been a hard year for her. For us. I heard her say, not quite into the phone, "Oh God, Oh God, Oh God, what am I going to do?" I tried to comfort her, but it was useless.

"I don't know . . ." she was saying, "I don't know . . ." She sounded like an animal in pain—she *was* an animal in pain.

"Nothing happened," I said. "Hey, babe, it's okay, I'm totally fine. I'm right here, I'm talking to you."

Through her tears she was trying hard to say something. She took a breath.

"I don't know what I would do if something happened to you. I don't know what I'd do without you."

I could feel my heart literally clench when she said that. I was speechless. I'd never heard her this upset and was completely unprepared for this late-night surge of raw emotion, for the unforeseen immediacy of that statement, *I don't know what I'd do without you.* When said in earnest this sentiment, abused in countless idiotic love songs, is startling.

It held a particular meaning for us at that time. A few months earlier she had moved to Philadelphia to begin medical school, to begin a new stage of her life. With the distance, our happy four-year relationship, for much of which we'd lived together, now had to justify itself. Was this a temporary separation, or the beginning of a serious drifting apart? It was clear that we couldn't float along forever on autopilot. Our relationship would require some sort of a decision.

One of the possibilities was marriage. At least this was how various friends and family advised me. But I couldn't shake the notion that Groucho Marx was right. "Marriage is a great institution," he'd said. "But who wants to live in an institution?" Especially given that I already worked in one. Aside from Groucho, the only guidance that grabbed my attention had come many months earlier, and from an unexpected source: Jessica.

I t had been a strange night in prison. Sunset had been awkward and inconclusive, the sky remained a shade of weak yellow tea through the night. Inside, things also felt off. It was as if a switch had been thrown in some corner of the prison, causing a widespread simultaneous unhinging. The previous night one of the women inmates had scuttled into the library, pounced like a feral lynx roughly four feet through the air directly *onto* the counter, arched her neck at disbelieving bystanders, crawled the length of the counter, almost bit a library detail member—who had made a valiant effort to prevent her advance—then pounced again, ambushing the magazine display I kept stashed safely (or so I'd thought) a full five feet behind the counter. Having missed her mark by a considerable margin, she proceeded to roll on the floor, giggling uncontrollably.

The following night, the library had been tranquil, suspiciously so, until the stillness was dramatically shattered by Janet Jackson's

"You Want This"—or was it "Throb"? It was hard to tell, it was so loud. A group of five lady inmates—the cool clique, the mean girls (which in prison meant *mean*)—had hijacked the back room and converted it into their own private club, complete with a bouncer. At the entry, they'd posted a lackey, a plus-sized woman who clung to the belief that she had a chance of earning her way into their bitchy graces. The fab five had gotten their hands on an ancient tape of music videos, which I hadn't known existed in the library, and were having themselves a retro dance party.

In a flash, I was on the scene, face-to-face with the large bouncer. I recognized her as the woman who'd recently been hauled out of her prison unit in tears and shackles after intentionally cutting herself. She tried to turn me away from the party, then thought better of it and let me through.

The dancers had refashioned their uniforms into club outfits: pants rolled high from the bottom, low from the top—shirts twisted and retied to bare midriffs. They were dancing for the gold, writhing around invisible poles and gyrating like strippers. Three of the five, I later learned, were strippers (among other things). One of these women—who told me that she used to moonlight as a Monica Lewinsky–impersonating stripper at private parties—was starting to inch her shirt higher and higher. It became immediately evident that there would be a topless prison inmate, who bore a slight resemblance to Monica Lewinsky, slut-dancing in my library. And if I had any doubts about this, the woman began shouting, "I'm gonna take this motherfucker *off!*" The other women watched in awe from the wings. Some joined in from afar.

They didn't hear me shout the first couple of times. I waited for the right moment, and made a wild dash between their squirming bodies, lunging at the old VCR, just barely reaching the stop button.

Perhaps they teach you these commando tactics in library school—I wouldn't know.

In the spirit of full disclosure I must admit that, in the past, I'd quietly permitted modest amounts of dancing in the library. Don Amato, the former prison librarian, would have strangled me. And my bosses would surely have scolded me. But I couldn't help it. It seemed cruel and unusual to offer music while demanding that people sit quietly (a clear sign, if one was needed, that I wasn't cut out for the librarian business). But still, this particular dance session was going a bit too far. I imposed a no-video punishment on the entire group for the rest of the evening.

The cool group of hookers regrouped, however, and exacted their revenge by relocating their party to the front counter. They demanded to know about my life. I told them to readjust their uniforms.

"Cut the shit, Avi," one of them said, folding her arms, tough-broad style, her bare midriff revealing a proud green shamrock, peeking out just over her underwear. I hadn't met this woman before and was taken aback that she knew both my name and how to pronounce it. And that I could see the tattoo on her thong-line.

"I know you're not married," she said. "But do you got yourself a cute little college girlfriend, or what?"

"Yeah, Halby," said another. "You got a wifey stashed back there?" She craned her neck and peered behind me, into my office.

Poor women. Forced in prison to live vicariously through the love life of a librarian. You may be a homeless heroin addict, you may be doing one of those unfortunate 125-year sentences, but surely this has got to be rock bottom.

"Fix your uniform," I said to the shamrock woman, trying hard to keep my gaze above her neck. "You trying to get me in trouble?"

"Maybe I am," she said, hands now on her hips, wielding her shamrock. "Unless you want to fess up."

I'm being shaken down by a brassy hooker, I thought with some amazement. In this moment of distraction, I lowered my gaze. All it took was a mere blink of the eyes.

"What're you looking at there, kid?" she said with a sly grin. This woman was a pro. She specialized in blinks. "You like that?"

I flipped my gaze over to the officers' post, outside of the library. Officer Malone had his attention elsewhere—more specifically, on a cute Boston College volunteer, whom he was merrily chatting up. Malone was acquainting her with the finer points of his walkie-talkie; he had her examining it.

I noticed Jessica making her way to the front counter. This was unusual. I'd seen her at the front counter once, but she had left after a minute, rolling her eyes at the endless jabbering. My initial impression of her as solitary, and that image of her in cold profile, had been borne out repeatedly. But that night she'd approached the counter with a rare smile on her face. She'd witnessed shamrock woman running circles around me. This apparently had enticed her to join the conversation.

"Yeah, Avi," Jessica said, as she placed herself at the counter. "You like girls?"

The crowd *oohed*, in accordance with the training they'd all received by daytime television.

"Damn, son," said another one of the mean-girl hookers, shaking her head at me. "You ain't gonna let her do you like *that*? You *got* to answer now."

The war of attrition on my male ego was now a concerted effort. Shamrock woman piped up. "*I* know he likes girls," she said.

Perhaps I was bored, or just a sucker for playing to a female audience, but I played along.

"I don't like girls," I said. "I like real, live American *women*."

A cheer went up from the assembled crowd. I immediately regretted my comment. Shamrock woman shot me a skeptical look.

"Tell us more!" came a hoarse little voice from the back.

"No, no," I said.

"C'mon, man," said the big bouncer lady, "you got a chick?"

I repeatedly invoked the fifth, an amendment with which these women were well acquainted. Unable to get me talking, the women proceeded to lecture me, about me. In the absence of any concrete facts about my life, the women instead adopted assumptions—challenging me to correct them—and then proceeded to voice strong opinions based on those assumptions. Perhaps they'd learned this tactic from cops.

"We *know* you got a girl," someone said.

"You got to marry her," one of hookers told me. "No offense, but don't be a pussy."

"No offense taken," I said.

"It's true," shamrock woman nodded gravely.

To my surprise, it was a position that adhered, in content if not in terminology, to my family's and former rabbis' view.

But that's where the similarity ended. What emerged from the next few minutes of conversation was that shamrock woman, who claimed to be an actress and high-priced prostitute, held three beliefs about marriage: 1) a man must marry or he's a pussy, 2) if the man doesn't also have extramarital affairs, he's a pussy, and 3) if he confuses these two things, he's a pussy.

According to her, a woman will love you if you propose and if you're a good husband/father, but she'll only respect you if you're the kind of guy who also gets some on the side. A hustler. (Of course, the wife wouldn't want to *know* about it . . .) There was a consensus of nods all around.

From the gallery one woman added, "Um-hm. That's on some *real* shit now."

"It ain't easy," I was told. "Most guys can't pull it off. But you want the truth? *That's* the truth."

I hadn't recalled asking for the truth.

"You got your work cut out for you, Avi," said Jessica.

"I don't think he can do it," the bouncer woman said.

"And another thing," said shamrock woman. "You *better* know how to please a woman. Do you know how to please a woman? 'Cause if you don't, that girly's out of there, believe me."

Again, I just made a face and glanced over at the guard's post. Officer Malone's lady friend was long gone. He was now staring at the ceiling. His walkie-talkie lay forlornly on his countertop.

"And *another* thing," said shamrock woman, who seemed to have an infinite store of these addendums. I braced myself.

"Fuckin' *Date Night*—you do Date Night with your lady, you're a confused little boy."

I probably looked perplexed, because she asked me, "You know what Date Night is? I hope not."

I told her I was familiar with the concept, yes.

"These girls here know what I'm talking about," said Shamrock. "Married guys come to you, and I'm talking regular clients, lawyers and businessmen and shit, kind of guys you probably went to college with, and they can't come to see me next Saturday night because," and now she switched into a tone of devastating mockery, "*that's Date Night.* Are you fuckin' *kidding* me?"

Her friends wailed in recognition.

"But lemme tell you something. These guys' *real* date night is with *me*, and with whatever other little thing they're chasing around. And that's the way it's supposed to be. You don't date your fuckin' wife, you fuckin' pussy."

"Is that what you tell them?" I asked.

"Not exactly," she said, lightening up a bit. "Not to a client. Unless of course I know he likes gettin' chewed out. Then I fuckin' tell him whatever I think."

It would have been easy to dismiss this shamrock-wielding woman's view as mere street cynicism. True, she may have had a skewed perspective—but it was hard to refute her contention that her clients, and their wives, also had a skewed perspective. Her opinion, at least, wasn't delusional. This woman worked in the trenches of marital warfare. She had something to say on the subject.

And to be honest, I agreed there was something awful about date night, and the entire *happy marriage* industry it represents. Every marriage propagandist seems to agree: the happy marriage requires "a lot of hard work." So, at the same time Americans are told that they work too hard, they're also enjoined to do more hard work. A lot of it. But who really wants to go home and begin a graveyard shift? Is it possible modern marriage requires so much hard work because it's a busted up and obsolete old machine? For all of Oprah's cant, her guides to Recession-Proofing Your Marriage, her enthusiastic advice to "Go Outside Yourself—*Often!*" one can't help wonder why people don't just follow Oprah's real approach, the one she herself follows: simply refrain from entering into the quagmire of wedlock to begin with. Why ruin a perfectly wonderful relationship by turning it into a marriage?

After the conversation in the library had ended—or rather, after

I had dispersed it—Jessica quietly approached the corner where I was shelving books. I could tell she had something to say. I figured it concerned the situation with her son. In a way, perhaps it did.

"I've been doing some thinking," she said. "You do have a girl-friend, don't you?"

"Yes," I said.

I was open because I knew and trusted her.

"You serious with her?"

"I am."

"So why don't you get married?" she asked.

I laid out my highly speculative cultural criticism. She cut me off somewhere during the Oprah oration.

"Awright," she said. "But at some point, when push comes to shove, remember what I'm telling you now: *it matters.*"

I shrugged. "I don't know—"

"That's right," she said. "You don't know. You got no idea what it's like to lose everything that matters to you, okay. I do. That's why I'm telling you."

I wasn't going to argue.

"I'm telling you this 'cause I know you listen. You take every-thing so serious. Too serious. I know. I can tell. So take this serious. And listen to what I'm telling you: *it matters.* Take a vow and mean it. Don't listen to those stupid bitches in my unit. Put it down on paper, sign that dotted line. Say it in front of your family and God—"

"I get the point," I said.

"I'm serious, Avi," she said. "Look at me, in my prison PJs. Why should you listen to me, right? It's true. I don't know nothing worth knowing—but that."

A few months later she was dead, the letter and drawing for her son ripped up and discarded. She had nothing left to say, and left no words of counsel, except those two: *it matters*. It had been the single piece of advice for which Jessica broke her silence. Perhaps she wanted urgently to convey this message to me because she knew she'd never deliver it, or anything, to her own son. Perhaps I was the only person available to receive her single scrap of wisdom.

But what had she meant by *it matters*. What matters? Why does it matter? I hadn't asked. Frankly, I hadn't wanted to know.

After Kayla's emotional outpouring the night of the mugging—the question of our relationship weighing heavily in the background—I couldn't fall asleep. Why had I thought it was a good idea to call her late at night, while she was alone hundreds of miles away, to tell her my "hilarious" story?

Male pride. Couldn't admit that I'd felt scared, that I'd just been in very real danger. I couldn't even admit it to myself. It took her sincere, emotional reaction to shake me into seeing, into feeling, what had actually just happened. I'd just encountered an armed, possibly intoxicated man. A knife-wielding ex-con with the upper hand and a motive to attack. It was not hard to imagine that this man might want to take revenge against a card-carrying agent of his imprisonment. I could have been hurt or killed. I'd decided to jump ahead, to use humor to deflect this discomfiting experience, to ignore the fact that my decision to work in prison had possibly just put my life in danger. My *life*.

Lying in bed, wide awake, I could see it. The mugger's knife. I could feel it. The chill of steel against my skin. The knife was inanimate, but the force behind it, the pressure of it, was not. That was alive. A human will, not my own, an outside agent whose motives were unknown to me. A stranger who could make the most important decision of my life. In that knife, I was given a hint of something more than fear. The sorrow of loss: for everything that my life could be, for me and for those who loved me, but wouldn't, if this man, by some inscrutable calculus, made that decision.

This was what Jessica had meant by *it matters*. There are things we don't control, decisions that are not ours to make—sometimes even the most important ones. For those we do control, Jessica had advice. *Sign the dotted line*, she'd said, *put it down on paper, take a vow, say it*. She wasn't evaluating the theory of modern marriage but was speaking to something primal. The need to protect one's most fragile possession, to put love into words, to commit those words to paper, to read them aloud, to store them for safekeeping.

This was something even a man with a knife could not take away—what Jessica herself, facing death, had tried but failed to accomplish for her son. As she had said to me, "You don't know, but I do." Life had imparted to her the knowledge of the knife. She'd tried to pass it on to me, but it took seeing the knife for myself to understand why *it matters*.

There had been something emotionally lacking in my attempt to spin the story to Kayla as a mere comedy. The more honest moment came in my impulse to call her. Instinctively I knew whom to call, even if I was confused about what needed to be said. But she was not. She wasn't afraid to bare her most vulnerable emotions. That was why I loved her, why I'd picked up the phone and dialed her number.

I turned on the reading light next to my bed. On a piece of paper I scribbled, *Listen to Jessica*, folded it up and stashed it in a book. Only then was I able to fall asleep.

Don't Know What

I wasn't able to say goodbye to Chudney in person. This was how it often went in prison: people seemed to appear and disappear at random. An inmate might think he was being discharged in a week or a month, only to get a knock on his cell at 5 a.m. and be told to pack it up immediately. Comings and goings happened at the whim of faceless, external forces. And it was usually in the interests of those forces to keep inmates, and nonessentials, in the dark.

Perhaps in anticipation of a sudden departure, Chudney wrote a note, which was delivered by his cellmate to the library. It was typed and formatted as a formal business letter.

Dear Avi,

Next time I write I WILL have good news. Don't know what it's gonna be but it's gonna be GOOD. I'm gonna start working construction or something soon and get in my applications. I got my plan. Pray for me. Just wanted to say THANK YOU THANK YOU THANK YOU!!!!! Here is a recipe. Don't steal it or I WILL find you.

He signed it:

Chudney Franklin © 2006

I waited for word from Chudney. It arrived one late-winter day. I was working with the library detail, entering books into our handy new database. Forest had just ordered Pitts to shelve books in the Gay section, as punishment for calling him "chunky" and for advising him, loudly and in front of a dozen inmates, to "get on that treadmill, man, get on it *immediately.*" The inmates and I were all very pleased with Forest's creative punishment—and in an odd way, it helped the inmate librarians warm up to the newly inaugurated Gay/Lesbian section.

When we announced the addition, they'd argued that it diminished the credibility of the library; though really, they felt it compromised their status among their fellow inmates.

"What are you trying to do to me, man?" Odum had pleaded during his brief stint on the library detail—Odum was let go after a few days when it was determined that not only was he incorrigibly lazy but he also didn't maintain a reliable grasp of the alphabet.

Everyone was having a good time heckling Pitts as he gingerly handled the gay books, mournfully reciting titles like, *Mondo Homo: Your Essential Guide to Queer Pop Culture* and *Talking Cock* while Fat Kat entered them into the database. Everyone, myself included, was thoroughly enjoying the spectacle.

Dice appeared from the back room and tapped me on the shoulder.

"I've been meaning to tell you," he whispered, "your friend from 3-1, the guy with all of the school applications—he got shot."

I was in the midst of laughing at Pitts and in the lightness of the moment, Dice's words didn't register.

"What?" I said, still smiling.

He repeated himself.

Officially Gay, I heard Pitts recite. The inmates burst out into a fresh peal of laughter.

Now the words settled into my mind. *He got shot. Chudney was shot.*

"I heard you the first time," I said.

"I'm sorry, Avi. That's some fucked-up shit, man. I know."

"Is he dead?"

"Yeah."

Queer Theory: An Introduction, Pitts bellowed, to more catcalls. "What the fuck—they got *theories* now?"

I became suddenly exasperated at the inmates' loud, crude laughter. I told Pitts that he was done, and retreated into my office.

CHAPTER 4

Delivered

There are various reasons to cry in prison.

Crying as initiation rite. Dice claimed that any inmate who tells you he didn't cry when he first came to prison is a liar. As he said this, the three inmates standing around us nodded. One of them confessed he was so stressed his first day in prison he could hardly breathe. When he heard the door of the cell bolt shut for the night, he panicked and began pacing, beating on the door and shouting.

"It's hard to explain it," he said. "It's not like I wanted out. I just wanted the door unlocked. Just knowing that the door was locked made me freak out. I'd never been locked in." His cellmate was an old guy who took pity on him. "He just said to me, 'Get into bed, son. Let yourself cry. There ain't no shame in that. Just do it, and then you'll be done with it.' And so that's what I did."

Thus he joined the club.

Bored to tears. A woman inmate told me this can literally happen.

Crying as a nightly sleep aid. "You can ignore shit during the day," a woman inmate told me, "you can just go about your business, pretend this is normal. But in bed at night, you do a lot of thinking." The only way to stop the thoughts and fall asleep is to give in and cry. She laughed and said that she'd developed the same habit as her baby daughter. "I can't fall asleep without crying first."

Crying to mark a season. "I cry every Christmas, Easter, birthdays, you name it," Jessica had once said. She thought she would cry on these days even when she got out. "This place gets you pretty well-trained."

Crying on cue. Prison life is full of Oscar-worthy moments. Some inmates become proficient at crying miserably at will, a skill they employ at various crucial moments: in court, in caseworkers' offices, to officers, to the parole board, to the prison librarian. A prison teacher who got fooled by one of these actors came to the library just to tell me the story. "I've been doing this for a long time now," she'd said, "I'm pretty hard to fool. This guy was *good*."

And just what is a good fake cry? The teacher explained: a professional sobber will:

a.   generate real tears, not simply bury his face and begin heaving
b.   not overdo it by moaning and wailing and the like
c.   not just begin sobbing but rather "try to hold it in," until, finally, he is simply overcome. This the Academy loves.

In defense of crying on cue, Martha the gossip explained that she legitimately cried all the time, but no one was there to see it. So when she fake cried, she was just showing a person something they weren't around to see for real. Her tears were a replica, not counterfeit.

"And once I get going," she said, "I feel it for real."

"But," I asked, "you are crying in order to get something from someone, right?"

"Well, yeah," she conceded.

Crying when it rains. "Just seems like the thing to do," a suggestible woman inmate told me.

Crying in your office. After Dice informed me of Chudney's death, I sat down at my desk and composed an email to my former obituary editor at the *Boston Globe*. For some reason, this had been my first reaction.

"I have an interesting, slightly unusual candidate for an obit," it began. I saved the email in my Draft folder.

Later, during my dinner break, I called the editor to make the pitch. He didn't respond immediately. I heard some typing. Then I heard him mutter, "yeah, hmm." He politely declined the obit.

"Looks like we already ran a piece on this story," he said.

He read the headline. Yes, he said, he remembered this article: local man shot, some vague details, a five-year-old boy left without a father, police investigating. I had read it, too.

Forced to make some small talk, the editor paused.

"How's, um, prison," he asked with a touch of irony.

"Fine," I said, suddenly regretting that I had made this call.

"See any *crazy* prison stuff?"

But before I could answer, he excused himself to take an urgent call. I was relieved to say goodbye.

After I hung up the phone, I Googled Chudney. There were exactly two hits. Twins, as it turned out: a notice of the murder on the Boston Police Department's website and the *Globe* article. *We already ran a piece on this story*, the editor had said. I focused on that phrase—*this story*. What, after all, was *this story*, the story of Chudney? To a coldly pragmatic newspaper editor, the answer was clear. The story *Globe* readers needed to read was the story of this person's murder, not of his life. Perhaps it was the correct editorial decision.

In writing obituaries for the *Globe* I always tried to include the subject's voice. I would try to read something he or she wrote—a letter, novel, essay, book, poem—and quote it in the story. For some reason, a recently deceased person's voice takes on strange properties. His words are finite and instantly more valuable. Sometimes they take on completely new meanings. This was certainly true of Chudney's last kite to me: *Next time I write I WILL have good news. Don't know what it's gonna be but it's gonna be GOOD.*

I looked at the doleful Google search page: two hits, one story. *This story*, the story of the murder, would be his story. That's it. There would be nothing else.

I got up and did something I hated to do. I locked the library. I did it instinctively, perhaps as a protest, a small labor strike. And then I continued shutting things down. In my office, I turned off the light. Locked my door. Exited the Google search page. Turned off the glaring monitor. Then I closed my eyes and was initiated into an ancient club: those who cry alone in the darkness of prison.

Stories on Walls

I walked into the prison Friday morning for the early shift with a copy of *Newjack* by Ted Conover tucked under my arm. The moment I'd discovered it in a used book store, I knew it had a place in the library. In the book, Conover, a journalist, tells the story of his year working as an officer in Sing Sing. As I walked through the sally-port, the long hallway, and the yard, I got all kinds of reactions to the book from passing officers. Some smiled, some gave me a wink or a thumbs up. More than one asked to borrow it. A few officers gave me dirty looks—though these particular guys always gave me dirty looks, so I didn't read anything into it.

When I caught a member of the Angry Seven looking at the book as I paused to unlock the library I seized the moment to reach out and resolve our lingering hostilities.

"It's the story of a year in the life of a CO in Sing Sing," I said. "It's supposed to be pretty good. Want to read it? I'll lend it to you, if you want."

He looked at me in disgust.

"Why the hell would I want to read about *that*?" he said.

As I walked into the dark library and flipped the light switch, letting loose a wave of fluorescence, I considered his point. Why the hell would an officer want to read about those things he knew so well? All too well. The stuff that had vexed him day in and day out for the last twenty years? Getting feces thrown at you, being cursed out, twisting your ankle and not getting enough time off to recover, not being able to afford living in the city in which you're a public servant. This was the last story he wanted to hear.

But I suspected that many officers were interested in the book for precisely that reason. For them, telling their story was essential. For many officers in South Bay, Sgt. Richard "Ricky" Dever, a colleague of theirs, was the hero of that story.

One night in late March, Dever had intervened in a bar fight. It was shortly after midnight at Sullivan's Pub in Charlestown. A drunk, abusive man named Francis X. "Kicka" Lang, recently released from prison, was making a big scene and harassing a bartender, a friend of Dever's. Lang was told to leave. Dever, trained to deal with violent assholes, gave the man an ultimatum, then escorted him to the door. Outside, Lang became enraged. Soon they were scuffling. Lang pulled out a knife and slashed Ricky's face. Then stabbed him repeatedly. Then bolted. Ricky staggered back into the bar. He was taken to Mass General. Shortly after 1 a.m., he was dead. The next day, police found Lang hiding in a basement crawlspace.

When I learned about Ricky's murder, I immediately thought of my own encounter with a knife-wielding ex-con. The officers, too, had their own personal take on it.

A veteran officer summarized it to me thus. "Ricky was a CO; the bastard who killed him was a con. Far as I'm concerned, it don't matter if neither of them was wearing their uniform. That's what it was: a good guy officer versus a shitbag."

Their confrontation could very well have been the resolution of an old prison beef. But it made no difference if it was or not. To them, Dever was the good cop, doing the right thing; Lang was a worthless con, a coward who would savagely kill another human being over the pettiest issue. Ricky had principles, Lang did not. There was no disputing that.

For a group of soldiers doing a dangerous, underpaid job—a line of work so routinely disparaged in society that some officers tell strangers that they "work for the city" or the state—this murder carried a great deal of meaning. The experience of victimhood cut to the core of their professional identities. They do right, toil and suffer, only to get shit on by society. It was unjust.

After Kicka Lang was handed his life sentence without parole, the harshest sentence in the state, a courtroom packed to capacity with Dever's family, friends, and hundreds of fellow officers erupted in cheers and applause. Given a chance to speak, a bespectacled Lang smiled broadly and was quoted as saying, "What I got is still better than what Ricky got." These remarkably inflammatory comments, unusual even for a murderer—and possibly indicative of clinical psychosis—made blaring front page headlines in the *Boston Herald*: Twisted Killer Taunts Victim's Family in Court.

As one enraged officer put it to me, "It was like a perfect ad for the death penalty. I mean this guy is Satan, for crissakes. No kidding. It sent shivers down my spine."

The *Herald* article featured a photograph of an off-duty prison officer jumping out of his courtroom seat, pumping his fist in celebration of the life sentence. But, even amid the feeling of vindication, none of the officers forgot what the murderer's statement had implied.

"What I got is still better than what Ricky got"—in other words, that life in prison is better than death. Some officers took this comment as something of a challenge.

An officer in the prison cafeteria told me that if Lang was under the impression that he had a fate better than death, he'd find out the truth soon enough: "The COs over there will give him what he fuckin' deserves. You can be sure of that," he told me, as we waited in line. "And I know guys in here who wish they could help out with that themselves."

The prison organized a giant memorial for Dever. It was held in the inmate visiting area, which doubled as an auditorium. The same space where, months earlier, the entire prison staff had been warned against behaving like Miller, the teacher who'd aided an inmate in disposing of a weapon—the meeting in which we were told to honor the two names on our ID cards: ours and the sheriff's.

Dever's prison memorial was a dizzying array of lapel pins. The visiting area was filled with people from all strata of local politics. City pols in fire-sale suits, state officials wearing imports. Full refreshments, fruit platters, veggies with ranch dressing, cheap diced cheese, cookies, brownies, coffee. The honor guard was present. Union heads, representatives of city and state cop outfits. Prison guards in dress uniforms. You could identify the members of Dever's family by the grim expressions of the people speaking to them.

I thought of Chudney's memorial. It had taken place months earlier during a poetry reading I'd held in the library. These open-mic-style events were often used by inmates as an improvisational platform to memorialize various people, friends and relatives, whose funerals they were unable to attend. Dumayne had stood up and offered a tearful eulogy for Chudney, his friend from childhood. "We all know you had big dreams, brother," he'd said. "We all know you wasn't able to finish your work here. There was stuff you wasn't able to accomplish in this world. Big cuz, I know you in heaven. I know you hear me when I say: I promise to be a better man because of the example you gave me. I promise to use my gift of life to finish some of your work. And I'm gonna take these words," he concluded, shakily holding up the paper from which he read, "and I'm gonna tape them to my wall, so I don't never forget." He ended by reading a poem Chudney had liked, something we'd read in class.

Speaking at the official prison dais, an officer told the story of how Dever was the only person in the prison infirmary, which had been his post, who'd been able to calm a certain terrified inmate. He'd established a rapport with her; she'd trusted only him. And he gained her faith, said the officer, "by speaking to her as a person, human heart to human heart."

All around the visiting area, fellow officers were nodding their heads. This was a rare opportunity to be known and understood on their own terms. The telling of this story was made a permanent prison fixture, nailed directly onto the institution's walls: the sign outside of the infirmary would now read, This Place of Medical Care and Healing is Dedicated to the Memory of Sergeant Richard T. Dever. This would be followed by a quotation from Andrew Jackson: "One man with courage makes a majority."

In his concluding remarks, the speaker offered his interpretation of the new sign. It wasn't remarkable, he said, for an officer to run into harm's way to break up a fight, as Dever had done that night at Sully's. That after all was his job, his training. But for him to find a way to be compassionate in an environment like prison, that was courage.

An Epi-Prologue

I revisited the C.C. Too Sweet question. To find compassion for someone guilty of C.C.'s crimes truly did demand some act of courage. A type of bravery I hadn't been able to muster, and had indeed tried to escape.

For a while, I'd been uneasy with how things had ended. We'd had a productive working relationship, a rapport. I'd become familiar with his story, his quirks, those things that draw people together in sympathy. I'd helped him find a picture of Nemo, the cartoon fish, so that he could design a birthday card for his five-year-old son. I knew too much about his life to simply dismiss him. Even though he'd committed some scumbag crimes, I wished him the best. In fact, I wished him the best precisely because he had done those things. He needed it more than most.

And I was still rooting for him to figure things out. His book, at least the parts I'd seen, were truly gripping. He had a valuable story to tell. I didn't want him to think I was trying to undermine his extraordinary resolve to see it through — but there was no way for me to explain my hesitations to him without making things worse.

At first, C.C. seemed to be doing just fine for himself. I watched as he set up a literary shop, standing with his arms crossed managerially, while two cornrowed young recruits simultaneously typed different parts of his manuscript. But soon his editorial process fell into the mire. Instead of revising and rewriting, he busied himself with trifles: choosing a pretty computer font, designing a book cover (maps, maps, and more maps). This was all an amateurish waste of time.

But it was the issue of the floppy disk that finally swayed me. Ever since our relationship had soured, he'd refused to use the disk I had stored in my office and which I'd been backing up. He now kept a contraband disk stashed in his Legal Materials folder, an infraction to which I turned a blind eye. It killed me that all of his work lived solely on this one terrifyingly unreliable disk. I begged him to let me back it up in some other way. He had refused. It was a matter of pride.

This had gone too far. C.C. Too Sweet was many things, including many extremely bad things, but he was earnestly trying to tell his story. It was a legal endeavor, and a worthy project. This wasn't a "tell-all"—it was a serious account of his life. Perhaps in telling his story he'd redeem that story. But even if he didn't, perhaps I still had a duty to help him try.

It wasn't my job to judge his past. For this, there were attorneys, judges, juries. If he wanted to do something creative, perhaps it was not only permissible for me to help, but actually my duty. After all, as the great Officer Chuzzlewit had said, this wasn't the Quincy Public Library. It was a *prison* library, the library for the bad guys. The beauty of this job, if there was beauty, was in giving people like C.C. a shot to do something right and do it well. To remind them that they're more than criminals, if they choose to be. In practice, this turns out to be harder and more complicated than it sounds.

When we first met I had asked why he wrote with such fervor. He didn't think for a second.

"The truth?" he'd said, leaning in close and whispering. "It's because I'm homeless."

That wasn't pimp talk. He'd whispered because he didn't want the other inmates to hear. This writing stuff wasn't a hobby for C.C. It was serious business. I decided to act, to do something I had been trained never to do in prison: apologize to an inmate. When I did, C.C. remained standoffish until I offered to write a prologue for his book. Before things between us had soured, this had been something he'd asked me to do for him—though he'd never straightened out the difference between a prologue and an epilogue. The prologue would be my small act of Dever-like prison courage, to attach my name to C.C.'s project.

The next week, when I handed him the prologue, which was really a glowing blurb, his face lit up. It seemed as though he wanted to jump over the counter and hug me. I wasn't expecting this sort of reaction. He read it again; then again, aloud.

"Thank you, man," he said.

There was a sincerity in how he said it that prodded my attention. It was like he was speaking in a different voice altogether. There was nothing Too Sweet about it.

"It was nothing," I said. And it really wasn't all that big a deal. The path of privilege, which I had treaded, was paved with bombastic recommendation letters. It was a pittance at this point. What actual difference, after all, did my blurb make? To what end, exactly?

"No, man. It really means a lot to me. I'm gonna show this to my mother."

Now he had my attention. After everything that had happened in his life, the abuse and the nasty crimes, perpetrated by and against him, the years hustling on the street, the homelessness, the lifetime in prison, it all came down to a simple thing: a good review. Possibly his first ever, possibly his last. All of it—the bogus talk of book deals, his fame, the constant macho posturing—it all amounted to a short, slightly balding guy wanting the approval of his momma. He was still that kid lying on the grimy hallway floor of the projects hoping his mother would appear and take him back gently into their home.

Prison Yard Lighting: A Queer Theory

It's odd to speak of outcasts in prison. Inmates live on the fringe of society. They are all, by definition, outcasts. But within the closed society of prison itself, there was mainstream, and then there was the fringe. The outcasts of the outcasts.

Katy was one of the more obvious examples. She was the coolest chick in Unit 3-2. She was also the only chick in 3-2. And technically she wasn't a chick. But she was part of 3-2 and would roll into the library, together with her fellow inmates in tan—uniform pants rolled up rakishly at her ankle—walk up to the front counter, comb her luxuriant locks from her face, and flash a weary half smile.

Dread seized the inmate librarians. It was palpable. Teddy, the young Muslim convert, crossed his arms and scowled through his beard. Stix looked at the ground and giggled. Pitts actually backed away slowly, as though beholding the glory of the Archangel Gabriel. Schofield, a library regular, smiled stupidly, a clear attempt to be affable, but he straightened his spine and puffed his chest out, as though trying to scare away a mountain lion. As usual, Fat Kat kept his face planted in a car magazine and just shook his head. Not in disapproval—though he did disapprove—but rather in neutrality.

The only inmate librarian who acted civil was Dice.

"What can I do for you today?" he asked her, with a smile.

Later Dice explained his attitude to me.

"Man, I was educated on Forty-second Street in New York in the 1970s," he said, his sunglasses flashing. "I've seen it all."

What Dice saw, or did not see, was of ongoing interest to me. With those sunglasses, and a slight migration of gaze when he spoke, he had the distinct mien of a blind man. Was he in fact blind? I sometimes wondered. Mostly I wondered how he'd managed to get sunglasses in prison.

"Those were some crazy times," Dice continued. "In my opinion, that's when New York was New York. I'll tell you what though, some of the best people I met on the street there was the transvestites, man. I ain't afraid to say that. These young guys here don't know shit about the world."

There seemed to be a generational divide on the question of Katy. Ironically, it was the elders who were more accepting. Boat, too, didn't seem the least bit put off. On the contrary.

"Toughest motherfuckers I met in the joint were the queers," he told me. "Fuckin' guys gotta be tough, you know? I knew this queer guy in Leavenworth. I'm talking *queer*. Didn't make no bones about it. You said something wrong to him, though, *Boom!* He'd fuckin' gut you. I got nothing but respect, nothing but."

Boat told me that the toughest motherfucker in South Bay was a queer. He'd introduce me. The next week, Brian showed up in the library. He was an intriguing character. By his own modest admission, Brian was "fuckin' *smaht*." With his cocky intelligence, his brash accent, and lapsed altar boy persona, he was the kind of wounded, tough Boston Irish kid Matt Damon has made famous. Brian was the son of a crooked Statie, and was full of self-serving stories about police corruption. He was also a tank. Probably about six foot three and solidly built. Giant hands. He was definitely not someone even a prison tough guy would cross.

Brian was more or less openly gay. Standing at the library counter, he told me, with a sly grin, that he'd seen a couple of prison guards in "my kind of club." When he said this, inmate eyebrows in the vicinity raised.

"I should probably watch myself," he said to me, without lowering his voice. He was, in fact, slowly raising his voice. "I'm not in hiding, you know, but I don't get much by advertising it, either. Especially with all the ignorant *fucks* in this place."

The inmates standing around regarded this comment for what it was: an open threat. Teddy didn't cross his arms and glare, Pitts didn't cower. Stix didn't giggle. Everyone just pretended not to hear. Brian smiled smugly.

Katy wasn't a hardass like Brian. At least that wasn't her persona. (I wouldn't tangle with her, though.) She wasn't a mean queer, but an old-fashioned queen.

And as a queen, she had a predilection for royalty. She was making her way through our small collection of books on the late Princess Diana. Every few days, she'd give me updates on the saga: the fairy tale courtship, divine wedding, the saintliness, the betrayals, the martyrdom.

After three books, Katy had all but tapped the library's Princess Di collection. I tried to meet her needs for a couple more weeks by pawning off books on other female monarchs in history. Mary Queen of Scots, Cleopatra, Isabella of Spain. But it wasn't the same. She wanted more Di. Needed more Di.

I looked for other titles of potential interest. The only thing I could rustle up was the autobiography of Shirley MacLaine. When I presented her with the book, she just looked at me and said, "Omigod, are you serious?" and then, catching herself, "I mean, that's *really* sweet of you, but puhleeze."

Instead she gathered a pile of women's magazines and went to the table, took a seat next to a couple of gangbangers, tossed her hair back, and started flipping through the glossies. The guys exchanged quick glances but went back to their own reading.

"Nobody talks to me," she confided to me once. "Not a word. But I guess I should be happy about it, 'cause I probably don't want to know what they're thinking."

Unlike most of the inmates, Katy's problem wasn't direct conflict, but extreme loneliness.

There was a more literal version of this prison-within-a-prison. One night, at about 10 p.m., after I'd lingered an hour or so after the end of my shift, I encountered it. As I walked out of the 3-Building, I saw a large group of inmates lining the prison yard. They were wearing gray uniforms. In over a year working in prison

I had seen exactly one inmate wearing a gray uniform. Now I saw probably sixty, standing in a line, shoulder to shoulder. There was something disturbing about this group. For a moment I paused to figure it out.

The men themselves seemed deeply unsettled. Under the brilliant stadium lights, some stared, bug-eyed and unblinking. Haunted. Some wrung their hands. Most of the men stood, shrinking, as though naked and cornered. A few shielded their faces with their arms or retracted their heads into their uniform tops, turtle style. A few mumbled to themselves, giggled, snickered, twitched. At the tail of the group, like a punctuation mark at the end of a long and bizarre sentence, a tiny sullen bald man held a basketball under his arm.

I'd heard about this unit. They were the inmates of the Protective Custody (PC) unit: the homos, snitches, psychos, and pedophiles. The outcasts of the outcasts, the freaks of prison, the queers of the queers. The inmates that the prison mainstream, criminals all, considered criminals. These men were—sometimes by choice, often not—kept completely separate from the rest of the prison population. This was done for everyone's safety. Katy and Brian were given the option of joining this prison unit, if they felt threatened.

Rarely did the inmates of PC ever emerge from their unit on the fifth floor of the Tower. Among inmates of the general population, a sighting of a PC freak held a nearly sacred significance. Once in a while, a PC inmate gained special permission to visit the library. When he did, all of the other inmates would be evacuated, though they'd try to linger for a moment, to catch a view of the mythical gray creature. Afterward they'd shower me with questions: *What was he like? What did he say? What did he look like? How did he seem? Did he try to touch you? Was he a total freak?*

The one man in gray I met was, in fact, rather disturbed. He had visited the library to do some legal work. After photocopying dozens of cases and laws, he told me, "I'm gonna nail the prosecution." With great care, he produced a document and asked me to photocopy it. It would, he told me, clinch his case, prove conclusively that a "lizard overlord" had arrived on Earth and, with the help of the CIA, quietly overthrown the U.S. government.

I glanced at the sheet. To his credit, the document, a printout from a website, did indeed say just that. I asked him how this was going to help his case. He sighed and gave me an exasperated look, like I was the most incorrigibly naïve person he'd ever met. "'Cause they don't got jurisdiction to try me if the Constitution and the government is controlled by a lizard." It was a logical argument, if somewhat misinformed.

Now here they all were, the entire gray ensemble, standing in the expanse of the prison yard, exposed to all. The curtain dramatically lifted. They were poised to play the most charged game of basketball since the infamous 1972 U.S.-USSR Olympic gold medal match. Under the heavy glare of the yard's stadium lights, it almost seemed as though that were the purpose: to place these men on center stage.

I looked behind me at the giant wall of cell windows, and up at the women's tower. Out of habit, my eye tended toward the eleventh floor, to the window from which Jessica used to watch her son in the yard. Jessica's window, a classroom window, was now dark. It belonged to the world of the daytime, to the concerns of business hours—but now it was night, afterhours.

The inmates' personal cell windows were all lit. Each had a silhouette or two or three in it. In the windows closer to the ground, it was easier to see the inmates pointing, laughing, glaring, watching with curiosity. Within a few minutes, word was out over the entire prison. *Every* inmate with a yard-facing cell, man and woman, was now standing at his or her window. The galleries were packed full. Inmates who didn't have a view would get detailed reports later. The PC inmates down in the prison yard could see plainly that they were being watched, discussed, reviewed, mocked.

This was a peculiarity of prison architecture. The late-eighteenth-century prison of Santo Stefano, near Naples, Italy, was constructed in a multitiered horseshoe shape, an architectural scheme borrowed directly from the theaters of that period. But that blueprint was only the most obvious example of a general phenomenon: Prisons are designed for optimal viewing, a security imperative that occasionally produces accidental live theater performances.

And this was one. It was a rare example of a collective experience in prison. The inmate general population, as one, was viewing a prison freak show under the blazing stadium lights, a spectacle that probably allowed them, as the audience, to feel less like freaks themselves.

As the painfully awkward basketball game commenced, I made my way along the edge of the yard—the last sight I caught, looking back over my shoulder, was a group of inmates in the 3-1 Unit, standing in a cell window literally falling on each other in laughter. This wasn't like Jessica, whose window gazing was an intensely private experience—and one that further locked her into her own loneliness. The PC freak show was something else. It was a cruel bonding experience for the inmate majority. A unique opportunity for inmates to look out of prison windows and feel better about their lot.

The prison's queers, the Brians and the Katys, are given the option to join this stage show. Or to be in the audience.

The next day I decided to put a Princess Di biography, and

other more directly gay books, on prominent display. My friend and coworker, Mary Beth, had told me of an inmate from 1-2-1 who had fashioned a skirt out of a towel during count time and pranced around like Josephine Baker, batting his eyes, pursing his lips, sidling up to inmates and officers alike. Everyone thought this was a hilarious act.

Later, when this young man came down to the library, I told him that news of his antics had made the rounds. I asked him if he was a performer.

"Nah, man, it was just a joke, you know to keep things light," he smiled.

Uninterested in my new display, he checked out an old battered copy of *The Shining* by Stephen King. Then he winked at me and went on his way.

The Narrow Place

One of the oddest people I met, the one who least fit in, was the most familiar. I first met Josh Schrieber during the library's 3:30 period, one wet and overcast afternoon. In our constant effort to lure inmates to the library we were screening *Superman II*.

I noticed him immediately. He had the appearance and demeanor that my grandmother would approvingly call *eidel*, Yiddish for *gentle*. A trim and gregarious twentysomething, boyishly handsome, close-cropped curly brown hair, and plastic-framed glasses. He reminded me of every boy from my yeshivas and Orthodox summer camps. In fact, he bore such a close resemblance to a certain kid from my yeshiva high school, in nearby Brookline, I wondered if perhaps they were related. It wasn't every day that a guy who looked like Josh Schrieber walked into the library. I was intrigued.

When the period ended and the inmates came to the front desk to collect their IDs, I couldn't help myself.

"Hey," I said, taking a look at his ID. "You know what *Superman* is *really* about?"

He smiled and shook his head.

"It was created by two Jewish guys from Cleveland. It's about how even a skinny neurotic with glasses can be a total badass sometimes. You with me on this one, Schrieber?" I said as I handed him his ID.

"Yeah, I'm with you."

It wasn't the right thing to say. I'd outted him. I shouldn't have said it in front of the other inmates. It had made him wince.

Later I asked Mary Beth, who worked in the prison's Offender Reentry Program, which was based in Schrieber's unit, "So who's the Jewboy in 1-2-1?"

She knew exactly who I was talking about and briefed me on his background. From the western suburbs. Into some bad stuff. Heroin. He was in for larcenies and breaking and entry, common charges for cash-strapped addicts. Within the month he would be wrapping up his bid to the streets, meaning he was being released, on probation, but left to his own devices. No halfway house or sober home.

She told me that he was a very friendly kid who got along well with everyone. A bit too well. Desperately eager to please, Schrieber carried out every order with conspicuous diligence. Never lingered when told to lock-in, never gave anyone any problems. Seizing on Schrieber's obedience—and sensing that he was different and without allies—a certain officer, had decided to take advantage of the situation.

In the presence of his fellow inmates, the officer had deputized Schrieber, bestowing on him the dubious honor of serving as the officer's sidekick. This meant doing tasks—tasks that were the job of the officer alone—such as summoning inmates from their cells, even aiding with lockdowns. Schrieber was caught in a no-win situation. He was too cowed to defy the officer. But, by following these particular orders, he was severely compromised among fellow inmates who could turn violent on him.

He'd been tenuously accepted by the white guys in his unit. By these semi-friends, he was routinely called, "the Jew," to remind him of his place. He wasn't a total pushover, but he also wasn't an Italian or Irish tough guy from the inner city. He was permitted entrance as a guest, but only by his strained effort to pass. Now, with his new deputy honor, he'd be officially isolated, and put in danger. Everyone would assume that Schrieber was not only a Jew lackey but a snitch.

This was the last thing Schrieber needed. He could get severely beaten or stabbed; once he hit the street it could mean getting shot. Indeed, it wasn't long before a fellow inmate turned hostile on him. He and the other inmate had to be separated to avoid a battle. His list of enemies, which is officially called "the keep separate from" list, was five names long, a high number.

I felt bad for Schrieber. He needed some allies. The next time I visited the 1-2-1 unit, I called on him. He seemed surprised to see me out of the library. I introduced myself.

"I hear you're a brutha," I whispered.

He smiled. "Yeah," he said.

I told him about my background, that I had been raised Orthodox and attended yeshiva in Israel. I told him that it was a good idea to roll with the Irish and Italian guys, but if he ever wanted to keep it real, he should come to the library some time and talk. I added the infamous Jewish nudge: "No pressure."

We agreed to meet. He seemed genuinely interested—though, of course, he was a pleaser.

But before we had a chance, he was released. I happened to have been passing through the prison's front lobby at the moment he was walking out to freedom. He was dressed in his street clothes, a sweater and jeans and a black leather jacket. We chatted for a moment. I wished him good luck. Just then, his ride showed up.

I knew this guy. He was a former inmate from 1-2-1, a junkie who used to steal newspapers from the library. It had been a running joke with him (I found it less funny). In the lobby he gave me a big, toothless grin. "Hey, Avi, got any Revere Journals fa' me?" he asked.

"Nothing changes, hey Hescock?" I replied.

It was all perfectly clear to me. Schrieber, despite what he had told Mary Beth and his mentors in the reentry program, was on his way to get high with his old buddy from 1-2-1. A little junk to celebrate getting out of the joint. I wanted to shake him. But instead I leaned in and said, "Avoid bad friends, it's the only way, Josh. Or you're going to end up dead—or, if you're lucky, back in this shithole."

I would never have spoken this frankly to an inmate when I first started my job. At this point, however, I felt not only able, but responsible to say such things. I'd officially turned into a tough-love prison-mentor type. He looked down at the floor. And that was it. He and Hescock went out together into the darkness.

Schrieber got lucky. A month later, he was back in prison. I was frankly surprised it took that long. That week, I visited him and arranged a meeting. He wanted to study Jewish texts, he said. He started with a question.

Why does the Jewish tradition require mourners to cover the mirrors in their house during the shiva?

A random query, but an interesting one. As a yeshiva-boy-cum-obituary-writer, I felt uniquely qualified to answer it. It is a strange custom and there was no obvious answer. I told him that there were undoubtedly some deep-seated folk fears regarding mirror images — especially in a house of mourning, which already has ghosts swirling around it. Mirrors exacerbate these anxieties.

But there was also a more directly psychological reason: to focus the attention of the mourners away from the world of appearances and into their thoughts, their memories, their souls, their mortality. They are not to concern themselves with the mundane during the shiva. Every worldly issue is handled by a friend. For seven days they inhabit an internal space and need not be concerned with their hair looking perfect. Or if their ass is too big.

Schrieber asked about the Passover Seder, which was imminent. I told him that to understand what leaving Egypt means to Jews, you have to know what the word *Egypt* means. In Hebrew it's *Mitzrayim*, which the rabbis interpreted, as usual, through a pun: it means the Narrow Space (*meitzar*). It's not a specific country that existed in the Iron Age or a historical event that may or (more likely) may not have happened. It's a state of mind.

"You know what I'm talking about, right?" I asked Josh. "*The Narrow Space*: You know all about it. It's a very hard thing to break out of. It's as hard as a miracle. But it can be done."

Ever since he was a kid, Josh told me, he had identified with the legendary second-century sage, Rabbi Akiva, particularly the story of the great rabbi's dramatic martyrdom.

This startled me. I'm not a shrink, but when an imprisoned heroin addict tells you that his hero in life is a righteous man who was arrested and thrown in prison, where his skin was flayed (meaning, peeled off layer by layer using red-hot irons), one gets to wondering.

What did Josh see in a man who refused to renounce his God even as he underwent torture?

Surely having a Rabbi Akiva–complex might be a sign that a person expects, perhaps hopes, to die soon. Considered alongside his question regarding mirrors in the house of mourning, it was all grimly revealing. This was a man, aged twenty-nine, deliberating over his own imminent death.

Something about Schrieber really got me. I felt a strong urge to watch out for him. A part of me felt guilty for these feelings. Why should Schrieber elicit any more sympathy than any other inmate? He, of all inmates, was lucky. Although deeply mired in addiction, he did have a loving family who cared for him. He spoke of them often. He had role models, knew what a stable life looked like. He wasn't an orphan of the streets like so many other inmates.

But I couldn't help it. We were roughly the same age. His sister and mine shared the same unusual Hebrew name. He grew up in a suburban community like mine, with the same expectations. The accent, the humor, the cultural references, the hangups were very familiar to me.

But there was something else about Josh that gave me pause. At my friend's wedding roughly two years earlier, my run-in with Rabbi Blumenthal had inspired me, half in jest, to consult the prophets regarding my decision to work in prison. It had occurred to me that many of the prophets were either criminals, or prisoners, or had spent time among criminals. It had seemed mysteriously significant.

Now, I couldn't help but wonder if it was related to this uncomfortable familiarity I felt with Josh. The prophets crossed the boundary into the realm of the criminal not to comfort themselves by discovering the essential humanity of the criminal—in that Hollywood way of ennobling the prisoner, of dramatizing how *they're just like us* — but rather to unveil the essential criminal in the human. To expose a darker truth: *We're just like them.* When the prophets crossed over, they discovered just how familiar it looked, how much it resembled the world of the supposedly upright.

Wasn't this the unsettling truth behind the theater spectacle that night in the prison yard? The prison mainstream got more than mere cruel pleasure in watching their own outcasts from the Protective Custody unit dramatically exposed under the lights; it allowed them to feel self-righteous. To feel less like outcasts themselves. Even criminals look for ways to conveniently distance themselves from criminals. When I looked at Josh, his face, his life, I wasn't able to conveniently distance myself.

Josh told me that he had been the quintessential "good Jewish boy." Everyone had loved him, all the community ladies wanted to set up their daughters with him. "I was a good catch," he said with a little laugh. The one problem: his secret hobby. Once he tried heroin in college, that was it. For a while he led a double life.

"At first," he said, "I was a put-together college guy. I was dating this great girl. A beautiful girl."

She'd had no idea that he was a dope fiend, until one night, when his secret spilled out. Literally. On a date, he excused himself to the bathroom, for a quick, surreptitious shooting session. Upon returning to the table, the girl stared at him as though she were beholding the devil. Her expression terrified him — recalling it still spooked him. This was his nightmare: to be recognized, exposed. He looked down and saw blood trickling out of the puncture wound on his arm. Right there, at the table.

That night, he lost more than the girl. The shame of that experience threw him into a crisis. "It changed everything," he told me. From then on, he no longer saw himself as Josh, from the Schrieber family, son, grandchild, friend, neighbor.

"When I made that decision," he said, "that I was no longer a part of that community, that I had let everyone down so fuckin' hard, that I literally wasn't that person they thought I was. That this was *who* I was. Who I *really* was: I wasn't Josh, I was a fuckin' dope fiend. When I made that decision, it was over. I became that person completely. I went from living a relatively normal life to fuckin' living in abandoned buildings downtown. Within one week, Avi."

He was crying now.

"Josh," I said, "it's true that you made that decision then, but listen to what you said: You made a decision. That means you have the *power* to make decisions. And that you can make other decisions now."

I wasn't sure whether this was a helpful or really idiotic thing to say.

Josh suddenly bolted up with an odd, slightly terrifying, fake smile plastered on his face.

"Hey," he said, adopting an upbeat, sporting tone, "did you see what Francona said yesterday?"

He was referring to Red Sox manager, Terry Francona.

"Um, no," I replied. "What did Francona say?"

"Ah, man," he said. "It was *hilarious*."

He launched into a manic monologue about all the wild shenanigans happening in the world of the Red Sox. He was all smiles now, spinning anecdotes and jokes, peppering his stories with commentary. Soon he was telling me about *this crazy girl* he once knew . . . He went on, breathlessly, until we were safely miles and an ocean away from our previous conversation. He simply didn't want to talk about his reality. Perhaps he thought I was preaching to him. Perhaps he was right.

As he walked out of the library that day, after successfully filibustering our conversation, he told me he wanted to apologize for abruptly and weirdly changing the subject. That he would like to continue "that conversation."

"Really?" I asked. "You don't have to, if you don't want to. And you don't have to apologize."

I wasn't good at the tough-love mentor thing; I considered giving it a rest. Giving us both an out. But this time, he persisted.

"No, I'm serious, I really want to. You'll be like my rabbi here." He said this with a wink.

I have to admit, this comment left a vomitty zing in my mouth. A rabbi was the last thing I wanted to be. He knew this. I'd told him as much. That's why he'd said it. A little revenge for making him cry.

As I stood momentarily locked in the sallyport—I was going to my parents' Passover Seder—I considered what the rabbis said about the holiday: that when you recount the story of the Jews' exodus from Egypt, you must feel as though you yourself made that journey. You must tell their story as if it had literally happened to you. The story of the Israelites' escape from Egypt is probably not factual. But it is factual that my family has been telling this story, in this way, forever.

Sitting in his cell upstairs, Josh would not be telling this story with his family. He was still deciding whether he could overcome his personal Narrow Place and live to tell the story.

I'd met many inmates who were figuring out their life story, determining their role in shaping that narrative. Some chose to leave it all behind, like Jessica. Chudney had emphatically decided to script his future, but the decision was ultimately clinched by someone else. Like Josh, Too Sweet was sitting in his cell at that very moment. He, however, was busy writing his story, page by page.

I waited for the sallyport to open. It seemed like I was always waiting for it to open. Even after almost two years, I was still awed at the simplicity of the machinery of imprisonment. There wasn't much that separated captivity from freedom. It was basically a switch and an aging steel door that hummed and rumbled as it opened, and slammed shut with a big metallic crash, just like in the movies. Even after all this time in prison, the daily relief of reemerging into the lobby, experiencing that small moment of liberation, never lost its effect.

The prison lobby was mostly empty that night, I slipped by Sully without a chat and was at my family's seder within the hour.

That Night

Chudney was sitting in the backseat. His seventeen-year-old brother, Darius, was in the passenger seat; Darius's girlfriend was at the wheel. It was just after 9:30 p.m. Late February in Boston. Roxbury. Icy streets, too cold for snow. They had to make a quick stop. Chudney needed something for lunch the next day. He'd just started a job working construction.

They pulled up to a bodega on the corner of Maple and Washington. Less than half a mile from their mother's home on Wharton Street, where Chudney was living at the time. They parked; Chudney ran in. Darius's girlfriend stayed in the driver's seat to make a phone call. Darius got out and struck up a conversation with some girls standing outside of the store. When Chudney emerged from the store he saw some young men hovering. They were glaring at his brother.

From his vantage point across the street, Chudney recognized the menace first—though they were a few blocks from their home, they were in enemy gang territory. Tensions were on the rise. Just then Darius noticed the men. He stiffened up and glared right back at them. Words were exchanged. Chudney jogged over to his brother. In one quick action, he grabbed the boy's arm and pulled him toward the car. He turned to the glaring young men and said, "It's cool, man. We out."

Darius reluctantly climbed into the front seat, Chudney got into the back and slammed the door shut. In the next moment four things happened simultaneously: Chudney shouted to Darius's girlfriend to drive, the car screeched, a shot went off, a glass window cracked.

The gunfire had been absorbed into the noise and commotion, like a tiny bit of poison dissolved into a drink. The car raced up Maple Street. Darius turned around to see whether they were being followed. The next minute was sheer panic. His eyes widened.

—Omigodomigodomigodshitshitshitshit.

—What? What! his girlfriend said.

He couldn't answer. He couldn't speak. Couldn't breathe. Couldn't move. Darius's girlfriend glanced in the rearview mirror.

—Oh shit, she screamed, and threw the wheel into a sharp turn, hastily parking the car a few blocks up Maple Street, across from Nazareth Baptist church.

Chudney was slumped over, the back of his seat soaked in blood. The bullet had entered his head from behind, almost execution style— he probably hadn't known what hit him. In the front seat, the two teenagers panicked. The girl was not from Boston and did not know the way to the hospital. Darius was in shock. Unable to think or speak *or blink or draw air into his throat. He managed to call 911. They waited, sobbing and hysterical. Chudney died in the backseat of the car, parked next to the church.*

Work to Do

The last time I saw Too Sweet, his smile was brief. From the moment he crossed into the library he was business. As he approached the front counter, I got a closer look. He was uncharacteristically disheveled, hair frizzed, uncombed and a bit long, beard coming in scraggily.

"What's good?" he said. He seemed exhausted.

He gave me some skin—and I, by instinct, glanced around guiltily. He got right to the point.

"Can't kick it today," he said. "I gotta get to work."

Standing alone at the counter, shaking his head and squeezing his lips shut, he said, "They're pinchin' me, man." He tapped his fingers on the library counter.

But suddenly and for no obvious reason his anxiety faded. He smiled and leaned back, an unmistakable prelude to one of his small dramatic performances. He threw a small air punch—more of a fist swat—and followed it with a verbal equivalent.

"They *pinchin'* a pimp!" he announced.

C.C. was in playland. He looked around to see if anyone caught his little turn of phrase. Nobody was around.

He embellished a bit: "Bitches be pinchin' a *pimp*!"

Still, no one heard him. But he didn't mind. C.C. thirsted for a large and adoring audience, but he would settle for just himself, if necessary.

He got serious again. "I got a lot of work," he repeated.

For some reason, I took this to mean he had a lot of law work to do. But, of course, out came the manuscript. I should have guessed: His main occupation was not his legal defense but his narrative defense. His apologia. With his back up against a wall, in the world of lawyers, judges, prison guards, and humiliating press coverage—in which his narrative was being shaped by people who despised him—he struggled to tell another version.

"Man, I got no love in court today, Avi."

"Are you scared?" I asked. This is the wrong question to ask in prison. But it was the best I had for him.

"Nah, man," he said, as he shrugged and looked away. "It'll be a' ight; ain't nothin for a real, live P-I-M-P."

I didn't press the issue. Instead I exchanged his ID card for an ink cartridge.

Deconstructing the Prison Library

The order came from on high. The Education Department wanted to update the library. The whole place had to be cleared: Every book was to be boxed; every bookshelf disassembled; every table, chair, and computer removed. The entire area was to be taken apart, piece by piece. And then, after the work was done, reconstructed. The library needed new carpeting.

My duty switched from the norm, such as it was, to the work of dismantling. It was an involved, dirty, and annoying responsibility.

But the order had been long overdue. The carpeting was in tatters. Nearly fifteen years and thousands of hours of prison traffic didn't look pretty. It was deeply stained and, in some spots, ripped to shreds and held together by duct tape. The smell was of rotting apples. As Dice had put it, "This carpet here is tainted."

And it was killing morale, sending the message that the library wasn't being watched. Across the prison, graffiti increased markedly when a space looked beaten up, and was usually a sign of lapsed discipline. And it was bad PR (the library, of course, was a routine stop for pols and other official visitors).

When we began the project, I'd estimated the work would occupy a day or two. In the end, it ate up almost two and a half (union) weeks. Reconstruction added another five days.

After a few officers sorted out among themselves who was boss—and one of them threw a mini-tantrum when his cause failed—the work commenced. At first, the only people working were the five members of the library detail, plus me and Forest. But after an hour or so the immensity of the task became clear and the officer in charge asked us to enlist more workers.

I was always hesitant about using prison labor. It felt dirty, too much like slavery for my taste. My staff, at least, got some compensation, meager though it was. But this overhaul job offered no pay for any of the inmates involved. When I mentioned this to one of my officer friends, he said, "You ever hear of cons 'paying their debt to society'? These guys should be working. It's good for them to be working. Nobody owes them nothing. *They're* the ones who owe something." When I continued to express my doubts, he said, "Look, these guys fucked up. You gotta give them a chance to earn trust back. You give 'em work and they do it good, they can walk out of here with pride and say, 'I did my time right.' Nobody can take that away from them."

As it turned out, inmates lined up for the work. After a day or two of backroom negotiations, when caseworkers and officers came into my office to advocate for their favorite inmates—guys they knew from the neighborhood or who they were rooting for or, even more

369

obscurely, owed a favor—we had a small workforce of about ten. This force grew as the need increased.

At first every book was taken off the shelf and stacked onto a linoleum-tiled patch of the library. There were twenty-thousand-plus books and we were trying to keep them roughly organized. Halfway through this massive job, we were informed that the library also needed to be repainted, and the books could not remain stacked on the floor. Now we needed to redo a couple days' worth of work and put every book into a box, again maintaining a rough order. We were awash in books; it was as if someone had made a small puncture in a dam. Once the shelves were down, the flow continued ferociously. Nobody could take a step without tripping over a pile of books.

Once the books were gone, each shelf of the floor-to-ceiling bookcases had to be unscrewed and removed. Then the steel frames of the cases had to be carefully felled. Fifteen men would have to carefully lower these surprisingly heavy beams down, unscrew them, and then haul them out or stack them. Hampered by the tight prison schedule and interruptions for lockdowns (following violence on the units), this effort dragged on for days.

The deconstruction of the steel bookcases required a careful amount of group coordination. This delicate effort had to be carefully organized or someone was certain to get hurt. As it was, an inmate was caught on the shoulder, very nearly his head, by a lowering beam and knocked down hard, the result of a miscommunication. When he fell, a few other men unwisely let go and jumped to help him, leaving the rest of us clinging to the hopelessly cumbersome shelf, nearly causing us to drop it. This could have been unfortunate for everyone, particularly for the man lying underneath it.

But this incident was the exception and served only to remind everyone what a good job the captain was doing coordinating the workers.

Captain Sweeney was a small, structurally sound balding man who chewed two sticks of gum with a crooked grin. Unlike many other officers, he didn't simply supervise work projects, standing at the side as the inmates toiled; he rolled up his sleeves and got to work. When he got sweaty, he'd strip down to his undershirt, and he encouraged the inmates to join him. The inmates respected him.

At the end of a particularly grueling workday, we all sat around the wreckage, chatting and bullshitting. At that point, it was five inmates, three officers, and me. An outsider walking in would not have been able to distinguish who was staff and who was a prisoner. And it wasn't just because we were stripped down to matching white undershirts and work pants. It was the familiar way in which the men spoke to one another, the casual way they reclined together at the work site. The body language here was clear. If the deputy had suddenly appeared, the officers would surely have jumped up and corrected their posture.

After the inmates departed for count-time, the officers discussed lunch. One suggested that we order the inmates lunch "from the staff line"—not four stars, but significantly better than what the inmates got for chow. Sweeney agreed, but when the other officers left, he came up to me and said, "You might wanna get the guys something at the end of the job. Something small, like Chicken McNuggets or fries or something—and make sure they eat it in here. And don't broadcast it." I wasn't surprised that Sweeney was a feeder; nor was I surprised that he delegated the task to someone else. He was kind but he wasn't stupid.

A few days after we completed the job, one of the inmate workers dropped by. "Man, I wish we were still working in here," he said. "There was, like, a different vibe last week." He was right. The rigidity of prison life had softened during the library deconstruction project. Never was the drama of prison more clear. The uniforms seemed like theatrical costumes. It was as if the dismantling of the theater set also undid the script. And people were free to fill it briefly with another reality.

But now the library had been fully reconstructed, the work accomplished, the food (secretly) shared. And now the uniforms stayed on. The set was reassembled, the roles reestablished. After a week or two, the pleasantly tart smell of fresh paint dissolved completely. People forgot that the place looked different—and actually much better than before. It was as if it never happened.

Joining Elia

The banter behind the library counter, the bar, was as boisterous as ever. There had been some turnover in the inmate work detail. Coolidge had been transferred to a different prison. Pitts had been released. So had Stix. Dice, Teddy, John, and others, had fallen prey to prison mischief and had their details revoked. The inmate staff was still captained by Fat Kat, who'd somehow regained his library job despite his violent actions in 3-2. As usual, Kat held silent sway, sitting placidly with his magazines, keeping a half-shuttered eye on operations.

Two newer detail workers had become inseparable. They formed a house comedy team: the wily old-timer, Boat, and the most recent addition, a young jester named Nequieste. They were an odd couple. Boat, a grizzled Irish Italian small-time mobster and possible ex-hit man, his legs numb with FBI ammunition—one bullet of which remained lodged—leaned on his cane, offering trenchant straight-man commentary.

Nequieste, a baby-faced twenty-year-old black guy who oozed intelligence and ingenuous criminal optimism, would run literal circles around Boat, doing brilliant impressions of inmates and prison staff. They were deeply entertained by their own duets.

Their routines were not unfunny. But most of the time, they were just loud. Their friendship was quickly turning into an irritating convict mentorship. Nequieste listened enraptured as Boat recounted the catalog of his old bank robberies, mob jobs, brushes with the notorious Stevie "Machine Gun" Flemmi and Whitey Bulger, one of the FBI's most wanted fugitives, whom he called by his neighborhood name, Jimmy.

I was getting tired of all the noise.

I ventured out into the stacks, where I found the detail's most elusive member, Elia. He was quietly shelving books. At first he looked annoyed to see me, but he was actually just surprised. He smiled shyly, sighed, and asked, "Finally had enough of them guys, huh?"

He said this with a touch of frustration, as though he'd been waiting, almost two years, for me to realize this and join him.

In the gaps through the shelves, I could just make out Nequieste on the other side of the room. He was hunched over, quaking, and with the help of Boat's cane, walking at an agonizingly slow pace and with theatrical feebleness. His pants were pulled obscenely high, and his uniform top tucked into them. He wore Boat's thick glasses pushed down all the way to the end of his nose.

I can't walk, I need my meds, where are my meds, I can't see, I heard him say, blending Boat's gritty Boston smoker's voice with, to my surprise, an old Jewish man's accent. *My bladder is* killing *me.*

His audience, including the now-blind Boat, giggled.

You fuggin' ass'ole, said Boat, approvingly.

I reached into the carton of books next to Elia and began shelving alongside him.

"You wanna see my kid?" Elia asked, in his usual whisper.

He held out his well-thumbed photo of the beaming four-year-old girl. Then, just as quickly, returned it to his chest pocket. And with it, his smile. We continued silently shelving. I asked him how he'd earned the nickname, "Forty." He paused for a long second and I knew I'd asked the wrong question.

"It's an old drinker's name," he said finally. "You know, like forty ounces? But I don't like it. I'm trying to live it down, okay? But it's the name I got."

We continued shelving books. Out of the corner of my eye, I watched his quiet labors. He would lift a volume, dust it off with his uniform top or with a little paper towel he kept folded in his pocket like an oldtime handkerchief. Or he would blow a soft breath over the book. Then he'd rest his eyes on the cover, squint, pronounce the title carefully to himself, compare it against a printout of the database. Then he'd use both hands to firmly install the book in its precise spot, in accordance with the Dewey Decimal system. Then he'd align the book on the shelf so that it looked comfortable and secure in its new home. Then he'd dust the neighboring books a bit and check their order and classification markings. He would pick up the next one and begin the process again.

The man was more than meticulous; he handled these books with love and elegance. I recalled all the times I had noticed him from afar, sometimes just merely detecting his movements at the outer reaches of the library. All those hours—how many hundreds of hours?—he had been engaged in this silent monastic repetition.

Fuuuck you, you fuckin' Jamaican, I heard Boat say from the other side of the room, *why donya get on a banana boat and go back to your fuckin' island.*

I spied Nequieste, feeling Boat's face like a blind man: *What did you say, young man? I can't hear good and my pants are soaking.*

More giggling.

I said, Fuck you, Jamaican.

I saw Elia tense up, close his eyes, sigh, and shake his head for a moment. Then he returned to his work, installing a book into its spot. I suddenly felt awful for all of the times over the years when his brittle equilibrium was disrupted by the frequent banter I'd permitted at the front of the library.

I apologized to him for it. He cocked his head at me and flashed a jagged smile.

"Aw, I don't mind," he said with a shrug. It was a friendly little lie that neither of us had any intention of correcting. "But thank you," he added.

We continued shelving books in silence. I didn't dare shatter his peaceful rhythm. He was among these shelves to escape talk. To let questions sit. We finished the carton and got another. It was a task with no end, the steady job of the old Jewish Messiah joke. This didn't seem to bother Elia, though. In fact he seemed comforted by it.

Time has its own peculiar meaning in prison. *All I got is time* was an expression Elia, and others, often used. In its everyday prison usage it means, *I'm in prison, I'm never too busy.* But it is always said with irony, in the sense of having *only* time and nothing else. Although a person in prison always has countless hours, he has no access to time's attendant meanings. When it comes to time, most inmates are like the tragic mariner: *water, water everywhere, nor any drop to drink*. There's endless time but not the nourishing kind, no seasons, no holidays, no cycles. At least, nothing that can be shared with others.

When snow collects in the yard—it is winter. When your cell-mate smells particularly rank—it is summer. But these things don't imply anything beyond themselves. Snow doesn't mean sledding with your children, or skiing, or playing football or going to concerts for Christmas. It means snow.

The closest approximation of seasons in prison are the gambling seasons. When the Super Bowl gambling crunch hits, it is winter; when the NCAA basketball tourney happens, it is spring. These are the Christmas and Easter of prison. Aside from these sad interludes, prison time is neither marked nor shared by a community. It is personal and moves toward one holiday: the end of one's sentence. Each individual follows his own private eschatological calendar, which has only one holiday, the Last Day, the End of Days.

This is a very practical matter for those who work in prison. When you leave before a holiday, a well-meaning caseworker instructed me, you don't say "Merry Christmas" to the inmates. It doesn't make sense and, as she added, "It's kind of a slap in the face." In prison, seasons are best left unmarked and unremarked upon. And indeed it was always poignant to close up shop before a holiday, or even before a weekend. The looks that came my way then were invariably pitiful, sometimes desperately so, and it was in those moments I got a sense of what the library meant to many of the inmates.

For the next few days, I imposed a no-noise policy. I joined Elia in the stacks. For hours, we'd shelve books wordlessly. I heard the textures of silence, like those in the recorded interview of my grand-mother. In the library one could hear the sudden crank and surge of nearby pipes. Digital squeaks. The low thrum, high hiss, of prison air pumping constantly from shafts in the ceiling—and the barely audible voices, occasional quiet shouting, from some far corner of the prison, all of it deposited into the library along with the processed air. These sounds were remarkable because they stream around constantly but are never heard.

This was the first real silence I'd experienced in the library since the night I showed up late after visiting Deer Island and the Liberty Hotel. And just like that night, the stillness of the library opened up the space in a new way.

Elia often used the phrase "doing time." I saw what he meant by it. Time in prison isn't celebrated, commemorated, or even lived in, but something *done* with your hands, a repetitive chore, like doing laundry or shelving books. There's a difference between *being in prison* and *doing time*. Elia was, I now saw, making masterful work of that task.

Every time Elia placed a book on the shelf, he acted in opposition to the order of prison. His labors involved small interpersonal acts he created for himself and which affirmed he wasn't merely an object with a number attached to it. No: *He* was the person, the subject, who imposed the order.

He dusted and arranged each book with deliberation and grace. Aware of his place in an infinite circulation, Elia was not in any rush, not concerned with *finishing* but only with *doing*. By dusting, then placing each individual book in its precise spot he was reaching out, anonymously and indirectly, kindly, to a stranger, perhaps even an enemy. He was making it possible for others to find what they were looking for. He was using the library to set things straight. Carton by carton, shelf by shelf, book by book.

He wasn't the only one. Everyone who enters a library is in search of *something*. It was right there, in the stacks, where Elia had made a home, where Jessica had sat for her portrait with a paper flower in her hair, where she'd given her anxious cellmate a comfort ribbon. It was where the young prostitute from Dunkin' Donuts had sat with her art books. Where Chudney had learned some of his first recipes. Where hundreds of inmates had paused and searched. Sometimes not even certain what they were looking for.

In the silence of those hours of shelving books I remembered I had also arrived at the library in that way. In search of something, not certain what.

After nearly two years, I was still trying to figure out the purpose of my job and of the library at large. For this, I needed only take Elia's example. He wasn't merely counting down the days with each book. His elegant librarianship, his hands deliberating over each title, the gentle way he dusted and kept notes and piles, the care with which he arranged the shelves, his silence, made me appreciate how order is created: Not through grand schemes—to which I was often drawn—but by small graceful actions, repeated often and refined with time.

Shortly thereafter, I found myself sitting on a grassy, wild-flower-covered hill on Deer Island, looking out at the Atlantic and eating tuna salad on a sesame bagel. I was serving my suspension without pay, my punishment for assaulting Officer Chuzzlewit. It was spring and almost starting to feel like it. Boston Harbor was fussy and uncooperative. The ocean loomed in the near distance, black and vast.

I finished my sandwich too quickly. Possibly due to the influence of haunted Deer Island—or possibly a lingering effect of the childhood trauma of trying to lose my Israeli accent by sitting for hours in a windowless room with a speech therapist who forced me to endlessly repeat the word *girl, girl, girl*—my thoughts turned toward the Apocalypse. I wondered which place would be first submerged by the great imminent deluge: Deer Island or the landfilled South Bay?

It was a silly question. Of course Deer Island would sink first. It sits directly in the harbor. The water level in nearby Hull was already rising. It was only a matter of time. I finished my pickle in two and a half bites. My back twinged. I laid myself out flat, in the yoga pose— or non-pose—known as the Dead Man. It was really the only position I could pull off.

I thought about the nineteenth-century prison that lay in ruins in the manmade hill upon which I was sitting. And the minimalist librarian job description from that departed era: *such provision of light shall be made for all prisoners confined to labor during the day as shall enable them to read for at least one hour each evening.* A *provision*, from the Latin for *foresight*. Listening to the waves, I thought about Chudney, survived by a five-year-old boy and a newspaper article about his murder. Even at the moment, Elia was in the South Bay prison, shelving books.

And Mike Pitts who had shown me the mug shot on his ID shortly before he was released, and proudly asked me to compare how much better he looked after years in prison.

"I'm not that fat dude anymore," he'd told me, "I'm trim, I filled my head with knowledge in this library, man, and I'm ready to *go.*"

But, one sunny day, months after his release, his photo appeared in the *Boston Herald*, bloated and miserable. The victim of a horribly botched liposuction.

And the great Coolidge, whose photo appeared in the *Boston Globe*, standing in Massachusetts Superior Court, wearing a crisp white dress shirt and tie. The article recounted the amazing story of how this man argued his own case, and persuaded two judges to ignore the fact that police found a treasure trove of stolen property from eight locations in his possession: ATM cards, purses, a rotary saw, a computer. A crime spree. According to court records, they also found "books on how to improve your writing."

The *Globe* reporter marveled that a lifelong street criminal had repeatedly bested professional prosecutors by "relying on a state law so obscure that several defense lawyers interviewed were unfamiliar with it." And just as Coolidge had promised me when we first met, he was planning to one-up Napoleon and take his arguments on the offensive: He was demanding $66,000 from the state, compensation for lost wages and a sum of money large enough to purchase a used SUV. He had other cases pending, though, and still faced a twenty-year sentence.

I thought of my friend Yoni, who discovered that he wanted to be an anthropologist studying hippies. Enrolled in a Ph.D. program, he could now live his dream of roving the remote hills of Arkansas—wearing only a sarong and a cowboy hat—going native with a group of stoned moon-worshippers. All in the name of science.

And what would my next step be?

I listened to the choppy sea, the rutted waves Sylvia Plath mournfully watched eat away at this sad little island. I imagined notes falling out of books, and the undelivered, unfinished letter: *Dear Mother, My life is*

I thought about Jessica's undelivered note. About how she left her son in a church, then met him almost two decades later in a prison. About Chudney's son trying to stop the waves. Jessica sitting silently, looking out of the window, her hands folded in her lap, watching from way up in the prison tower. Doing what mothers do, what she never could do herself: Watching her son play in the yard. Just watching. How she made herself pretty for the portrait she would never give him. I thought about Elia placing books and books in their proper order.

Books, it was written on Amato's immovable sign, *are not mailboxes.*

A provision of light.

I synchronized my breath with the waves. A decision fixed itself to my mind. I had an unfinished piece of business.

The Diameter of a Sunday

Marcia Franklin, Chudney's mother, cried on the phone when we spoke. I'd told her what I had for her. She invited me to her home in Roxbury—where Chudney had been living when he was shot.

I got an early start that day. It was a Sunday. Our meeting had been planned for the early afternoon to give Marcia time to return from church. Before the meeting, I took a short driving tour of Roxbury. I knew of only a few sites connected to Chudney. The prison, his mother's house, and the corner store where he was shot. And a few other places he had mentioned. Most of what I knew about Chudney concerned his imagined future, not the streets of his actual life. Driving around his neighborhood I realized how little I knew of his life outside of prison, even though we had spent much time in conversation.

The site of the shooting was across from Crispus Attucks Place, a small street, more of a glorified parking lot, named for the most famous of the five people killed by English gunfire during the Boston Massacre of 1770. In American mythos, Attucks was "The First to Defy, The First to Die," the first casualty of the Revolution. A large mural nearby depicted Attucks—an iconic African American—not as the civilian he actually was, but rather eyes ablaze and musket bayonet poised, charging into an apocryphal battle.

Further down the street, a minute or so away, was 72 Dale Street, where Malcolm X lived as a teenager. And around the corner in the other direction, the home where Martin Luther King Jr. lived during his years as a seminary student at Boston University. These streets were heavy with the ghosts of martyrs.

While Chudney's mother prayed in church, I decided to pick my own text for meditation. Mine wasn't from the Bible but from Hebrew poet Yehuda Amichai. I read "Diameter of a Bomb" with all of my writing classes. It was the poem Dumayne had read in memory of Chudney, after his eulogy at the library poetry reading:

The diameter of the bomb was thirty centimeters
and the diameter of its effective
range—about seven meters.
And in it four dead and eleven wounded.
And around them in a greater circle
of pain and time are scattered
two hospitals and one cemetery.
But the young woman who was

buried where she came from
over a hundred kilometers away
enlarges the circle greatly.
And the lone man who weeps over her death
in a far corner of a distant country
includes the whole world in the circle.
And I won't speak at all about the crying of orphans
that reaches to the seat of God
and from there onward, making
the circle without end and without God.

The poet's method of cold, numerical measurement is an appropriate way to begin dealing with the horror of sudden violent death. It gives the mind something concrete, objective, to grasp when trying to contemplate the enormity of murder. But as the poet concludes, taken far enough the dimensions of these measurements become too vast, too mysterious, for either human or divine calculus.

As I drove around Roxbury, I used my odometer to take some preliminary measurements of my own. Chudney was shot a quarter of a mile from where he lived with his mother, where he had once seen a deer run through the middle of the city; a rough mile from the market where he bought ingredients for his banana pudding; three and a half miles from the nearest market that sells fresh rosemary; less than two miles from where he had been imprisoned; probably about a mile and a half from where he was born and a mile or so less than that from where he had gone to school. He died one mile from the Greater Love Tabernacle Church, where his mother was praying for his soul. And about a mile from Roxbury Community College, where he was applying to begin his new career with a certificate course in Food and Beverage Preparation. His sister lived roughly twenty miles away in the quiet suburb of Wellesley; about seventy miles away, in a Connecticut town, lived his five-year-old son, who—according to the *Boston Globe* article about Chudney's murder—had asked his mother "why God called him."

How far did this circle of loss extend? I certainly didn't know. Ultimately, as the poet said, it was a "circle without end," fundamentally a mystery.

As I drove up Chudney's street, I looked down at the sheets of folded printing paper sitting on my empty passenger seat. These were Chudney's writings: now in the form of a kite. A small letter, written and then left behind in a hidden corner of the library. The kind of thing I was trained to discard. But I was very pleased with this breach of my job description. I had intercepted so many misguided notes, witnessed so many unfinished, unsent, impossible letters—here was one good one, as complete as it would ever get, that I might see properly delivered. It was a small thing, but at least it would arrive. For Chudney's family, and especially for his son, a modest provision of a few words for the coming eternity of silence.

Books are not mailboxes—*yes they are*. It was a bit of graffiti I had often imagined scrawling in the margin of Amato's sign.

My trip to visit Marcia was unusual for a variety of reasons. First, I was a youngish white guy, well-dressed (in honor of Marcia), in the heart of the hood driving a (borrowed) Saab with Cambridge parking stickers. Any illusion that this was a neutral event was banished when I parked the car and walked up to Marcia's apartment building: People literally stopped what they were doing to stare at me. Some with contempt, most with curiosity.

Old men repaired a rusty car. Young men in hoodies, bedecked in clanging jewelry and sneakers whose gleaming white stood in stark relief to the garbage-lined street, sat on stoops and strutted for each other in front of the boarded-up and graffitied liquor store on the corner. All watched me as I walked up to the building.

But what made my visit even stranger was that I was a prison worker making a house call to the family of a former inmate. This didn't happen every day.

Marcia buzzed me into the building and welcomed me with a big smile. She wore sweatpants tucked into her socks and a billowy extra-large T-shirt with a picture of her slain son, *RIP* and his birth and death dates printed on it. There are shops in town that specialize in the paraphernalia of street-corner martyrdom. In the picture, Chudney's arms are fully extended out at his sides, his palms facing up in a jaunty "bring it on" sort of pose. His head was slightly cocked and he wore the face of tough-guy indifference.

For me, it was a jarring way to encounter Chudney for the first time in his regular clothes, not in his prison uniform. He looked different. Healthier.

Marcia's apartment was small and neat, shades drawn, dim lighting. Framed and unframed family photos and religious quotations adorned the walls. Nearby loomed a small, square mirror with a prowling black panther painted on it. A murky fish tank gurgled and hummed in the background. The TV, tuned to BET, remained on. Later, when Marcia and I went into another room to retrieve old photos, I noticed another TV that she'd left on. She lived alone in an apartment full of the commotion of television voices. Perhaps this helped her alleviate loneliness.

She sat in an easy chair; I took a spot on the couch across from her. She turned down the volume on the TV. Hip-hop music videos, specters of scantily clad women fawning over cocky young men continued to flicker next to us as we talked.

I took out Chudney's writings, the kite he'd left in the library. She read it for a long time. As tears filled her eyes, Marcia gently folded up her son's words and placed them on the coffee table.

"I'm gonna have this laminated," she said.

She told me that her son's murder was ordained from on high. "The Scripture tells us that we don't know the hour and we don't know the place," she told me. "And that's exactly how it was with Chudney."

I told her that I believed a little haiku-like piece that Chudney had written was in fact a religious poem. She picked it up, looked at it again, and read it aloud slowly.

> plane flying high in the sky,
> me standing alone,
> sunday morning in the yard.

"Why do you think it's religious?" she asked.

I told her that I had assigned the class to write this little three-line poem and to give them a leg up, had furnished them with the last line. The line I suggested, which I had scrawled on the board, was *monday morning in the yard*, meaning the prison yard. I'd picked "Monday morning" because of that moment's proverbial connotation of working week dread. Monday morning is also a frenetic time in prison, when inmates are released from extended weekend lockdowns.

But Chudney had changed my line to "Sunday morning," a

moment of the week with vastly different connotations. I'd noticed this alteration when he made it and had wondered if it had anything to do with Sunday as the Lord's day. I had meant to ask him, but forgot.

But it wasn't just that. The images in this lonely Sabbath morning encounter with the sky also suggested a spiritual meditation. The contrast between the plane soaring, an image of heaven-bound freedom and power, and with his own radical feeling of earthboundness—standing alone, static, in captivity, in the prison yard. There was some kind of longing in that. It was the quiet fire that burned under *The Plan*. He rarely spoke of it. But it was understood.

Chudney's mother told me that she found comfort in the fact that he had died next to a church. "It might have been the last thing he saw on this planet," she said.

Marcia told me that, as a child, Chudney had wanted to be a clown. He had made her look in the Yellow Pages for clown jobs. He loved making people around him smile.

The second oldest of five, he would do anything for his mother: cook, clean, put the children to bed. And when he did these things, he went all out. He didn't just clean the oven, he would take it apart and scrub it clean. He would make sure that the house looked presentable and cozy when his mother returned home from a long day of work as a janitor at Beth Israel Hospital.

"You know when you come home, you want everything to look right—Chudney always made sure that happened, even without my asking him. There were some things he just knew to do."

After he was released from prison, he began working in construction. Every night before he went to bed, he'd make his lunch for the next day. He'd make his tuna sandwich with great care and would wrap it with great care. Each part of his lunch was placed together in the refrigerator, ready for him to grab it on his way to work, she told me.

When she returned from the hospital after he was pronounced dead, Marcia opened the refrigerator. There was his sandwich—still fresh—meticulously made and wrapped, ready for him to grab on his way out. She picked it up and examined it: it was put together so thoughtfully, by his living fingers, only hours ago.

There were questions about Chudney's death that I didn't dare ask his mother and she probably wouldn't have known the answers in any case. Did Chudney know the killers? Was this the result of a previous conflict? The prison beef? And how many people had witnessed this murder but were bound by the code of silence—or were too scared to talk?

Was the bullet intended for Darius? Was Darius in a gang? Was Darius plotting revenge? For all I knew, he'd already taken it. For all I knew, Chudney's killer would walk into the library next week and ask for a good book.

A few weeks later I dropped by Marcia's home again to chat and to look at photos. I stayed for a while and when I finally left, it was dark. As I walked out of the apartment complex, I heard a voice behind me.

"Hey, you from South Bay?"

I turned around. A man, whom I did not recognize, was sitting on the stoop. He was glaring at me.

"Yes," I said. "I'm not *from* there, I work there. You don't seem happy to see me." This was my attempt to be friendly. He continued to stare.

"Yeah, I remember you," he said. "You're the guy in the library."

"That's right. What's your name?"

He smiled sarcastically and shook his head. Even through the shadows I sensed his truculent eyes searching me.

"I remember you, you didn't let me make some important copies. You were just like the rest of them."

Yes, now I did remember him. He had made a big scene in the library about how I was trying to prevent him from doing some important legal work, because I hesitated to make him sixty pages of copies. The library's policy was no more than ten pages per person at a time, which I extended within reason. We were perennially short on paper and ink.

As I stood on a dark side street of Roxbury, this anonymous man began berating me about how his rights were violated again and again in prison, how I had no idea about the abuse he suffered in there. He told me that there were some people from prison—both inmates and staff—whom he had vowed to "fuck up" if he ever caught them on his turf.

It occurred to me that if I were one of those people, I was in serious trouble. If anything did happen to me, the cops would undoubtedly have wondered why I thought it was a good idea to be in this neighborhood at this hour. There wasn't anyone nearby, just me and a belligerent and possibly intoxicated ex-con.

I thought about turning around, going straight to my car and booking it the hell out of there. But then I remembered what happened to Chudney. Turning my back to him would be a sign of blatant disrespect and also make me vulnerable. The less risky option was to try to have a conversation with him. I took a step toward him.

I apologized to him and said, "The only reason that I denied you copies was that we are always short on paper, crazy as that sounds. If I give you all those pages, it means someone else doesn't get anything. And you know what the person will say to me? *You're prevent-*

ing me from doing my legal work—and he'd be right. My job is to make sure each person there has equal resources."

He continued to stare.

"You chose to be a part of that system," he said, "you profit off that system, man—you gotta answer for it. And then you be coming into this building up in here . . . Why you here?"

I didn't like the way this conversation was going. I devised an exit strategy: to talk like a telemarketer.

"I appreciate your criticism," I said absurdly. "Whether you believe me or not, I do try to make the library a place that goes above and beyond. If I'm performing under par, please tell me how to improve. I welcome it."

I extended my hand to him. He looked at it in disgust but took it, squeezing a bit harder than he needed to.

"I need to run," I said.

Never had those words been so true.

"But thanks for your comments. I'm always trying to improve the library."

"Yeah," he said.

"My name is Avi Steinberg, by the way."

"My name is Mike. Mike Tree," he said, as his eye caught a tree. *Really original*, I thought.

"Nice to meet you again, Mike *Tree*," I said as I walked toward my car.

As I drove home, I felt as though I were surreptitiously slipping back across a border at midnight. Two cop cruisers tore past my car in full shriek and throttle.

Picking up some new library patrons, I thought.

As I drove past the corner where Chudney was shot, I flicked my odometer to zero. I thought of Chudney's final poem, with its longing for a realm apart from our fallen world. As I drove, I recalled the poem Chudney wrote about his baby son, a poem heavily laden in question marks. I decided to commit it to memory:

Where did you come from?
No Place that I know.
A place full of the love
And the glory of pure joy.
Where did you come from?
Where is this place?

When I got home, I looked down. I lived 3.4 miles from the corner where Chudney was shot.

Prologue

Shortly after I left the prison for the last time—which had the miraculous effect of instantly healing my back—I found myself in Copley Square, walking toward the stately Boston Public Library. It was late May. In some corners of the city, the scent of lilacs could hold its own against rush hour's amassed fumes. The flower of Boston's spring is short-lived, a life-span of mere hours, but it was in full bloom that day.

I thought of Hawthorne's description of the wild roses blossoming next to this city's first prison, "which might be imagined to offer their fragrance and fragile beauty to the prisoner as he went in, and to the condemned criminal as he came forth to his doom, in token that the deep heart of Nature could pity and be kind to him." His prison rose bush struck me as a fine metaphor for a prison library, freely giving a small gift of beauty to a criminal. And as Hawthorne, a fellow fatalist after all, had also noted: this tiny, freely given object of beauty, a rose (or a book), was fragile, a mere token—and probably nothing more.

It had been almost a month since I had walked into a library. I missed it. I mounted the steps of Boston's great marble hall of books. All across America public libraries were, and are, being shut down, while prisons—with libraries—were, and are, being built. This has been a choice the American public has been making for over thirty years. Even in his fatalism—envisioning the New World Utopian dream dashed early by the grim necessity of building a prison—it is doubtful Hawthorne would have imagined so *many* prisons, the biggest penal system in the history of the world. America has 5 percent of the world's population, 25 percent of the world's prison population. A population the size of an American city left without a vote. If, as Hawthorne wrote, prison was the "black flower of civilized society," how would he describe the modern American penal system?

The central Boston Public Library however was still open, and lovely as ever. Inside, I discovered a crowd that was somehow familiar to me from prison and was suddenly struck by the universal culture of daytime libraries, both those in prison and in the free world: they are havens for all variety of loners and outcasts.

There were manic scribblers, filling legal pads with their musings; schizos, the obsessive and the compulsive; conspiracy theorists sitting with piles of books filling notecards in a careful effort to document their revisionist views of history; skeletal women grimly surveying massive tomes with magnifying glasses; an ancient gentleman smartly attired in a fedora and necktie (with tie clip), shuffling by at a glacial pace. His houndstooth sports jacket may have fit him handsomely during the Johnson administration but now came almost to his knees. There were others. Angry, bearded weirdos. Nap seekers. Grad students with Macs. A librarian snickering over an email.

All were equal in the main reading room, Bates Hall, with its magnificent fifty-foot vaulted ceiling and arched windows set high upon the wall, carefully placed, so it would seem, to remind one that the effulgence pouring through streamed directly from the heavens. Rows upon rows of reading tables dotted in glowing green lamps, like the wonderful affirmation signaled by the endless chain of green traffic lights that occasionally turns Broadway into a joyride through Manhattan.

Somebody stirred nearby.

Psst.

I turned around. I was being summoned with a smile and an elaborate gesture. This man knew me, which meant I probably knew him. But I didn't recognize him. Not until I got close.

"*Maestro,*" he whispered fervently. It was Al, the above-ground swimming pool salesman I'd met in the prison library during the winter.

"You don't recognize me!" he said, as I took a seat next to him. "I remember *you*, Mr. Prison Librarian."

"Of course I remember you," I said. "How could I forget?"

I might have been forgiven for not immediately identifying him. He was generously cloaked, wizard-like, in a fluttering, immaculately white Arabian thobe, with equally well-scrubbed white Air Jordans on his feet. There were the beginnings of a beard.

I remember he once told me that he wore the cap of whatever baseball team was currently the World Series champion. This was a man intent on partaking of greatness. Perhaps there was something like optimism in that—though, as a baseball fan myself, I tend toward more loyal forms of optimism. True to his word, though, he was wearing a new, red St. Louis Cardinals cap that day.

His head was the site of much activity. Over the Cardinals cap was a hood from his red sweatshirt, and thick headphones connected to an iPod. Under the cap, a white silken do-rag. And under that, a white kufi. The final tally: five items wrapped around this man's cranium. Until I arrived, he'd been hunched over an Arabic Quran, with facing English translation. An Arabic-English dictionary sat nearby.

The process of saying hello was pleasantly delayed by his methodical effort to remove each piece of headgear. He peeled off each layer, and with it, an entire persona. First, he doffed the hoodie, headphones and cap, his city garb. He was now left in a white do-rag that clung tightly to his hair and dangled nobly down his right shoulder. Together with the white robe, he was a jewel-encrusted dagger away from being a proud Moorish sentry. Then he ran his hand under the do-rag, removing it, and revealing the hand-knit kufi. Now he was a pilgrim on the hajj.

I told him I hadn't known he was a devout Muslim.

"Is the pope Catholic?" he said to me. "Then why can't I be Muslim?"

As usual, I couldn't quite tease out whether this was wit or sheer nonsense.

"What about Marx?" I asked. "I remember you were into the whole religion thing as a false ideology designed to keep the masses—"

"Fuck that," he whispered. "Man's *got* to believe."

I asked him about his star-selling business and about the swimming pools. He seemed uneasy with the questions. I got the sense he'd moved on from these things, or that it had gone sour. Or perhaps it had been nothing more than prison talk.

"I can still get you one . . . if you want," he said, referring to either a star or an above-ground swimming pool. Possibly both. I didn't ask.

"Nah," I said, "I'm all set."

After playing a bit of prison geography, I told him about my worries regarding Josh and other inmates with whom I was trying to stay in touch. He re-outfitted himself, wrapping and rewrapping his head. We floated out of the reading room together. He told me that he still remembered the jokes I told in the writing class (I would often start the class with a joke). I thanked him for saying that.

"No man, I'm *serious*," he told me, as we rounded down toward the grand staircase. "I wrote them all down, that was some serious shit you was spinning."

"That's true," I said. "Jokes are serious. I'm glad you agree."

We turned through the triumphal arch, past a clutter of columns and parapets, into the soft yellow, Siena marble arcade. The grand staircase. Under the murals of Aeschylus, Virgil, and Plato, we began our descent. He grabbed my arm, apparently in need of help balancing. We walked past the stone library lion—libraries really do need lions to protect them, the way that Officer Eddie Grimes had once told me, "the sword protects the pen."

I continued telling him about my issues. It wasn't clear that he was listening. We passed through the arched front door. It felt strange to walk about freely with an ex-inmate, with nobody watching, no restrictions or checkpoints. We stood under the heavy wrought-iron lanterns on the building's facade. Through the warm air, a swirl of scents reached us, cotton-candy, burgers, and buses. A twist of sewage. It was a Saturday—and even though I no longer kept the traditions, I resolved to observe the loveliness of this particular Shabbat day, to walk the forty-five minutes home.

As I rattled on about my concerns for the various people I had left behind in the prison, Al stared out over Copley Square, toward Trinity Church and the reflection of Trinity Church in the mirrored John Hancock building.

Finally, he cut me off.

"Let me tell you a good one," he said. "*You* told me this one. But I think you need to hear it again."

He told me the joke, getting it mostly right.

A merchant bought a sack of prunes from his competitor.

I smiled. I knew where this was going.

Opening the sack, he saw that the prunes had begun to rot. He went back to the seller and demanded his money back. The seller refused, and the two men went to see the rabbi to settle their dispute.

The rabbi sat down at a table between the two men and emptied the sack in front of them. Then he put on his glasses, and without saying a word, he went to work, slowly and carefully tasting one prune after another and each time shaking his head.

After some time had passed, the plaintiff finally spoke up, "So, Rabbi, what do you think?"

The rabbi, who was about to consume the last of the prunes, looked up and replied sharply: "Why are you fellows wasting my time? What do you think I am—a prune expert?"

"You *did* write those jokes down, didn't you?" I said.

"I told you, man, that's some deep shit."

"What do you think it's about?" I asked.

"I've thought about it," he said, "and I'll tell you exactly what it is: in this life, a man don't got to have all the answers."

"That's funny," I said, "I thought it was about a hungry thief who calls himself a rabbi."

"Nah, man. Shit. You missed the whole point."

He seemed genuinely agitated.

"It's about a smart guy, okay, but he ain't smart in the *right* way, see? Just 'cause you think about something a lot don't mean you know anything about it. Maybe you went to rabbi school, or you're an imam, or whatnot, but that don't mean you know shit about no damn prunes."

He gave me a stern look. We descended a few more steps. And I decided to accept his interpretation.

At the curb, Al released my arm—only when he finally let go did I realize how tightly he'd been clutching me. He gave me the Islamic farewell. I followed his lead: we alternated pecking each other's cheeks until he seemed satisfied that the gesture had been properly executed, after what felt like forty, possibly fifty turns. Then we thug hugged. Then fist bumped. Then we shook hands, and parted ways. He in a cab, I by foot.

Acknowledgments

My thanks to the following people who, in different and indispensable ways, helped make this book possible.

To Deena Croog, Steve Fredman, Jesse Kellerman, Anita Leyfell, Lorna Owen, Jed Perl, Marcie Richardson, and Sasha Weiss; to Jennifer Lyons, for her patience and wisdom; to my brilliant and clairvoyant editor, Ronit Feldman, Lauren Lavelle, the hard-working staff at Doubleday, and of course to the inimitable Nan Talese.

To Cathy, Charlie, Dottie, Forest, Kamau, Kelly, Mary Beth, Ming, Rick, Yoni, and all of the good people at the Bay.

To Kayla Yonit, *yonati b'chagvei ha-selah*. And to Abba, Ima, and Adena for, you know, everything.

DATE DUE
